CURRENCY CONFLICT AND TRADE POLICY

A NEW STRATEGY FOR THE UNITED STATES

Bergsten and Gagnon have written a very interesting and provocative book about currency manipulation and what the United States should do about it.

—Ben Bernanke, former chairman of the Federal Reserve Board

Based on rigorous analysis and their deep understanding of the dynamics of real-world international trade, Bergsten and Gagnon forcefully explain why understanding and resolving currency conflicts is essential to the future of globalization. They not only document the problem of currency conflicts in today's international trading system but also offer detailed, workable solutions. For those of us who recognize the benefits and costs of international trade, this is required reading.

—Jared Bernstein, former chief economist to Vice President Joseph Biden

"Currency conflict" and "manipulation" have bedeviled policymakers, political leaders, and publics since the beginning of the modern era of floating exchange rates. Bergsten and Gagnon offer a principled basis for assessing manipulation and recommend a practical tool to counter exchange rate distortions. In doing so, they have identified the missing link between IMF rules on exchange rates and WTO strictures on barriers to trade.

—Robert Zoellick, former president of the World Bank and US Trade Representative

Bergsten and Gagnon are long-time trusted authorities serving as thought leaders on the critically important issues of international financial and exchange rate policies. In this comprehensive study, they describe the "Decade of Manipulation" from 2003 to 2013 and its significant contribution to US job loss and to the financial crisis and recession. They leave no doubt that we must act to prevent it from happening again. We need structural reform to address not only the problem of currency manipulation but also the problem of inadequate efforts to address it. This book outlines a number of thoughtful proposals and should spark a serious dialogue about how best to move forward.

—Rep. Sander Levin (D-MI)

In a comprehensive analysis, Bergsten and Gagnon show why the problem of trade imbalances has not gone away. Fortunately, neither have they. So read this book to understand what has gone wrong with the world economy and how to put it right.

—Lord Mervyn King, former governor of the Bank of England

In recent years, Fred Bergsten and Joseph Gagnon literally defined the terms of the policy debate over how countries should and should not manage their exchange rates. Their views directly influenced the path-breaking macroeconomic policy declaration that the Obama administration negotiated alongside the Trans-Pacific Partnership. Going forward, it is hard to imagine the United States entering any new trade agreements that do not explicitly prohibit currency manipulation.

—Rory MacFarquhar, former special assistant to President Barack Obama for international economics, and visiting fellow, Peterson Institute for International Economics

Bergsten and Gagnon provide a thorough examination of the economic implications of currency manipulation and possible policy responses. In particular, they help us understand how foreign official reserve accumulation has significant implications for international financial flows and current account balances. This timely book is sure to stimulate debate and reflection.

—Douglas Irwin, Dartmouth College

CURRENCY CONFLICT AND TRADE POLICY

A NEW STRATEGY FOR THE UNITED STATES

C. FRED BERGSTEN AND
JOSEPH E. GAGNON

Peterson Institute for International Economics
Washington, DC
June 2017

C. Fred Bergsten, senior fellow and director emeritus, was the founding director of the Peterson Institute for International Economics (formerly the Institute for International Economics) from 1981 through 2012. He is serving his second term as a member of the President's Advisory Committee for Trade Policy and Negotiations. He was chairman of the Eminent Persons Group of the Asia Pacific Economic Cooperation (APEC) forum (1993–95) and assistant secretary for international affairs of the US Treasury (1977–81). He has authored, coauthored, edited, or coedited 44 books on international economic issues, including *International Monetary Cooperation: Lessons from the Plaza Accord after Thirty Years* (2016), *The Long-Term International Economic Position of the United States* (2009, designated a "must read" by the *Washington Post*), and *The United States and the World Economy: Foreign Economic Policy for the Next Decade* (2005).

Joseph E. Gagnon is senior fellow at the Peterson Institute for International Economics. He was visiting associate director, Division of Monetary Affairs (2008–09) at the US Federal Reserve Board, where he was also associate director, Division of International Finance (1999–2008), and senior economist (1987–90 and 1991–97). He has served at the US Treasury Department (1994–95 and 1997–99) and taught at the Haas School of Business, University of California, Berkeley (1990–91). He is the author of *Flexible Exchange Rates for a Stable World Economy* (2011) and *The Global Outlook for Government Debt over the Next 25 years: Implications for the Economy and Public Policy* (2011).

PETERSON INSTITUTE FOR
INTERNATIONAL ECONOMICS
1750 Massachusetts Avenue, NW
Washington, DC 20036-1903
(202) 328-9000   FAX: (202) 328-5432
www.piie.com

Adam S. Posen, *President*
Steven R. Weisman, *Vice President for Publications and Communications*

Cover Design by Peggy Archambault

19   5   4   3

Library of Congress Cataloging-in-Publication Data
Names: Bergsten, C. Fred, 1941– author. | Gagnon, Joseph E., author. Title: Currency conflict and trade policy : a new strategy for the United States / C. Fred Bergsten and Joseph E. Gagnon. Description: Washington, DC : Peterson Institute for International Economics, [2016] Identifiers: LCCN 2016035211 (print) | LCCN 2016048684 (ebook) | ISBN 9780881327267 | ISBN 9780881327250 Subjects: LCSH: Foreign exchange rates—United States. | Balance of trade—United States. | Devaluation of currency—United States. | Monetary policy—United States. | United States—Commercial policy. Classification: LCC HG3903 .B47 2016 (print) | LCC HG3903 (ebook) | DDC 332.4/50973—dc23 LC record available at https://lccn.loc.gov/2016035211

This publication has been subjected to a prepublication peer review intended to ensure analytical quality. The views expressed are those of the authors. This publication is part of the overall program of the Peterson Institute for International Economics, as endorsed by its Board of Directors, but it does not necessarily reflect the views of individual members of the Board or of the Institute's staff or management.

The Peterson Institute for International Economics is a private nonpartisan, nonprofit institution for rigorous, intellectually open, and indepth study and discussion of international economic policy. Its purpose is to identify and analyze important issues to make globalization beneficial and sustainable for the people of the United States and the world, and then to develop and communicate practical new approaches for dealing with them.

Its work is funded by a highly diverse group of philanthropic foundations, private corporations, and interested individuals, as well as income on its capital fund. About 35 percent of the Institute's resources in its latest fiscal year were provided by contributors from outside the United States. A list of all financial supporters is posted at https://piie.com/sites/default/files/supporters.pdf.

Contents

Tables

Figures

Boxes

Preface

Currency issues regained their political and economic salience in the years since 2000. Heavy intervention in the foreign exchange markets by a number of countries, most extensively by China, led to widespread charges that such currency manipulation was adversely affecting other economies and the United States, in particular. The record trade imbalances of the first decades of the new century illustrated and fed these concerns about stealing demand and competitive devaluation, especially when global demand was shrinking during the global financial crisis and slow recovery.

From a longer-term perspective, the unilateral exercise of currency intervention highlights the recurring and seemingly inherent failure of the international monetary system to achieve effective adjustment on the part of surplus countries. G-7 and G-20 compacts on exchange rate policy as well as subsequent shifts in countries' relative economic fortunes have meaningfully diminished the exercise of manipulation since 2012, but the underlying problem and risk of renewed tensions remain.

Currency has also become a central issue in the debate over trade policy in the United States, and remains so. Congressional and other critics of further trade liberalization, most notably of the Trans-Pacific Partnership, cited the manipulation issue as a major reason for their opposition, with some justification (as well as some opportunism). New legislation was passed to govern US currency policy, and potential TPP partners and others were prepared for a more forceful approach. The topic was prominent as part of the broader attack on globalization by candidates of both parties during the US political campaigns in 2016, and it has remained on the agenda of the Trump administration and is even higher on the agenda of trade-concerned Congress members of both parties.

This book analyzes the economics and politics of the currency issue, globally and with respect to the key individual countries that engage in repeated intervention or feel its effects. It shows empirically the strong connection between official foreign exchange intervention and trade imbalances, using new reproducible econometric research. The authors also create a practical definition of currency manipulation, with a relevant objective test of exchange rate policy that the official sector can use for fair assessment (and which the US Treasury has already largely adopted). The book assesses the effects on trading partners of countries that intervene, with a focus on effects on the United States.

The authors argue that currency manipulation accelerated the already rapid technology-driven loss of manufacturing jobs prior to the Great Recession and slowed the economic recovery afterwards. On their estimates, the degree of manipulation-induced dollar overvaluation kept US unemployment higher than it otherwise would have been by roughly a million jobs from 2009 through 2013. To put this impact in perspective, that direct harm came in a US economy of more than 150 million jobs, of which 12.4 million are in manufacturing. That is worth addressing since those manipulation-induced job losses should have been completely avoided, but it was not the primary determinant of US economic outcomes. That said, currency manipulation against the dollar at its height was meaningfully harmful, not least to the support for globalization and trade openness by being visibly unfair. Arguably, China's peak currency manipulation in the years leading up to the 2008 crisis caused much of the currently discussed additional job dislocation in the United States blamed on China. While expanding open and fair trade with China itself inevitably brought some industrial adjustment in the United States, it delivered considerable aggregate income gains. The unfair large-scale currency manipulation pursued by the Chinese government in the early 2000s, however, subtracted from US income and employment with no shared gains and was intentional grabbing of demand rather than the result of market competition. This dynamic underscores why a systemic lasting solution to currency manipulation and conflict is in all countries' long-term interest.

The authors' US focus of analysis and policy recommendations reflects the central role of the dollar, such that interventions and any manipulation primarily target the dollar, and that US policy responses could set rules for or disrupt international trade and currency markets. Starting systemically and analytically, the book develops norms for trade imbalances and recommended limits for currency policies. Importantly, it also explores alternative policies that the key currency-intervening countries could have adopted to achieve sound economic growth and price stability, without reliance on excessive foreign exchange intervention. Smaller open economies must be offered an alternative path to legitimate goals for domestic economic stability if they are to reduce or foreswear currency manipulation. The authors also explore a wide range of potential policy responses in the G-20 and via the International Monetary Fund (IMF) for the United States and other affected countries to undertake to prevent future currency conflict.

Bergsten and Gagnon make innovative proposals for US policies to deter such currency manipulation in future and thereby address constructively one of the more justified congressional concerns about trade liberalization. They propose that the United States take advantage of the current lull in currency intervention to announce a new policy of "countervailing currency intervention," by which the United States would commit to offsetting the effects of future currency manipulation by any G-20 country through equal purchases of that country's currency. The United States should also pursue the adoption of stronger and more objective rules, which the authors propose on currency intervention, both in the IMF and in the context of future trade agreements. The authors argue that a strong and credible policy approach now would help to prevent currency conflicts from heating up again and help to safeguard the global trading system.

The Peterson Institute for International Economics is a private nonpartisan, nonprofit institution for rigorous, intellectually open, and in-depth study and discussion of international economic policy. Its purpose is to identify and analyze important issues to making globalization beneficial and sustainable for the people of the United States and the world, and then to develop and communicate practical new approaches for dealing with them.

The Institute's work is funded by a highly diverse group of philanthropic foundations, private corporations, public institutions, and interested individuals, as well as by income on its capital fund. About 35 percent of the Institute's resources in our latest fiscal year were provided by contributors from outside the United States. This study received generous support from the Smith Richardson Foundation for independent research on this crucial topic. A list of all our financial supporters for the preceding year is posted at http://piie.com/institute/supporters.pdf.

The Executive Committee of the Institute's Board of Directors bears overall responsibility for the Institute's direction, gives general guidance and approval to its research program, and evaluates its performance in pursuit of its mission. The Institute's President is responsible for the identification of topics that are likely to become important over the medium term (one to three years) that should be addressed by Institute scholars. This rolling agenda is set in close consultation with the Institute's research staff, Board of Directors, and other stakeholders.

The President makes the final decision to publish any individual Institute study, following independent internal and external review of the work. Interested readers may access the data and computations underlying the Institute publications for research and replication by searching titles at www.piie.com.

The Institute hopes that its research and other activities will contribute to building a stronger foundation for international economic policy around the world. We invite readers of these publications to let us know how they think we can best accomplish this objective.

ADAM S. POSEN
President
April 2017

Acknowledgments

The authors gratefully acknowledge support for this project from the Smith Richardson Foundation. We received helpful comments and advice from Andrew Baukol, Tamim Bayoumi, Olivier Blanchard, Chad Bown, William Cline, Richard Cooper, Caroline Freund, Morris Goldstein, Gary Hufbauer, Douglas Irwin, Takatoshi Ito, Olivier Jeanne, Karen Johnson, Steve Kamin, Jacob Kirkegaard, Robert Lawrence, Mary Lovely, Rory MacFarquhar, Marcus Noland, Adam Posen, Changyong Rhee, Jeffrey Schott, Brad Setser, Mark Sobel, Ted Truman, Steve Weisman, Yu Yongding, Zhu Min, and Robert Zoellick. Owen Hauck provided capable research assistance. Madona Devasahayam, Barbara Karni, and Susann Luetjen provided thorough and professional editorial and graphical assistance. Jill Villatoro managed the project expertly for the authors.

1

Introduction

Tensions over exchange rates have been a recurrent feature of the world economy for at least 80 years. They helped provoke the disastrous trade wars that intensified the Great Depression of the 1930s. They brought about the collapse of the Bretton Woods system of fixed rates in the early 1970s, ushering in an extended period of financial and economic instability.

The Plaza Accord in 1985 was required to correct the largest currency misalignments in modern history, which spawned intense protectionist pressures in the United States that threatened the global trading system. The capital flows associated with record trade imbalances, caused largely by a decade of currency manipulation after 2000, contributed significantly to housing bubbles in deficit economies, the bursting of which sparked both the Great Recession and the euro crisis. Currency manipulation greatly intensified the "China shock" that has eroded political support for globalization and new trade agreements in the United States and elsewhere, destroying the prospects for realization of the Trans-Pacific Partnership (TPP) and threatening to reverse some of the most important trade liberalization of the past.

Policy responses in each of these episodes have been too little and too late. The international rules and institutions, particularly the International Monetary Fund (IMF) and the World Trade Organization (WTO), have faltered badly. National policies, including in the United States, have not fared much better. Each episode has been exceedingly costly—for the world economy, for the United States, and for the credibility of the global monetary and trading systems.

Currency manipulation went largely into remission in 2014. However, it could resume at any time. Moreover, the political backlash against it and against globalization more broadly, has escalated to levels that are unprecedented in the postwar period. New policies, at both the national and international levels, are essential to deter and remedy future currency conflict.

The Concept of Currency Conflict

Currency conflicts occur when countries seek an advantage in international trade by positioning their currencies at a level lower than justified by fundamental economic forces and market outcomes. They can do so by directly weakening their currencies through excessive (and thus competitive) devaluation of a fixed exchange rate or depreciation of a flexible exchange rate. More subtly, but now more frequently and with similar economic effects, they can block adequate (or any) upward revaluation of a fixed rate or resist market-driven appreciation of a flexible rate, a practice that has come to be called *competitive nonappreciation*. Such "competitive" outcomes are pursued primarily through direct intervention in the foreign exchange markets, which is often labeled "manipulation." It is sometimes argued that quantitative easing and other manifestations of unconventional monetary policy by the Federal Reserve and central banks of other advanced economies also represent "manipulation," but those policies are very different from direct intervention and should not be viewed as similar, as described below.

Currency manipulation improves a country's competitiveness by reducing the prices of its exports and raising the prices of its imports relative to the levels they would reach under market conditions, enabling it to expand exports and substitute domestic production for imports. An increased trade balance increases domestic output and jobs in tradable goods and services sectors. It will create jobs on balance if the economy is not already at full employment and therefore has unused resources that can be activated in those sectors and in others that serve their increased demand.

Countries also seek to run surpluses to build their national reserves (previously gold, now mainly foreign exchange) and to defend themselves against future external shocks. The old doctrine of mercantilism still has adherents, who believe that a nation's economic, political, and military power are enhanced by running large trade surpluses, particularly in manufactured goods and related services.

Exchange rates matter a great deal for countries' trade positions and thus their economies. The IMF (2015c) and Cline (2016) show that every 10 percent move in the trade-weighted average of the dollar prompts a shift of about $300 billion in the US trade balance in the opposite direction (i.e., dollar depreciation of 10 percent leads to a trade balance that is $300 billion stronger, and dollar appreciation of 10 percent produces a trade balance that is weaker by a similar amount). Such changes can move US GDP by as much as 1 to 2 percent, depending on the state of the economy and the macroeconomic policy response. As every $1 billion of trade links to roughly 6,000 jobs, the impact on the economy can be substantial.

From an international perspective, trade and current account *balances* are a zero-sum game—unlike trade and current account *flows*, which are generally a win-win proposition (in the aggregate). Surpluses and deficits across countries must balance out and add to zero (although statistical discrepancies sometimes produce a "global surplus" or "global deficit"). Hence a strengthening of one country's external balance must be mirrored by a weakening in the balance of one or more other countries. For this reason, when competition takes on extreme or unfair characteristics, "competitive devaluations" can produce serious international conflict and even be described as currency wars. The never-ending search for a level playing field among trading nations must therefore encompass currency issues.

There is nothing inherently good or bad about a trade or current account surplus or deficit of modest magnitude, or maintaining an exchange rate that will sustain one, as explained in chapter 2. However, large and persistent deficits can generate two types of unsustainability. First, they can become difficult to finance. Second, they can adversely affect important sectors of domestic production and employment, which in turn can undermine domestic support for open trade and economic policies. Large and persistent surpluses can generate inflationary pressures and, of particular importance, make it more difficult for deficit countries to correct their imbalances. Both types of imbalances distort the allocation of resources in ways that reduce efficiency and welfare over time in both surplus and deficit countries.

High-income countries have traditionally generated high rates of saving and thus tended to export corresponding amounts of capital and run external surpluses. Poor countries have offered good opportunities for investment. They therefore tend to import capital and run current account deficits to help fund their development. There are major exceptions to this pattern, however, notably contemporary China (which runs surpluses) and the United States (which runs deficits). Currency manipulation by China and other countries is an important reason why this anomaly has persisted, with wide-ranging economic and policy repercussions.

Historical Background

Currency conflict plays a central role in the traditional narrative of the 1930s and its lessons for future generations (Eichengreen 1992, Irwin 2011). All the major countries of the period—especially the United Kingdom, the United

States, and France—devalued sequentially and substantially in an effort to extricate themselves from the deep recessions of the day. The devaluations against gold ultimately raised prices worldwide and helped lift the world economy, and the abandonment of overvalued pegs freed monetary policy to stimulate economic expansions. In the early stages, however, countries that remained on fixed gold parities suffered from the devaluations of their neighbors. In response, some raised tariffs, which, along with the recessions, cut world trade by a quarter in three years, offsetting much of the benefit of easier monetary policy and prolonging the Great Depression.

The disastrous impact of competitive devaluation and beggar-thy-neighbor policy was a—probably the—central lesson policymakers gleaned from the interwar years. Prevention of a repetition was thus the cardinal goal of the international economic order that was constructed at Bretton Woods for the postwar period. The Articles of Agreement of the IMF explicitly ban competitive devaluation and currency manipulation. The charter of the General Agreement on Tariffs and Trade (GATT), now the WTO, contains a similar proscription of "exchange practices that frustrate the intent" of the agreement. A central purpose of the entire postwar structure was to avoid renewed resort to currency conflict.

Periodic currency conflict nevertheless recurred throughout the postwar years. As the United States began running overall balance-of-payments deficits in the 1960s, requiring sales of US reserves (mainly gold) despite steady current account surpluses, and the United Kingdom ran chronic deficits, countries with growing surpluses—mainly Germany, some other European countries, and increasingly Japan—resisted revaluing their exchange rates as the adjustment process required, becoming early practitioners of competitive nonappreciation. Largely as a result, the United States concluded that it had to abrogate some of the fundamental rules of the system, by terminating the convertibility of dollars into gold for foreign monetary authorities and imposing an across-the-board import surcharge, to enable it to restore equilibrium by negotiating a devaluation of the dollar. Its actions in essence destroyed the original Bretton Woods system of "fixed" exchange rates.

The major players grudgingly agreed to the initial realignment of parities in 1971, although most of them, especially France and Japan, pushed back hard against the US initiative by intervening to keep their own rates from rising further (Volcker and Gyohten 1993)—what is now called manipulation. The second realignment in 1973, and the shift by most major countries to flexible exchange rates, followed the same pattern. There was much grumbling about a "third devaluation of the dollar" after fixed parities were finally abandoned.

The widespread adoption of floating exchange rates by the major industrial countries in the 1970s was partly intended, and presumed by many, to preclude future competitive currency behavior by governments by turning the determination of exchange rates over to markets. But markets make major mistakes, too, as they did when they pushed the dollar to absurdly overvalued levels in the middle 1980s, inviting governments to resume their intervention. Moreover, in practice no government was willing to permanently absent itself from influencing a price that was so important for its economy. The United States, one of the most vocal proponents of "letting the market decide," intervened heavily to shore up a plummeting dollar in 1978–79, to drive down a hugely overvalued dollar in 1985, and to stabilize the dollar when it dropped too rapidly in 1987. In the late 1970s, the Europeans, unhappy over the frequent downward swings of the dollar and related rises in their own currencies, began the movement toward a common internal currency that eventually produced the euro two decades later.

Three chronic problems soon reemerged, keeping alive both the risk and periodically the reality of currency conflict. One was the revealed reluctance of deficit countries to reduce their imbalances by depressing their domestic economies. This tendency was particularly strong in the United States, a large and relatively closed economy in which, because of occasional overheating and the generation of fiscal deficits, such correction would sometimes have been desirable on domestic as well as international grounds. The result was that the United States relied on currency depreciation to achieve adjustment when it became necessary, either because foreign financing threatened to dry up or, more frequently, in response to domestic political reactions. The ensuing outbreaks of protectionism placed its liberal trade policy and thus the global trading system at risk.

The second problem was the revealed reluctance of surplus countries to undertake any substantial initiatives, including currency appreciation, to correct their imbalances. Deficits, of course, cannot be corrected without parallel reductions of the corresponding surpluses, so surpluses cannot escape the adjustment process. But the locus of the adjustment measures makes a big difference in both economic and political terms. The persistent competitive nonappreciation by surplus countries forced most or all of the adjustment initiative on deficit countries, which often had to restrain their growth (despite their own preferences) and impart a deflationary bias to the world economy.

The United States was able to resist this pressure more easily than other deficit countries because the dominant international role of the dollar channeled capital to the United States and helped finance its deficits. The domestic protectionist pressures triggered by the industrial decline associated with those deficits, however, could demonstrably become an even greater effective constraint. When it did, the desire of the United States to adjust by weakening the dollar clashed directly with the desire of the surplus countries to avoid strengthening their currencies.

This fundamental asymmetry of the adjustment process became the most glaring shortcoming of the global monetary system. It magnified the importance of the third chronic problem facing the system: the inability of the IMF to promote timely and sustainable correction of international imbalances. The IMF was not very effective during the postwar period of "fixed" exchange rates (really, adjustable pegs) either, but it did then have a clearly defined and authorized role. Once floating began, despite the adoption of amendments to its Articles of Agreement and some elaboration of its operating procedures, the Fund became largely a bystander in managing the nonsystem, as it came widely to be called.

Any cooperation that occurred was worked out mainly informally by the G-5 (for the Plaza and Louvre Accords in the 1980s) and by the G-7 (for the Asian and related crises in the 1990s). These groups have been vigilant, and largely successful, in trying to prevent competitive depreciations.

The largest currency misalignment of this period was by far the massive dollar overvaluation of the 1980s, which was driven by market forces (including rampant speculation) rather than manipulation by officials in surplus countries. It was resolved through cooperative intervention without any charges of currency warfare when the major countries realized that the most likely alternative was an outbreak of trade protection in the United States that would threaten the entire global trade regime (Bergsten and Green 2016).

The "Gs" were less effective in fending off competitive nonappreciations, especially with respect to one of the two chronic surplus countries of the period: Japan. Although its exchange rate did fluctuate widely, and it played by far the largest role in carrying out the Plaza Accord, Japan intervened periodically in the currency markets to keep the yen undervalued, cumulating more than $300 billion in foreign exchange by 2000 as a result of this activity. The other main surplus country, Germany, did not pile up nearly as high a level of reserves and even ran deficits for a while. But it achieved the equivalent of competitive nonappreciation by subsuming its exchange rate in the euro area and enjoying the weakness of that currency (relative to an independent Deutsche mark) caused by the poor economic performance of other members of the currency union.

While all this was going on at the international level, most members of the European Union—the world's largest economic area—were moving toward creating a currency union. Their chief goal was to avoid changes in exchange rates that would disrupt the level playing field they were developing internally with free trade and eventually the single market—that is, to prevent currency conflict within the union. The idea was almost as old as the original Common Market itself, with the concept for monetary integration dating back to the Werner Plan in 1970. The move intensified after the abandonment of the pegged exchange rates of Bretton Woods in the 1970s and especially the repeated depreciations of the dollar, which created fluctuations among European currencies and generated upward pressure on all of them. The initial European Monetary System, a regime of small and frequent changes in parities, commenced in 1979.

Germany, as the traditional surplus country and paymaster of Europe, played the central role in these developments. It was probably modestly overvalued within the euro at its outset and, partly as a result, paradoxically became the sick man of Europe in the early 2000s. It adopted a strategy of wage suppression and labor market reforms that produced a sizable "internal devaluation" thereafter and, by sharply undermining the competitiveness of its EU partners, sowed the seeds for the later euro crises. At the same time, the weakness of the common currency in global markets—as a result of the weakness of many member countries—enabled Germany to achieve and maintain the world's largest current account surplus without experiencing the subsequent currency appreciation that in pre-euro days had always forced it to accept at least some adjustment (Bergsten 2016). As a member of the euro area, Germany was thus able to benefit from depreciation, or at least nonappreciation, that stemmed from its membership in a currency union that added a subtle but very important new dimension to the problem of currency conflict.

Recent Developments: Renewal of Currency Conflict

Over the past two decades, four major developments have restored the centrality of the currency conflict issue.

Asian Financial Crisis of 1997–98

The Asian financial crisis led virtually every Asian country and some countries in other parts of the world, whether or not they were victims of that crisis, to resolve to build their foreign exchange reserves to far higher levels to shield themselves from any repetition of such an event. They sought to buttress their defenses against future market pressures, which could demonstrably derail even such major economies as Korea and Indonesia, and to their again becoming beholden to the strictures of the IMF, which they detested.

The result was that virtually all Asian countries sought to run very large current account surpluses for a decade or more. They succeeded spectacularly: China's reserves (including its sovereign wealth fund) eventually peaked at more than $4 trillion, and a number of much smaller economies, including Hong Kong, Singapore, Korea, and Taiwan, amassed war chests of several hundred billion dollars each. These surpluses were triggered in large part through currency nonappreciation, engineered largely through manipulation, as demonstrated in chapter 4. International imbalances escalated sharply as a result, with the US current account deficit rising to a record $800 billion (6 percent of GDP) in 2006.

The pursuit of adequate precautionary balances is understandable in a world of high capital mobility and volatile markets. The reserve buildups and consequent current account surpluses during this period climbed much too far, however, producing reserves that were greater than needed to meet even the most extreme possible circumstances. They created global imbalances that contributed to the onset of the financial crisis and Great Recession in 2007–08 and undermined support for open trade and globalization more generally. Currency conflicts had again become a major phenomenon.

Chinese Currency Intervention

The second important development, which overlapped but went far beyond the first, was the enormous and highly contentious intervention by China to keep its currency from rising at all before 2005 and during 2008–10 and by much less than it should have when the authorities were allowing it to appreciate gradually. By the beginning of the new century, China had adopted a development model that relied heavily on integration with the world economy and rapid export growth. This strategy included extremely healthy aspects, such as China's aggressive use of the rules of the WTO to promote controversial reforms at home. But it also produced steady and substantial rises in China's external surplus, which reached an astonishing peak of almost 10 percent of its GDP in 2007.

China's export surge generated enormous pressure on the economies of the United States and other deficit countries, especially on their low-skilled workers and their communities (Autor, Dorn, and Hanson 2016). These pressures from the "China shock" became a major factor in the narrative that undermined support for globalization (especially trade agreements) in the United States and some other countries and may have had a decisive impact on the 2016 US presidential election (Autor et al. 2017).[1]

---

1. Support for leaving the European Union was much stronger in localities in the United Kingdom where industries faced greater competition from Chinese imports (I. Colantone and P. Stanig, "Brexit: Data Shows that Globalization Malaise, and Not Immigration,

The huge buildup of Chinese foreign exchange reserves that resulted from its currency manipulation also produced large flows of capital into the United States that contributed to the easy financial conditions there in the mid-2000s that facilitated the housing bubble and ultimately brought on the financial crisis and Great Recession, as discussed in chapter 4.

China achieved its entire external surplus throughout the "decade of manipulation" through its massive and sustained intervention in the currency markets. It pegged the renminbi to the dollar in 1994 and rode the dollar's appreciation upward until 2002, including by maintaining its peg unchanged through the Asian crisis, then rode the depreciating dollar down substantially against all currencies when its superior productivity growth suggested that the renminbi should have instead been appreciating by several percentage points per year (what Bhalla 2012 calls "standing-still depreciation"). Its intervention averaged more than $1 billion per day for several years—almost $2 billion per business day at its peak—keeping the renminbi from rising against the dollar and other currencies despite the soaring current account surplus and sizable inflow of direct investment capital. The United States (especially Congress) and some others complained loudly and increasingly frequently, as described in chapter 5. China let the renminbi rise gradually from 2005 until the outbreak of the Great Recession in 2008 and again from 2010, but its dramatic surpluses and reserve accumulation, driven by its currency manipulation and the inability of the IMF and the United States to do much about it, brought the issue of currency conflict back onto the front burner.

China was by far the most important currency manipulator, but it was hardly the only one. Half a dozen other Asian economies conducted similar policies, significantly contributing to the impact of the group as a whole on global imbalances. A number of oil exporters and a few other countries—notably Switzerland, which became the largest manipulator in 2012—were active as well. Manipulation became a wide-ranging systemic problem of consequential magnitude that revealed the failure of the international rules and institutions to offer an effective response.

China eventually let the renminbi rise substantially, by more than 50 percent on a real trade-weighted basis and about 35 percent against the dollar, to its recent peak in 2015. Largely as a result, its current account surplus dropped to less than 3 percent of GDP in 2015-16. Market pressures on the renminbi reversed course in 2015-16, and China intervened heavily to limit its depreciation, selling more than $500 billion of its reserves, thus helping rather than hurting the competitiveness of the United

Determined the Vote," *Bocconi Knowledge*, July 12, 2016, www.knowledge.unibocconi.eu/notizia.php?idArt=17195).

States and other deficit countries. But its manipulation throughout the previous decade severely distorted world trade, transferred large amounts of production and employment away from deficit countries, left lasting effects on national competitive positions, and triggered strong antiglobalization politics in some of the advanced economies that continue long after the manipulation itself ceased. The episodes revealed once again the weaknesses of the international monetary system and the instabilities that result.

The surpluses of the oil exporters have dropped as well, as a result of the sharp fall in the price of oil. But surpluses of many other manipulators have remained large or risen further, despite a sharp drop in currency intervention. Private financial flows have boosted the exchange rate of the dollar and allowed former manipulators to maintain their surpluses without intervening. The problem of manipulation has thus become less compelling for the moment—though the problem of imbalances is likely to grow and the domestic backlash in the United States against past manipulation, if anything, has intensified.

Unconventional Monetary Policies

A third, and potentially powerful, source of currency conflict was initiated with the adoption by the United States and United Kingdom, and subsequently by the euro area and Japan, of unconventional monetary policies, especially quantitative easing, in response to the Great Recession. It was, in fact, the upward pressure on Brazil's currency, driven primarily by quantitative easing in the United States, that led its finance minister, Guido Mantega, to inject the term *currency wars* into the contemporary lexicon in 2010 (see Prasad 2014 for a useful review of the history surrounding these events). Some observers have viewed these developments as presaging a new phenomenon of "monetary policy wars" (Taylor 2016).

A number of European political as well as financial leaders expressed considerable unhappiness when the Federal Reserve launched its extensive quantitative easing program, which pushed the dollar down in 2008–09, despite the likely benefits to their own economies from faster US economic growth. Japan engineered a sharp depreciation of the yen with the aggressive quantitative easing mandated by the new Abe government in early 2013. The depreciation was exacerbated by the "oral intervention" with which it anticipated that policy shift around the time of the election in late 2012 (which led the G-7 at its meeting in February 2013 to welcome the quantitative easing but criticize the oral intervention and insist that Japan recommit to avoiding manipulation and competitive depreciation).

The central banks have not exacerbated the currency conflict in any substantial way. Their governments continue to respect their independence, but their ventures into the largely uncharted waters of unconventional monetary policies raise the prospect of another possible source of currency conflict. China, with support from Brazil and other emerging-market economies, has threatened to insist on including unconventional monetary policies in any new international process to assess the effects of, and consider sanctions against, currency manipulation. Though the threat is based on faulty analysis, as described in chapter 2, and thus unlikely to lead to restrictions on unconventional monetary policies, US officials cited the fear of future constraints on Federal Reserve policy in justifying their unwillingness to push for new international currency disciplines in, for example, the negotiations over the TPP (some members of Congress also cited these concerns in resisting the efforts of their colleagues to require the administration to seek such disciplines).

Frustration with US Failure to Curtail Currency Manipulation

The fourth key element in renewing the currency debate—and the main driver for new policy action as this book was being completed in early 2017—was the sharp increase in dissatisfaction in the US Congress and the US body politic with the unwillingness of the administrations of George W. Bush and Barack Obama to adopt more effective responses to manipulation, mainly by China and to a lesser extent by Japan and Korea. Dollar over-valuation and the resulting trade deficits have always been major drivers of protectionism in the United States; the risk that such sentiments would prevail motivated the aggressive strategies to weaken the exchange rate in 1971 and especially 1985. In the current period, when the main thrust has been to oppose new trade agreements and perhaps also to roll back previous liberalization, members of both houses and both parties promoted legislation to deal with currency manipulation throughout and indeed well beyond the "decade of manipulation."

These initiatives reached partial fruition in 2015 and 2016, when Congress adopted two important pieces of legislation that President Obama signed. The first, the Trade Promotion Authority bill, instructed US negotiators of the TPP and future free trade agreements (FTAs) to seek to ensure that partner countries avoid currency manipulation. In response, the Obama administration, for the first time with respect to any trade agreement, negotiated a side agreement to the TPP on the currency issue. That agreement recommitted all TPP members to avoid manipulation and added new disclosure requirements on intervention and related policies for some of them.

The second new law, the Trade Facilitation and Trade Enforcement Act of 2015, established new requirements for the implementation of US currency policy by future administrations based on clear criteria defining "manipulation" and timelines for responding to it (as described in chapters 4 and 5). The Treasury Department subsequently published its interpretation of the new criteria as a guide to its future policies.

Congress has proposed tougher measures, such as the import surcharge that was prominent in the initial debate on currency manipulation in 2005–07 but dropped thereafter because of its clear violation of US obligations under the WTO. All of the various proposals could be characterized as defensive reactions by the world's largest deficit country to manipulation by China and others. However, the rest of the world could well have viewed adoption of any forceful step by the United States as an escalation of, rather than a legitimate response to, currency conflict, because the US economy was doing relatively well and the dollar remains the world's key currency. Containment of congressional pressure for such steps by the Obama administration prevented a possible ratcheting up of that conflict.

These pressures broadened considerably with the political campaigns of 2016. For the first time in recent US history, trade became a central element in the presidential battle and some congressional contests. Both major presidential candidates, and several of the contenders for each party's nomination, explicitly opposed the TPP (Donald Trump also called for renegotiation of the North American Free Trade Agreement [NAFTA] and the United States-Korea Free Trade Agreement [KORUS]). So did key senatorial candidates, such as Republican Rob Portman of Ohio, a former US Trade Representative who supported the Trade Promotion Authority bill in 2015 but felt compelled to oppose the TPP in 2016 in order to hold his seat. All of these candidates cited the currency issue as an important reason for their skepticism and pledged to address it if elected, with Trump indicating repeatedly that he would "name China as a manipulator on his first day in office" (despite the total reversal in China's intervention policy, as described above, which presumably persuaded him not to fulfill that pledge).

The issue thus became much more politicized in the United States than ever before. Despite the recent remission in manipulation, it will play a major role when the administration and Congress address trade and globalization policy more broadly. President Trump has expressed far greater concern over manipulation than any of his predecessors, publicly indicating an intention to address the issue forcefully. Of all the issues critics of FTAs have cited, none has been mentioned more often than currency manipulation.

Any effort to revisit the TPP, or pursue new bilateral agreements with countries such as Japan or the United Kingdom (post-Brexit), could well seek to include "enforceable currency disciplines." During the campaign, both presidential candidates expressed their dissatisfaction with the absence of such disciplines. Many members of Congress have done so as well and could condition their support for any future agreements on their inclusion. The administration and Congress might also adopt new unilateral US policies, such as countervailing duties and countervailing currency intervention, through which the United States would buy offsetting amounts of the currencies of manipulators to neutralize their impact on exchange rates, described in chapters 5 and 6, to deter and deal more forcefully with currency manipulation. Depending on the nature of those measures and how they are implemented, such action could mark either a sharp escalation of the international currency conflict or a constructive new approach to reduce such conflict in the future.

This book focuses mainly on "currency conflict" and the economic distortions and policy problems that can result from government intervention in currency markets. It also pays some attention to the even broader misalignments of exchange rates and international imbalances, often driven by market forces such as changes in interest rates and underlying economic fundamentals, about which both authors have written extensively (see, for example, Bergsten 1996 and Gagnon 2011). After the "decade of manipulation," during which official intervention played a major role in many of the currency markets, such market-driven movements returned to primacy in 2015–16. Governmental intervention declined sharply, reflecting at least a temporary remission in manipulation and a return of currency misalignments and trade imbalances stemming from the more traditional movers of markets.

Since 2011, and especially in late 2014 and early 2015, the exchange rate of the dollar rose substantially for market-related reasons. Though not booming, the United States has been growing considerably more rapidly than Europe and Japan, the issuers of the other key currencies. The Federal Reserve stopped easing US monetary policy—and indeed began to tighten modestly—in late 2015 and again in late 2016, while the European Central Bank and the Bank of Japan were continuing to expand their quantitative easing programs. China's slowdown and renewed capital flight pushed the dollar up against the renminbi. Safe-haven money periodically flowed into the dollar, still the world's dominant currency, around events such as the Chinese mini-devaluation in August 2015 and the Brexit vote in June 2016.

As a result of this market-driven appreciation, as of early 2017 the dollar was overvalued by 10 percent (Cline 2016) to 20 percent (Bergsten 2016), depending upon whether one wants simply to restrain the US current account balance deficit within 3 percent of GDP or to eliminate it entirely. The overvaluation may push the deficit back toward 5 percent of GDP over the next few years, moving it toward $1 trillion. These growing misalignments and imbalances have been subtracting about 0.4 percent per year from real US growth, beginning in 2015 and running at least through 2017 (Stockton 2016).

These developments will increase concern, in Congress and elsewhere, about the impact of exchange rates and the trade imbalance on the economy, including via any new trade agreements that might be considered. It was just such market developments in the first half of the 1980s, and the demonstrable risks of congressional reaction via restrictive trade policies, that drove the Reagan administration to abandon its "benign neglect" of the dollar and initiate the Plaza Accord, which pushed the trade-weighted dollar down by 30 percent over the following 18 months. Donald Trump expressed considerable concern about the trade deficit throughout his campaign. Especially as his projected fiscal (and possibly tax and trade) policy could lead to further dollar appreciation, he may need to address the exchange rate himself.

It is remarkable that Congress paid scant attention to the dollar's rise during its debate on TPA in early 2015, just when the sharpest rise was taking place, a response that lies in stark contrast to its very intense focus on the issue in 1984–85. Congress instead focused exclusively on manipulation as an unfair trade practice. It is, of course, possible that the two issues will become conflated in the future, intensifying the likelihood that the United States will adopt new policies in response. With or without this "new" element, it is clear that US domestic politics have embraced the issue of unfair trading practices in general, and currency manipulation in particular, as never before and will push hard for more forceful national policies to address it.

Plan of the Book

This book analyzes the components of currency conflict. It places them in the context of both the global economy and the domestic scene in the United States and proposes new policy measures—at both the national and international levels—that would supplement the international monetary system created at Bretton Woods by effectively deterring and, when necessary, countering manipulation. The plan of the book is as follows.

Chapter 2 provides the basic economics of the issue. It defines trade and current account positions, identifies their immediate and underlying determinants, and traces their interactions with exchange rates. It links macroeconomic policies, especially monetary policies and official financial flows (notably currency intervention), to exchange rates and current accounts and demonstrates that reserve buildups in a number of countries, obtained through currency manipulation, have been key drivers of current account surpluses.

Chapter 3 addresses important normative questions, including current account targets for individual countries and their international compatibility. It documents a fundamental asymmetry of international financial markets, which limit the ability of countries to run up large negative net international investment positions but place no comparable restrictions on large positive net positions. The chapter relates these considerations to currency policies, suggesting where intervention is internationally justified and where it is not.

Chapter 4 describes the "decade of manipulation" (2003–13). It identifies the countries that intervened excessively (i.e., manipulated) and quantifies the size and economic impact of intervention on both the manipulators and, especially, the United States and their main trading partners. It derives new norms that might be adopted in fashioning future rules or understandings governing buildups of foreign exchange reserves and intervention policy, along with alternative policies that would permit past manipulators (especially China and Japan) to achieve their legitimate national goals without creating problems for other countries and the global monetary system.

Manipulation has been largely in remission since 2014. (The primary exceptions are certain financial centers, such as Switzerland and Singapore, for which we propose alternative policies going forward.) But other developments of acute relevance, including the congressional and broader US political debate over currency policy, are clearly not in remission. Chapter 4 examines the recent increases in market-driven exchange rates and current account imbalances, which are not caused by manipulation but raise related questions that may become relevant for currency policy.

Chapter 5 lays out the policy options for addressing the several aspects of the currency problem. It distinguishes between macroeconomic/monetary and trade policy possibilities and contrasts multilateral, plurilateral, and unilateral approaches. It provides detailed analyses of a wide range of specific measures, ranging from the "private diplomacy" of recent US policy through efforts to mobilize international rules and institutions (the IMF and WTO) and perhaps negotiate the inclusion of "enforceable currency disciplines" in trade agreements. It considers the use of fiscal and monetary policy, countervailing currency intervention, reforms of the international monetary system to encourage stabilizing intervention in the foreign exchange markets, the deployment of new capital controls to deter investments in the dollar that push its exchange rate up, and specific trade policy measures, such as countervailing duties and import surcharges.

Chapter 6 summarizes the analytical findings and offers policy recommendations. It concludes that manipulation is the main element of the currency conflict issue that needs policy attention, both to protect affected countries and to fill the most important gap in the international monetary and trading systems. The absence of effective policies to address manipulation raises the prospect that the resulting large external deficits in the United States and perhaps other countries, and the application of such illegitimate and unfair policies by major trading countries, may become unsustainable for domestic political reasons and lead to renewed outbreaks of widespread protectionism (or at least an unwillingness to adopt new trade agreements or expand globalization).

The most promising policy alternative is an announcement by the United States, ideally supported by others, that it will henceforth apply countervailing currency intervention against any G-20 countries that meet a clear set of objective criteria (excess reserves, excessive current account surpluses, excessive intervention in the currency markets) to determine "manipulation." This policy could be carried out under current legislation, although it would be desirable for Congress to authorize it explicitly, as the Senate did in a currency bill it passed in 2011, and provide adequate resources (carrying no budgetary costs) in order to make it fully credible. This proposal focuses on the world's most important economies. It builds on a commitment to which they have already agreed in numerous G-20 statements. As of early 2017, no G-20 country met these criteria, so there would be no immediate "indictments" under the new policy. If backed by sufficient resources to be fully credible, countervailing currency intervention should deter and indeed end the practice of currency manipulation (and thus never have to be used), indefinitely extending the current remission of that practice.

To help multilateralize the new policy, IMF policies should encourage intervention by surplus countries to strengthen their currencies. Taking major manipulators to the WTO and including currency disciplines in future US trade agreements could supplement countervailing currency intervention. Monetary policy, fiscal policy, and more sweeping trade policies, such as import surcharges, should not be deployed for these purposes. Indeed, doing so could intensify rather than curtail the currency conflict. It is highly likely, however, that unilateral steps by the United States will be necessary to start correcting this major gap in global monetary arrangements and in the economic policy arsenal of the United States itself. The United States should begin taking them as soon as possible.

2

Key Conceptual Issues

This chapter describes the forces that move the trade balance in the short run and the long run. At the broadest level, a country's trade balance reflects the difference between saving and investment within its borders.[1] Countries with excess saving have trade surpluses; countries with excess investment (in housing, factories, and infrastructure) have trade deficits. Macroeconomic and financial policies, including exchange rate policy, have important effects on saving and investment and thus on the overall trade balance.

Currency intervention was an important—probably the most important—driver of the record global trade imbalances in the first decade of the 21st century. Other important fundamental influences included business cycles, fiscal policy, demographics, and trend growth rates. In addition, excesses in private financial flows that are not well explained by fundamental influences have often led to large swings in exchange rates and unsustainable imbalances in trade. Because one country's trade surplus must be associated with trade deficits elsewhere, one country's policies or financial excesses have important effects on other countries.

---

1. Saving is defined as income that is not consumed immediately. Investment includes purchases of productive equipment and structures plus housing construction. For the world as a whole, saving equals investment.

The Trade Balance and the Current Account Balance

In this book we use the terms *trade balance* and *current account balance* almost interchangeably. For most countries, including the United States, the two concepts amount to almost the same thing.

The trade balance is defined as exports of goods and services minus imports of goods and services.[2] Economic growth is typically measured as growth in the production of goods and services, also known as gross domestic product (GDP). In the economic accounts, GDP is measured as total domestic spending plus exports minus imports. Imports subtract from GDP because they are produced outside a country's borders; an increase in "net exports of goods and services" adds to GDP growth and a decline in them reduces GDP growth. GDP, in turn, is a key driver of employment. Sizable and prolonged weakening of the trade balance can have a sufficiently negative effect on production and employment for a time to threaten the domestic political sustainability of a country's international economic policies.

The current account balance is the trade balance plus the balance in other transactions that reflect income paid to, or received from, the rest of the world. It is what matters for the financial sustainability of a country's international economic position, because its cumulation over time determines whether a country is a net creditor or a net debtor to the rest of the world.

Trade is by far the largest component of the current account for most countries. Movements in the current account balance are closely correlated with movements in the trade balance. Policies that affect the current account work largely through their effect on trade.

Definitions

The current account is the net balance between all income received from foreigners and all payments made to foreigners. Income or payments may arise from trade (in goods or services), returns on existing investments (dividends and interest), wages earned in a foreign country, or unilateral transfers (charity or remittances to family members).

The other main category of international transactions is the financial account, which includes all purchases and sales of real or financial assets. It includes direct investment by multinational corporations, portfolio in-

---

2. The goods, or merchandise, trade balance used to receive more attention than the overall trade balance, in part because it was reported earlier and because services were considerably less important than they are now. The US Census Bureau now releases monthly data on trade in goods and services at the same time.

vestment by individuals and financial institutions, and the extension and repayment of loans.

A surplus in the current account means that domestic residents are receiving more income from foreigners than they are paying to foreigners. A country with a current account surplus is acquiring financial assets in the rest of the world; it has a net financial outflow. In accounting terms, a net financial outflow is a surplus in the financial account.[3]

In principle, the current account must equal the financial account. In practice, some transactions are not reported or are misreported. A category called "errors and omissions" is created to ensure that the accounts balance.

What Moves the Current Account?

Models of the current account are typically based on its trade components: exports and imports of goods and services. In the standard model of trade, known as the elasticities model, imports respond to the exchange rate and domestic economic activity (GDP) (Armington 1969). Exports respond to the exchange rate and foreign GDP.

A simple model of the current account is given by

$$CA = a - bRER + cGDP^* - dGDP + U$$

where CA denotes the current account; RER denotes the real (inflation-adjusted) exchange rate; GDP^* denotes foreign GDP; U denotes a residual that allows for other factors that affect the current account; and lowercase letters denote model parameters (or elasticities). All of the parameters are positive. An exchange rate appreciation tends to reduce the current account, because it makes domestic goods more expensive to foreigners and foreign goods cheaper for domestic residents. Higher foreign GDP increases the current account, because it increases the buying power of foreign consumers and thus boosts exports. Higher domestic GDP reduces the current account, because it increases the buying power of domestic consumers and thus boosts imports.[4]

The business cycle has an important effect on the current account. A burst of spending (public or private) that pushes up domestic GDP tends

---

3. In some presentations of the accounts, a financial outflow is negative and the current account and financial account sum to zero. We prefer to present outflows as positive, because it makes the exposition of the relationship between net official flows and current account balances simpler.

4. A more detailed model would differentiate between trend and cycle in GDP. These effects are strongest for cyclical deviations in GDP from trend. The effects of trend GDP are smaller and may depend on other factors, such as the creation of new product varieties (Krugman 1989, Gagnon 2007).

to reduce the current account, and a burst of foreign GDP growth tends to increase the current account. In addition to these direct effects, business cycles may have indirect effects through the exchange rate. A country experiencing a boom typically will have an appreciating exchange rate, which will further depress its current account. However, as shown below, it is possible that the boom may be associated with a currency depreciation, in which case there are opposing influences on the current account and the net effect could go either way.

The other, nontrade, components of the current account tend to be more stable than trade flows, but to some extent they are also affected by the same factors in our simple model. For example, exchange rate appreciation increases the value of domestic payments to foreign workers and investors relative to foreign payments to domestic workers and investors, which pushes down the current account.[5] These effects on net foreign income operate both directly and indirectly through multinational corporations, whose foreign profits denominated in the domestic currency decline when the domestic currency appreciates relative to foreign currencies. Similarly, exchange rate appreciation increases the value of unilateral transfers to foreigners relative to the value of foreign transfers to domestic residents, pushing down the current account. Higher domestic GDP tends to boost profit payments to foreign owners of domestic capital and unilateral transfers to foreigners, both of which push down the current account.

For simplicity, the model does not include a time dimension. In reality, there is a lag in the response of the current account to these factors, especially the exchange rate. Most studies find that it takes up to two years for most of the effects of a change in the exchange rate to show up in the current account, and some effects take even longer (Goldstein and Khan 1985, Cline 2005). There are three time lags: from the change in the exchange rate to the change in the product price, from the change in the price to the change in orders for the product, and from the change in orders to the change in actual shipments (and entry into the trade data). Different types of goods and services are affected at different speeds, based on whether they are routine or infrequent purchases and how long it takes both domestic and foreign producers to adapt their operations to the new relative prices. For example, a stronger dollar may make it profitable for a foreign producer to sell in the United States for the first time, but building the capacity to produce extra products for export takes time, especially if the product needs design changes to suit the US market.

---

5. This effect is reduced in the case of countries that borrow in foreign currencies.

Box 2.1   A stylized model of the macroeconomy

Current account	$CA = a1 - a2\ RER + a3\ GDP^* - a4\ GDP + U1$
Financial flows	$FF = NPF + NOF$
Net private flows	$NPF = b1 + b2\ RER + b3\ (IR^*-IR) + U2$
Consumption	$C = c1 + c2\ GDP + U3$
Investment	$I = d1 - d2\ IR + U4$
GDP identity	$GDP = C + I + G + CA$
BOP (balance of payments) identity	$CA = FF$
Saving	$S = GDP - C - G$
GDP identity implies	$S - I = CA$

Endogenous variables: CA (current account), FF (financial flows), NPF (net private flows), C (consumption), I (investment), GDP (output or income), RER (real exchange rate), S (saving).

Policy variables: IR (interest rate), G (government spending), NOF (net official flows).

Exogenous variables: GDP^*, IR^* (foreign); $U1$, $U2$, $U3$, $U4$ (shocks) ($U1–U4$ are random shocks and economic forces outside of the model; they are not to be confused with the different measures of the US unemployment rate, sometimes referred to as $U1–U6$).

Parameters: a1, a2, a3, a4, b1, b2, b3, c1, c2, d1, d2.

Endogenous Interaction between the Exchange Rate and GDP

The simple elasticities model explains how exchange rates and GDP play key roles in determining the current account balance. However, the model reflects only part of the workings of the economy. In a broader model of the overall economy, the current account has important effects on the exchange rate and GDP.

Box 2.1 displays a stylized macroeconomic model that includes our simple elasticities model of the current account as well as feedback from the current account onto exchange rates and GDP. An important addition is international financial flows, which also influence the exchange rate. The current account equation is the simple elasticities model discussed above. The second equation is net international financial flows. Net financial flows reflect the balance between domestic acquisitions of foreign assets and foreign acquisitions of domestic assets. Acquisitions include outright purchases as well as reinvested interest and dividend payments. A net financial outflow occurs when domestic acquisitions of foreign assets exceed foreign acquisitions of domestic assets; in this case financial flows are positive. A net financial inflow occurs when foreign acquisitions of domestic assets exceed domestic acquisitions of foreign assets; in this case financial flows are negative. Financial flows include both net private flows and net official flows.

An increase in the exchange rate makes foreign assets more attractive relative to domestic assets and thus raises net private flows, both because foreign assets become cheaper in terms of domestic currency and the likelihood of a future decline in the exchange rate (which would raise the future returns on foreign assets relative to domestic assets) increases.[6] A higher foreign interest rate (IR^*) also raises net private flows, because it raises the return on foreign assets. A higher domestic interest rate (IR) lowers net private flows, because it raises the return on domestic assets. (For simplicity, we assume that inflation is stable over time and equal at home and abroad.)

Net official flows are another direct component of financial flows. They are the net acquisition of foreign currency assets minus the net incurrence of foreign currency liabilities by a country's official, or public, sector.[7] The main type of net official flows for most countries is foreign exchange intervention. The second most common type of net official flows derives from sovereign wealth funds, which have grown enormously in recent years. Some public pension funds also invest in foreign assets. Foreign currency borrowing by governments is a negative form of net official flows that used to be fairly important for developing economies but has declined over time.

Consumption responds positively to GDP, and investment responds negatively to the domestic interest rate. We could have included an interest rate effect on consumption and a GDP effect on investment, but doing so would have increased the complexity of the model without changing any of its fundamental properties.

The model in box 2.1 is more complex than the simple elasticities model of the current account, but it still omits many underlying factors behind current account balances. These factors ultimately influence the current account through their effects on GDP, IR, and the shocks U1–U4. For example, demographic factors such as population aging affect desired saving and can thus be viewed as operating through the shock to consumption (U3). A country's long-run potential growth rate affects GDP directly,

---

6. In a more general model, financial flows would depend on the expected change in the exchange rate. However, if the shocks and policies in this model are assumed to be temporary, no explicit future term on the exchange rate is necessary, because it will return to steady state and thus be incorporated into the constant (b1).

7. Unlike the sum of current accounts or net financial flows across countries, net official flows do not necessarily sum to zero across countries, because net official flows are defined only with respect to the public sector of the country in question. Thus Chinese official purchases of US assets (both public and private) give rise to positive net official flows for China but negative net private flows for the United States. Chinese purchases of US Treasury securities are not an official flow for the United States, because they are denominated in US dollars.

but it also affects desired investment and thus may also operate through the shock to investment ($U4$). Fiscal policy may operate directly through government spending, but it may also operate through tax rates, which are not in the model and can be thought of as influencing the shock to consumption ($U3$). Monetary policy operates through the interest rate. Trade policies, such as tariffs and nontariff barriers, may affect the shock to the current account ($U1$) or the parameters in the current account equation (a1–a4). Policies that restrict financial flows (capital controls) may affect the shock and parameters of the net private flows equation, $U2$ and b1–b3. A key property of the model is that the real exchange rate is free to adjust as needed to maintain equality between the current account and net financial flows.[8]

The model is completed with two accounting identities. The *GDP* identity is that total spending equals total production. The balance-of-payments identity is that the current account is financed by net financial flows. A current account surplus implies a surplus in net financial flows, which in turn implies rising net claims on foreigners (i.e., a growing net creditor position with respect to the rest of the world). A current account deficit implies falling net claims on foreigners (rising net foreign claims on domestic residents). Current account deficits thus lead to a growing net debtor position.

A country's current account balance equals the excess (or deficiency) of its saving net of investment. Saving is production minus private and public consumption. The *GDP* identity can be rearranged to show that saving minus investment equals the current account.

The only way that domestic residents can acquire more claims on foreigners than foreigners acquire on domestic residents is for the country to run a current account surplus. Conversely, if the total domestic assets foreigners want to buy exceed the total foreign assets domestic residents want to buy, the country must run a current account deficit. Ultimately, the exchange rate is the price that clears the market and keeps the current account equal to net financial flows. Although the current account is by definition equal to net acquisition of foreign assets, the net value of foreign assets can change without any current account surplus or deficit owing to changes in market prices, including in the exchange rate for assets denominated in foreign currency. Thus a country's net international investment position changes from year to year in response to both the current account, which reflects the net flows of asset acquisition, and any valuation changes in the existing stocks of assets and liabilities.

---

8. Indeed, the volatility of the exchange rate is evident in economies with a flexible exchange rate. For economies with a fixed exchange rate, other variables, such as GDP and prices, have to do more of the adjustment. GDP and prices typically are more volatile when exchange rates are fixed (Gagnon 2011).

When domestic residents want to buy more foreign assets, they bid up the values of foreign currencies (depreciate the exchange rate), which encourages exports and discourages imports, thus creating a current account surplus.[9] Conversely, when foreigners want to buy more domestic assets, they bid up the value of the domestic currency (appreciate the exchange rate), which discourages exports and encourages imports, thus creating a current account deficit. During the late 1990s, foreigners were attracted to the booming US stock market and sought to disinvest in the crisis economies in Asia and Latin America. They pushed the dollar up, widening the US current account deficit to 4 percent of GDP by 2000. During the early years of the 21st century, Chinese and other monetary authorities intervened directly in the currency markets to hold the dollar up, widening the US deficit to a record 6 percent of GDP by 2006.

Over time, current account imbalances lead to shifts in the allocation of financial assets between countries that may feed back into desired financial flows and the exchange rate. For example, a prolonged current account deficit may satiate the appetites of foreign investors for domestic assets, depreciating the exchange rate and returning the current account toward balance, thereby stabilizing the pattern of asset holding across countries. However, deliberate exchange rate policies sometimes act to frustrate this natural adjustment process. For example, when Swiss investors cut back on foreign investment and foreign investors increased their purchases of Swiss assets, the Swiss National Bank stepped in to offset these private flows, thereby maintaining Switzerland's large current account surplus over the past eight years.

The factors driving financial flows are generally more volatile than the factors driving the current account. It is useful to think of financial flows as the proximate driver of current accounts, operating through exchange rates.

---

9. The fact that financial flows change more rapidly than trade complicates this process. An incipient desire by some domestic residents to invest in foreign assets initially depreciates the exchange rate by more than necessary in the long run. This overshooting induces other investors, both domestic and foreign, to take offsetting positions in financial assets. At first neither the financial account nor the current account moves, although elements of the financial account may move in offsetting directions. Over time the depreciated exchange rate moves the current account into surplus, allowing the financial account to move into deficit (net outflows).

Factors Underlying the Current Account

Economists have studied the current account equation, or similar treatments of its components (goods imports, services imports, goods exports, etc.), for decades (Goldstein and Khan 1985, Marquez 2002, IMF 2015c).[10] The sizes of the coefficients vary across countries, depending on how exposed they are to international markets and what types of goods and services they produce and consume. Typically, a 10 percent depreciation of the exchange rate raises the current account balance by 1 to 2 percent of GDP after two years or so. The effect on GDP depends on the state of the business cycle. Trend growth typically has little effect on the current account, but domestic growth above trend tends to lower the current account and foreign growth above trend tends to raise the current account.[11]

The current account equation by itself does not reveal much about the underlying drivers of trade balances, however, because these underlying factors also have important effects on GDP, the exchange rate, and the shocks to the current account equation. The volatility of the exchange rate, as it plays its role of equilibrating trade and financial flows, makes it especially difficult to estimate its direct effect on the current account (parameter $a2$ in box 2.1). For example, an import tariff or other trade barrier tends to increase the current account for a given level of the exchange rate and GDP. However, the market outcome may instead be a permanent appreciation of the exchange rate that keeps the current account nearly unchanged. A statistician would observe an increase in the real exchange rate but no change in the current account, thus concluding that $a2 = 0$ when it does not. Economists call this the "simultaneity problem."

There is a constant interplay between the current account and the financial account. The exchange rate moves to reflect the balance between these forces. If all the underlying muscle were on the financial side, the current account would move passively in response to the exchange rate, and it would be easy to measure the coefficient $a2$. If all the muscle were on the trade/current account side, financial flows would move passively in re-

---

10. The feedback between the trade balance and the exchange rate, and the lags in these effects, can make it difficult to get sensible estimates of the direct effect of the exchange rate on the current account. A thorough study by the IMF (2015c) shows that despite the rise of imported inputs in the exports of most countries, there is no evidence of any growing disconnect between exchange rates and trade balances, as some observers have suggested.

11. Countries with high trend growth tend to have lower trade balances, but they do so as much from higher investment demand working through interest rates and exchange rates as from a direct effect of GDP on the trade balance. China and other East Asian economies represent notable exceptions to this general result; in these economies, exchange rate policies (net official flows) play an important role.

sponse to the exchange rate, and it would be easy to measure the coefficient b2. In practice, both set of forces are at work, and it is difficult to separate them out. If economists could readily observe all underlying factors and had a complete and accurate model of how they affect the current account, they could solve the simultaneity problem. But they lack good measures of many factors, including many trade barriers, which may arise for technological or competitive reasons as well as from official policies.

In response to the simultaneity problem, Chinn and Prasad (2003) began a line of research that focuses directly on the underlying policies and exogenous factors (the shocks in box 2.1) that move current account imbalances. This literature recognizes that the same underlying factors affect exchange rates and cyclical movements in GDP. Instead of estimating the simple elasticities model of the current account, this literature regresses current account balances directly on the underlying factors without including exchange rates and GDP. The approach uses data on dozens of countries over many years to maximize the available statistical information.

Early studies of this type did not include exchange rate policy in the explanatory variables. Gagnon (2012, 2013) and IMF (2012a) were the first to include measures of exchange rate policy in the form of net official flows. IMF (2012a) excludes countries with some of the largest net official flows (Persian Gulf oil exporters) and uses an incorrect measure of official flows in some countries with large current account surpluses, such as Norway and Singapore. It finds a statistically significant effect of net official flows on the current account balance, but the size of the effect is implausibly small and limited to countries with low capital mobility.[12]

Gagnon et al. (2017) show that correcting these errors and allowing capital mobility to have a pervasive effect on all coefficients leads to sensible and robust coefficient estimates. Table 2.1 presents results from a regression on 141 countries using available annual data for 1985–2014. The regressions are based on the current account minus investment income, which is subtracted for two reasons. First, an important explanatory variable in regressions of the overall current account is a country's net foreign assets. Countries with positive net foreign assets tend to have positive net investment income, which is part of the current account balance. Excluding net investment income from the regression eliminates the need to include net foreign assets and allows inclusion of a subset of net foreign assets (net official assets) to capture the portfolio balance effect of past official flows. Second, the current account minus net investment income is almost equal to the trade balance, which aligns a bit more closely with the concept of

---

12. The IMF also used inappropriate instruments to control for endogeneity of net official flows, which biased the coefficient downward (Gagnon 2013).

Table 2.1 What moves the current account balance?

Dependent variable: (Current account – net investment income)/trend GDP

Variable	Countries with lowest capital mobility	Countries with highest capital mobility
International capital mobility [0–1]	–0.01	0.05**
International financial integration [0–1]	0.01	–0.11**
Per capita GDP relative to United States	0.03	–0.02*
Projected population aging	2.79	1.51
Lagged five-year growth rate	0.04	–0.61**
Net energy exports/trend GDP	0.27**	–0.01
Cyclically adjusted fiscal balance/trend GDP	0.17**	0.54**
Net official flows/trend GDP	0.72**	0.31*
Lagged net official assets/trend GDP	–0.01	0.03**
R^2	0.49	
Observations	2,053	

* and ** denote coefficients that are statistically significant at the 5 percent and 1 percent levels, respectively, based on the averages of the standard errors in the two underlying regressions.

Note: Table presents averages of coefficients from instrumental variables regressions shown in the middle two columns of table 2 in Gagnon et al. (2017) with the addition of the financial integration variable. The current account is regressed on the variables listed on the left as well as the products of each of those variables and the index of capital mobility. The first column displays the coefficients on the listed variables; the second column displays the sums of the coefficients in the first column and the coefficients on the listed variables times capital mobility. The figures in the first column thus reflect the effects of the listed variables when the capital mobility measure is 0; the figures in the second column reflect the effects of the listed variables when the mobility measure is 1. For countries and years with mobility measures between 0 and 1, the implied effects lie between those of column 1 and column 2. All regressions include a full set of year effects. Instrumental variables for net official flows are the nonreserves portion of net official flows and a dummy variable for external crisis in the previous three years (Laeven and Valencia 2012). Sample includes 141 countries over the period 1985–2014. Many countries are missing data for some years.

Source: Gagnon (2016).

balance, which matters for economic growth and employment (and thus the domestic politics of trade issues).

An important feature of table 2.1 is that the effects of these underlying factors are allowed to vary with the degree of international capital mobility, as measured by an index of legal restrictions on private financial flows across a country's borders (Aizenman, Chinn, and Ito 2015). This measure equals 1 when there are no legal restrictions and 0 when there are important restrictions on all classes of financial flows. However, a value of 0 does not mean there are no private financial flows, and a value of 1 does not mean that flows across borders are as cheap and easy as flows within borders. The median value of capital mobility across countries is 0.45. About 5 percent of the 2,053 available observations have the minimum value of 0, and 25 percent have the maximum value of 1.

The left side of the table lists the variables that are used to explain current account balances. The first column in table 2.1 displays the estimated effects of these variables in countries and years when the capital mobility measure is 0; the second column displays the estimated effects when the capital mobility measure is 1. In most countries and years, the mobility measure lies between 0 and 1; the estimated effect thus lies between the values shown in the two columns. In many countries capital mobility has risen over time.

The first two explanatory variables in table 2.1 are measures of capital mobility and financial market depth and integration with the rest of the world. The expected signs of the coefficients of these variables are theoretically ambiguous. Demographic and other structural and policy factors determine a country's desired saving and investment rates. It is the difference between savings and investment that drives a country's current account balance. However, openness, depth, and integration of capital markets are critical factors in determining the extent to which these underlying factors are able to influence a country's current account. If private agents are not allowed to borrow or lend across borders, a country will not be able to run a current account in surplus or deficit, even if the underlying factors would call for one. In these financially closed economies, interest rates and other yields on financial assets will differ from those in the rest of the world. Any current account surplus or deficit would have to be financed by the government through official financial flows.

The first coefficient in the first column implies that in countries with the tightest restrictions on capital flows, increasing capital mobility has a tiny and statistically insignificant negative effect on the current account. At some point, however, the effect of removing capital flow restrictions turns positive; by the time all restrictions are removed, the effect is modest but significant, because outflows rise more than inflows.

The second variable is based on the depth of a country's financial market integration with the rest of the world. It is defined as the share of private financial transactions in total cross-border transactions (including exports and imports). It is another measure of the ease of borrowing and lending across a country's borders. The correlation coefficient between the two variables is 0.36. Because it is constructed as a share, financial integration is bounded between 0 and 1.[13] High integration is associated with a

13. The median value in the estimation sample is 0.10; 95 percent of observations take values less than 0.27.

slightly higher current account when mobility is low. The effect of financial integration declines and becomes significantly negative as capital mobility increases, because capital inflows rise more than capital outflows. For many countries with high capital mobility and high financial integration, the negative effect of financial integration mainly offsets the positive effect of capital mobility, so that the overall effect of these two variables for most countries is small.

The third variable is per capita GDP relative to the US level. This variable has a very small negative effect on the current account under high mobility.[14]

The fourth variable is the projected change in the ratio of the population over the age of 64 over the subsequent 10 years. It has an economically important but statistically insignificant positive effect on the current account. A projected increase in the older population 10 years ahead presumably increases desired savings for retirement now and thus increases the current account balance.

The fifth variable is the lagged five-year economic growth rate, which is meant to proxy for trend growth potential. Rapidly growing countries are expected to borrow more, because they have more investment opportunities. They thus have lower current account balances. This effect is especially important when capital markets are more open for external borrowing. Under high mobility, a 1 percentage point increase in trend growth reduces the current account by 0.61 percent of GDP.

Many Asian economies had both high growth rates and large current account surpluses in the 2000s. As shown below, these surpluses were driven by net official flows (foreign exchange intervention), which secured export-led growth. This fact is particularly remarkable given that most rapidly growing economies tend to have current account deficits.

The sixth variable is net energy exports. It has a moderate positive effect under low mobility and no effect under high mobility. Under low capital mobility, a $1 increase in net energy exports increases the current account by $0.27.

---

14. The sign of this coefficient under high capital mobility is the opposite of its expected value, although the magnitude is small. The result may reflect some collinearity between per capita income and the other independent variables, such as aging and trend growth rates.

The seventh variable is the cyclically adjusted fiscal balance.[15] A higher fiscal balance (smaller government budget deficit) is associated with a higher current account balance. As expected, this effect is larger when capital markets are more open. Under high mobility, a $1 increase in the fiscal balance increases the current account by $0.54.[16] (We return to the effects of fiscal policy later in this chapter.)

The eighth variable is net official flows (including foreign exchange intervention).[17] For each $1 of net official flows, the current account increases by $0.72 under low mobility and by $0.31 under high mobility. The effect of net official flows is expected to be larger under low mobility because private capital flows are small, leaving official flows as the main factor capable of moving the current account. As capital mobility increases, financial markets are free to arbitrage rates of return across countries closer toward equality. In so doing, private financial flows undo some—but not all—of the effect of official financial flows. Even in economies with no legal restrictions on capital mobility, the effect of net official flows remains significantly positive.

All of the variables in table 2.1 influence the current account in part through their effect on the exchange rate, but it is net official flows that are most closely associated with official policy toward the exchange rate. These coefficient estimates imply that official flows have a greater effect on the exchange rate when capital mobility is low, reflecting the reduced ability of financial markets to substitute between assets in different currencies. As capital mobility increases, financial markets are able to substitute one currency for another, but even when capital mobility is high, that substitutability is not perfect. In the jargon of finance, international financial markets are not fully efficient.

The regression uses instruments to control for endogeneity of net official flows to exchange rates. The instruments are a dummy variable for financial crises in the previous three years and the part of net official flows that does not arise from foreign exchange reserves. The first instrument captures a higher propensity to build up foreign exchange reserves following a crisis episode. The second reflects official saving or borrowing that

---

15. In order to remove any endogenous policy response, this variable is the residual of a regression of the fiscal balance on the level and change in the output gap. The output gap is the deviation between real GDP and a centered 11-year moving average of real GDP, using IMF projections for GDP beyond 2015.

16. This result rejects the proposition of Ricardo neutrality, which argues that private saving behavior fully offsets any saving or borrowing by governments.

17. Box 2.2 (on page 37) discusses sterilized versus unsterilized intervention. The vast majority of net official flows in our data are sterilized, as central banks have generally succeeded in controlling inflation. The regression results are not noticeably affected by including a control for monetary policy (and thus unsterilized intervention) in the growth in central bank assets.

is not motivated by exchange rate movements; countries that stabilize their exchange rates use foreign exchange reserves for that purpose.[18] This instrument primarily reflects flows from sovereign wealth funds and official development loans that reflect longer-term saving and investment motives. Although in some cases these flows respond to oil exports, we assume that oil exports are exogenous and control for any effect of oil exports on the current account in our regression to avoid endogeneity bias. Gagnon et al. (2017) show that external saving out of oil revenues is a policy decision that differs markedly across oil exporters and does not reflect an endogenous response to the current account. Indeed, for a given level of oil exports, countries have higher current account balances only when they choose to save the revenues abroad. Oil exporters without significant net official flows (e.g., Angola, Canada, and Nigeria) do not have current account surpluses.

Together these instruments explain a significant amount of the movements in net official flows while excluding movements that might be endogenous reactions to the current account or exchange rate. Moreover, the results are robust to alternative specifications. The net official flows coefficients are little affected by replacing the instruments with a dummy variable for each country or adding a country fixed effect (with the original instruments).[19]

The ninth variable reflects the persistent effect of past official flows. For each $1 of the net stock of official foreign assets (including foreign exchange reserves) the previous year, the current account is little affected under low mobility and increases by $0.03 under high mobility. Because the lagged stock of net assets is often many times greater than the net flows in a given year, this stock effect is important when mobility is high.

We believe that the coefficient on lagged net assets arises purely from portfolio balance, which relates to the stocks of assets people own. Accumulation by the government of a large stock of foreign exchange (paid for out of domestic currency) puts upward pressure on the value of foreign currency and downward pressure on the value of domestic currency. As long as the government retains the foreign currency assets, private portfolios have less exposure to foreign currencies than they would otherwise have. This ongoing scarcity of foreign currencies keeps them highly valued. Without private capital mobility, the portfolio balance effect cannot operate, which explains why the coefficient on the net asset stock increases with capital mobility.

---

18. Because China did not have a financial crisis during the sample period and the vast majority of its net official flows were in foreign exchange reserves, it has essentially no effect on the estimated coefficients.

19. Previous research shows that the effect of net official flows on the current account is significant when using other instruments as well (Bayoumi, Gagnon, and Saborowski 2015).

The coefficient on the net official flow combines a portfolio balance component (this year's stock equals last year's stock plus this year's flow) with a direct effect that arises from imperfect capital mobility. As expected, when the mobility of private capital is very low, the coefficient on net official flows is close to 1. As private capital mobility increases, this coefficient decreases (as shown in table 2.1), but it remains positive even at the highest levels of capital mobility. This result suggests that financial markets are not fully efficient, even when allowed by law to operate unfettered.

Gagnon et al. (2017) find that monetary expansion has a small and marginally significant positive effect on the current account when capital mobility is low and that this effect disappears as mobility increases. As they note, there is some question as to whether the estimated monetary effect under low mobility arises spuriously from the effect of financial crises. The results under high mobility are consistent with the view (discussed later in this chapter) that the effect of monetary policy on the current account is ambiguous and relatively small because the exchange rate effect is offset by a domestic spending effect. In light of the small and uncertain effect of monetary policy on the current account, we do not include it here.

An appealing property of the coefficients in table 2.1 is the joint behavior of the coefficients on net official flows and the fiscal balance. The fiscal coefficient captures the effect of government saving in the local currency. The net official flows coefficient captures the effect of government borrowing in the local currency to invest in foreign currency. The sum of these coefficients captures the effect of government saving entirely in foreign currency. With low capital mobility, the sum of these coefficients is 0.89, most of it arising from the net official flows effect. With high capital mobility, the sum is 0.85, most of it arising from the fiscal effect. Regardless of the degree of capital mobility, a government's decision to save entirely in foreign currency has a very large—nearly one-for-one—effect on the current account.

In many countries with large sovereign wealth funds, net official flows and the fiscal balance are nearly identical, implying that governments are saving almost entirely in foreign currency. In Norway, for example, the current account moves closely with net official flows and the fiscal balance, consistent with the sum of the coefficients being close to 1 (figure 2.1). Norway's central bank has successfully targeted inflation and has a floating exchange rate with very little foreign exchange intervention. There is thus little reason to believe that net official flows and the fiscal balance are directly affected by the current account there. Rather, the causality runs entirely from oil exports to net official flows and the fiscal balance and then to the current account.

Figure 2.1   Current account and policy variables in Norway, 1993–2015

percent of GDP

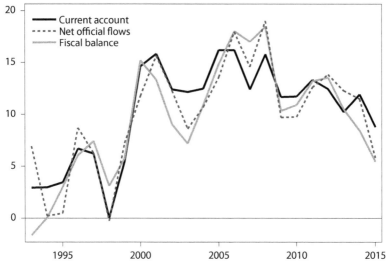

Source: Authors' calculations based on data from sources listed in appendix A.

Table 2.1 does not address dynamic adjustment or lags. Although the effect of intervention on the exchange rate is expected to be essentially simultaneous, the effect of the exchange rate on trade and the current account is generally believed to take place gradually, over a period of about two years. In the annual data, some of the effect of intervention ought to show up in the same year as the intervention, but some ought to occur in the following year and a small amount might even linger into a third year. The residuals of the regression in table 2.1 suggest that such dynamics may be important, but we were unable to model them successfully, because they appear to differ across country and across independent variables (the first-order autocorrelation of the residuals in table 2.1 is about 0.7). The coefficients are best interpreted as capturing the long-run effect of intervention and other factors, not the immediate effect.

Economic Policies and the Current Account Balance

Monetary Policy

Monetary policy has two opposing effects on the trade balance. First, lower interest rates make domestic assets less attractive to foreigners, thus pushing down the exchange rate. A depreciated exchange rate boosts exports and dampens imports, increasing the current account. This effect is known as the *expenditure-switching effect*. Second, lower interest rates encourage more domestic investment and consumption, increasing GDP. Higher GDP boosts imports and reduces the current account. This effect is known as the *expenditure-augmenting effect*. The expenditure-switching and expenditure-augmenting effects push the current account in opposite directions.

Macroeconomic models disagree on which effect is stronger, but whether the net effect of monetary policy on the current account is positive or negative, it is typically small. In the Federal Reserve's FRB/US model of the US economy, an increase in the US short-term interest rate of 1 percentage point causes the US current account to rise by only 0.03 percent of GDP after two years.

In the regression of table 2.1, only the exogenous component of policy can be included as an explanatory variable. We were unable to construct useful measures of exogenous, or cyclically adjusted, interest rates to include in the regression. As an alternative, Gagnon et al. (2017) use the cyclically adjusted change in central bank domestic assets. This measure has the appealing property that it captures the unconventional monetary policy known as quantitative easing, which the United States and some other major advanced economies adopted in recent years. Gagnon et al. find that this measure of monetary policy has no effect on the current account in countries with high capital mobility, which includes the countries that adopted quantitative easing.

Figure 2.2 displays the behavior of current account balances in the United States and the United Kingdom, which adopted quantitative easing policies beginning in 2009, and Japan, which adopted quantitative easing in 2013 (implementation of significant quantitative easing in the euro area is too recent to have had any effect on the data). The deep recession narrowed the US current account deficit in 2009; the collapse of US import demand transmitted that recession to its major trading partners. This narrowing occurred too early to have been plausibly caused by quantitative easing, which started only in 2009. After 2009 the current account balance was steady for several years; lately the deficit has begun widen. The UK balance has trended downward since the adoption of quantitative easing in 2009. In Japan quantitative easing had little initial effect on the current account balance. The increase in 2015 mainly reflects the global fall in the prices of oil and other commodities that are major components of Japanese imports.

In its analysis of the effects of quantitative easing in the United States on other countries, the IMF (2011b) finds little effect on current account balances and a moderate positive effect on GDP in other countries. Perhaps most important, it finds no evidence that quantitative easing operates differently from conventional monetary policy. The effect on foreign GDP

Figure 2.2   Current accounts in major quantitative easing episodes, 2004–15

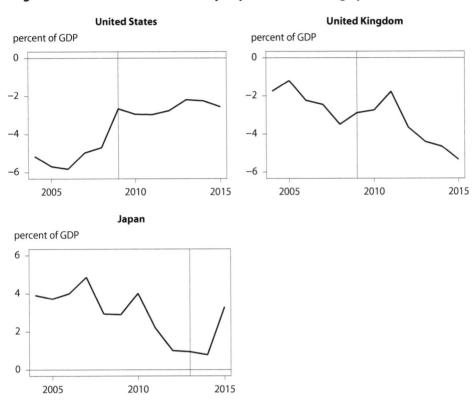

Note: Vertical lines denote the launch dates of quantitative easing policies. Data are from sources listed in appendix A.

arises because lower bond yields in the United States led to lower bond yields and higher stock prices in other countries, which boosted their domestic spending. To a large extent, these spillovers reflect a policy decision in other countries to follow US monetary policy, in part to reduce the appreciation of their exchange rates.

This episode highlights how difficult it can be to disentangle the effects of individual policies on the global economy. Too many other factors, including how policymakers in other countries react, are at play. In many cases policymakers may overrespond to upward pressure on their currencies. The effect of US quantitative easing on exchange rates is highly salient in many foreign countries, whereas the effect on US consumption, investment, and imports is less obvious.

Fiscal Policy

Fiscal policy operates through taxes and government spending. More expansionary fiscal policy (lower taxes or higher spending) pushes up GDP, increases imports, and thus reduces the current account. Tighter fiscal policy has the opposite effects. In the Fed's FRB/US model, an increase in government spending sufficient to lower the fiscal balance by 1 percent of GDP reduces the current account by 0.3 percent of GDP after two years. This simulation assumes no monetary response, but the effect on the current account is broadly similar if monetary policy tightens in response to fiscal loosening, because monetary policy has only a small effect on the current account. In the IMF's Flexible System of Global Models, a permanent reduction in the fiscal balance of Japan equal to 1 percent of GDP lowers the current account by 0.5 percent of GDP after two years (Andrle et al. 2015).

The effect of fiscal policy on the current account in the FRB/US model is slightly less than that implied by the fiscal coefficient in table 2.1 for a country with highly mobile capital. The effect in the IMF model for Japan is essentially identical to that implied by table 2.1, whereas the spillover of fiscal policy for a country with median capital mobility is 0.3 percent of GDP for each percentage point increase in the fiscal balance.[20]

Official Financial Flows

The largest component of official financial flows for most countries is foreign exchange intervention, which consists of official purchases or sales of foreign currency intended to affect the exchange rate. Financial flows are typically the most important drivers of the exchange rate and the current account. Foreign exchange intervention is a financial flow conducted by the public sector. It is part of a broader category of official financial flows, which includes external public borrowing and investment by sovereign wealth funds. As discussed in box 2.2, most official flows are conducted independently of monetary policy and thus have no direct impact on monetary policy.

The results in table 2.1 document the important effect of net official financial flows on current account balances. Other recent studies support this result. They confirm that official purchases of foreign exchange tend to depreciate a country's exchange rate, relative to what it would otherwise have been, consistent with a positive effect on the current account balance of a magnitude comparable to that shown in table 2.1 (Adler, Lisack, and Mano 2015; Blanchard, Adler, and de Carvalho Filho 2015; Saborowski and Nedeljkovic 2017).

---

20. The capital mobility variable equals 1 for Japan and the United States.

Box 2.2   Sterilized and unsterilized intervention

Most intervention is "sterilized," meaning that the central bank takes steps to insulate domestic monetary conditions, typically short-term interest rates, from any effect of intervention. Most central banks use the short-term interest rate as their monetary policy instrument; sterilization of foreign exchange transactions is thus automatic.

Other types of official flows tend to be conducted by agencies other than central banks. Because these agencies typically obtain the funds for their net official outflows from sources other than money creation, these flows are effectively a form of sterilized intervention.

Unsterilized intervention implies a sustained expansion of the monetary base to purchase the reserves. This expansion drives down domestic interest rates. Unsterilized intervention can be viewed as a combination of sterilized intervention and a loosening of monetary policy. Unless otherwise specified, our discussion of the effects of intervention and other official flows is based on the assumption that these flows are sterilized.

Under the assumption (widely but not universally held) that monetary policy has a small and ambiguous effect on the current account (because of opposing exchange rate and domestic spending effects), the effect of unsterilized intervention on the current account should be roughly similar to the effect of sterilized intervention. Sterilized intervention operates entirely through the exchange rate and thus unambiguously increases the trade balance.

Over time unsterilized intervention (loose monetary policy) leads to higher inflation. Given that central banks in the advanced economies and most emerging-market economies have achieved low and stable inflation for many years, monetary policy appears to have been focused on domestic stabilization and thus has not been excessively loose. In these circumstances foreign exchange intervention cannot be viewed as having been unsterilized in the long run.

These relatively recent results on the effects of foreign exchange intervention are only beginning to come to the attention of academic economists and policymakers. The conventional wisdom within the profession has long been that intervention has only a small and temporary effect on exchange rates and thus little effect on current accounts. This view reflects the results of studies in the 1990s that found small effects of intervention that were often not statistically significant (Edison 1993, Dominguez 2003). However, the interventions covered by these studies were much smaller than those after 2000, and their effects are difficult to distinguish from random variation in the data. The apparent success of the Plaza Accord probably reflects the change in market expectations about future policies and the possibility of future intervention rather than the actual intervention conducted, which was rather small. The much larger interventions since 2000 provide much more statistical information, or signals, which stand out among the noise.

When they are determined to fix the exchange rate, as China was during the 2000s, policymakers must choose between using interest rates or net official flows to achieve that objective. As long as the exchange rate is fixed, interest rates or net official flows respond endogenously to shocks to the current account and net private flows. The regression of table 2.1 uses instruments to remove the effects of this endogeneity. In particular, China, which has the world's foremost tightly managed exchange rate policy, has essentially no influence on the regression coefficients. The interpretation of the coefficients for a country like China is that if the exchange rate had been allowed to float before 2015 and net official flows had been reduced, the exchange rate would have appreciated and the current account would have declined. For commodity-intensive countries with fixed exchange rates, such as Saudi Arabia, the effects of domestic spending on imports are very large. A decision not to send money abroad as official flows but instead to spend it domestically directly increases imports and reduces the current account, even with a fixed exchange rate.

Official financial flows and fiscal balances constitute two of the most important policy factors behind the large current account imbalances of the first decade of the 21st century. Panel A of figure 2.3 displays the current account balances of the four largest economies and panel B displays the current accounts of other countries with large surpluses or deficits. The dark bars are the actual current account balances in 2007, the year of peak imbalances. For the world as a whole, net official flows in 2007 equaled 2.5 percent of world GDP; total net official stocks equaled 14 percent of world GDP; and total fiscal deficits equaled 0.6 percent of world GDP. One way to show the effect of policy differences across countries is to calculate what current account balances would have been if all countries had had official flows, official stocks, and fiscal balances equal to the world average in 2007. This exercise is motivated by the symmetry of current account balances, which add up to zero across all countries; differences in underlying economic factors and policies thus drive imbalances.

The medium grey bars display the current accounts that would be predicted if all countries had equal net official flows and stocks of net official assets as a percent of GDP, based on the coefficients in table 2.1.[21] The light grey bars display the current accounts that would be predicted if all coun-

---

21. Because the countries with small official flows tend to have more open capital markets, the direct effect of raising their official flows on their current account balances is somewhat smaller than the direct effect of reducing official flows for countries with large official flows. To maintain the global current account identity, we allocated half the aggregate discrepancy between rising and falling current accounts in proportion to nominal GDP and half in proportion to the reported currency denomination of foreign exchange reserves as of 2010 (IMF Currency Composition of Official Foreign Exchange Reserves database).

Figure 2.3   Actual and hypothetical current account balances, 2007

a. Four largest economies

current account balance (billions of dollars)

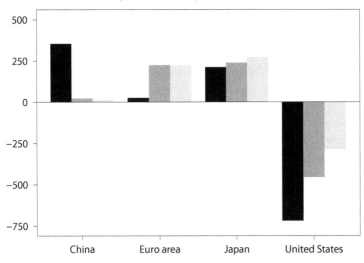

b. Other economies

current account balance (billions of dollars)

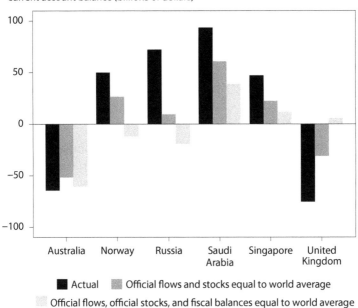

■ Actual   ▨ Official flows and stocks equal to world average
▨ Official flows, official stocks, and fiscal balances equal to world average

Source: Authors' calculations based on data from sources listed in appendix A.

tries had equal fiscal deficits (as percent of GDP) in addition to equal official flows and stocks.[22]

For China a reduction in net official flows and stocks to the global average would have reduced the current account surplus from $350 billion to $20 billion. For the United States, an increase in net official flows and stocks to the global average would have reduced the deficit by about $235 billion.[23] Because the euro area and Japan had very low net official flows in 2007, raising them to the global average would have increased their current accounts by about $180 billion and $25 billion, respectively. For the next-largest deficit countries, the United Kingdom and Australia, moving to average net official flows and stock would have reduced their deficits. For most of the next-largest surplus countries—Saudi Arabia, Russia, Norway, and Singapore—moving to average net official flows and stocks would have reduced their surpluses. The main exception is Switzerland (not shown), which had the sixth-largest surplus in 2007 but did not have large official flows that year and would have seen little change.

Figure 2.3, panel A, indicates that the fiscal deficit contributed about $190 billion to the US current account deficit in 2007. Both China and the euro area had fiscal balances close to the world average in 2007, so there was little impact on their current accounts. In contrast, Japan had a modestly above-average fiscal deficit that year; its current account surplus would have been even larger if the fiscal balance had been at the world average. The fiscal deficit contributed significantly to the UK current account deficit. Fiscal surpluses contributed importantly to the Saudi, Russian, Norwegian, and Singaporean current account surpluses. If Norway and Russia had had net official flows and fiscal balances at the world average in 2007, their surpluses would have turned into small deficits.

Capital Flow Measures

Restrictions on capital mobility range from outright prohibitions or quotas on purchases of specific assets to taxes on certain categories of transactions. Once anathema in discussions of sound economic policy, capital flow measures have achieved a measure of respectability in recent years. Staff at the IMF have described how such measures may be useful in limited and specific circumstances (IMF 2012b, Ostry et al. 2011).

---

22. We allocated the small additional discrepancy between rising and falling current account balances from fiscal adjustment across countries in proportion to nominal GDP.

23. Historically, the United States has had very small net official flows. One interpretation of this alternative scenario with significant US net official flows is that it might reflect a US policy of countervailing currency intervention, discussed in chapters 5 and 6.

The results of table 2.1 suggest that overall openness to capital flows, as measured by both legal restrictions on mobility and observed financial integration, has a small and ambiguous effect on the current account. However, openness to capital flows works primarily through changes in the effects of other factors on the current account, hence the differences between the coefficients on the right and left sides of table 2.1. A fiscal deficit or a demographic difference has less impact on the current account when capital mobility is low. Overall, restrictions on capital mobility tend to reduce current account surpluses in countries that have surpluses and to reduce deficits in countries that have deficits. Capital flow restrictions thus keep current account balances closer to zero.

In principle, it is possible to design capital flow measures to discourage inflows without discouraging outflows or vice versa. In practice, such asymmetric measures are rare and their effects not well known. Examples may include the variable tax rate imposed on capital inflows by Brazil or the holding periods on capital inflows once imposed by Chile.

Tariffs and Trade Barriers

In the popular imagination, tariffs and other import restrictions have an important effect on the trade balance and thus on the current account balance. Most economists, however, believe that such policies mainly affect the exchange rate, with little effect on the current account, except in countries with a fixed exchange rate. Even with a fixed exchange rate, the effects are mainly temporary, as we explain in the next subsection.

Consider a permanent increase in an import tariff. The increase makes imports more expensive for consumers and drives the current account up, other things equal. However, if a tariff change does not affect private financial flows—as economists typically assume—the exchange rate appreciates to offset some of the price increase in imports, making exports more expensive to foreigners. The combined effect of the tariffs and exchange rate change is to reduce imports and exports equally; there is no net effect on the current account balance.

In practice, the assumption of no effect on financial flows may not hold. If investors interpret a tariff increase as a signal of bad future economic policies, financial inflows may fall, preventing the exchange rate from appreciating and thus allowing the current account balance to rise. If, however, some investors decide to build factories to avoid the trade barriers, as many argue Japanese auto manufacturers did in Europe and the United States in the 1980s after they accepted "voluntary export restraints" on their sales to those markets, the tariffs may cause net financial inflows to increase. If they do, the current account balance will actually fall—the opposite result of what was intended! Another possibility is that a tariff increase is a signal that a country's leaders are serious about reducing its trade deficit. The tariff may be an opening gambit to negotiating a devaluation of the exchange rate, as happened with the Nixon tariff of 1971.

Bayoumi, Gagnon, and Saborowski (2015) review the recent literature on the determinants of current account balances. None of the studies they review attributes any role for tariffs or other trade policies in explaining the current account.

Figure 2.4 displays the correlation between the current account balance and the tariff rate across countries, using data for 2003-14. The figure reveals a negative effect: A higher tariff is associated with a lower current account balance. For example, Brazil had an average tariff of 13 percent and an average current account deficit of 1 percent of GDP. Singapore had an average tariff of less than 1 percent and an average current account surplus of 21 percent of GDP. To the extent that countries with current account deficits raise tariffs in a fruitless effort to restore balance, this negative relationship may reflect reverse causality.

To explore further, we added measures of average tariffs to the regression in table 2.1. By controlling for various important underlying factors behind current account imbalances, the regression framework may be able to identify a positive effect of tariffs that is not apparent in the simple correlation of figure 2.4.

The effective tariff (total tariff revenue divided by total imports) has a small and statistically insignificant coefficient. The simple average tariff (the tariff rate averaged across all import categories with equal weights) has a larger and marginally significant effect.[24] An across-the-board tariff increase of 10 percentage points—equivalent to the Nixon surcharge of 1971[25]—is estimated to raise the current account by 0.1 to 0.3 percent of GDP, depending on which regression coefficient is used. This effect is fairly small for such a large policy change (for comparison, a 10 percent depreciation of the exchange rate typically is estimated to raise the current account balance by 1 to 2 percent of GDP—about 10 times as much). The fact that the estimated tariff effect is not robust to including a complete set of country fixed effects raises the possibility that tariffs are spuriously correlated with some other factor that differs across countries in a way that is stable over time. Countries that generally have higher tariffs also have slightly higher current account balances, after controlling for other effects, but there is no evidence

---

24. Separate regressions were run for each tariff measure. The t-statistic on the simple tariff coefficient is 2, significant at the 5 percent level but not the 1 percent level.

25. The Nixon tariff did not cover nondutiable imports, such as petroleum and most services.

Figure 2.4   Correlation between average current account balances and tariff rates, 2003–14

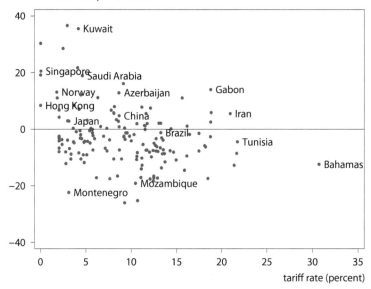

a. All economies

current account as percent of GDP

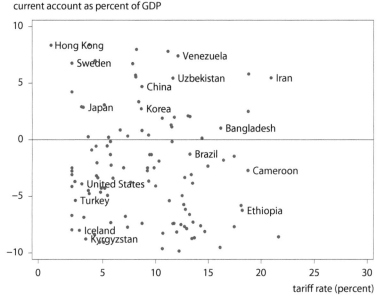

b. Economies with current account balances between –10 and 10 percent of GDP

current account as percent of GDP

Note: Tariff rate is unweighted average across import categories.
Source: Authors' calculations based on data from sources listed in appendix A.

that a change in tariffs leads to a change in current accounts in any predictable direction.

Trade policy does have important effects. Tariffs on specific goods reduce imports of those goods. But tariffs also affect exchange rates in ways that tend to offset any effect on the overall balance of trade.

The entire postwar global economic order has been premised on achieving the maximum flow of international trade, based on the view that doing so will enhance global economic welfare and minimize the risk of political conflict. Barriers to trade have been relegated to the end of the queue as potential adjustment devices. Free trade has become a nearly universal norm of the international system that, if not always observed in practice, has strongly deterred any sizable deviations, even at times of acute distress, such as the Great Recession. It is a model for the type of new international norm that we would like to propagate against currency manipulation.

Exchange Rate Regimes

Up to now we have assumed that the exchange rate is flexible. A country may, however, try to stabilize its exchange rate by using either its interest rate or its net official flows. Both policy tools operate through financial flows. An extreme example of a fixed exchange rate regime is a currency union, in which a country subordinates its monetary policy to the control of an areawide central bank. Box 2.3 describes recent developments in the world's foremost currency union, the euro area, and their implications for current account balances both inside and outside of the euro area.

When faced with upward pressure on the exchange rate, the central bank may lower interest rates to make domestic assets less attractive to foreigners. Interest rate policy thus operates through private financial flows. Alternatively, the central bank may intervene by buying foreign currency and selling domestic currency, a net official outflow.

When the exchange rate is fixed, trade policies do have effects on the current account. For example, raising an import tariff when the exchange rate is fixed makes imports more expensive without affecting the competitiveness of exports (except to the extent that exports include imported content). The current account therefore rises. To maintain the fixed exchange rate with a higher current account, the central bank could reduce interest rates to encourage private financial outflows to increase. However, lower interest rates would exacerbate any overheating of GDP already caused by the rise in the trade balance. Over time higher GDP would put upward pressure on prices, including the prices of exports. Higher prices raise the real exchange rate, despite the peg of the nominal exchange rate. Our simple model does not include this inflationary effect, but it is the real

Box 2.3   Germany and the euro area

Germany had the world's second-largest current account surplus in 2015, at $284 billion (China was first, at $331 billion). Many observers have criticized the policies that drive Germany's surplus.[1] But Germany has very small net official flows (even after including reserves at the European Central Bank). Moreover, it does not make sense to look at the members of the euro area separately in any analysis of current account adjustment, because they share a single currency and exchange rate movements thus affect them all equally. In the regression of table 2.1, the euro area is treated as a single economic unit.

During most of the "decade of manipulation," the euro area current account was close to balance. It reflected a large surplus in Germany, however, and large deficits in peripheral countries like Italy, Spain, Greece, and Ireland. To a large extent, Germany was financing a housing boom in the periphery that was brought on by the equalization of interest rates after the establishment of the euro in 1999. Periphery borrowers responded to lower interest rates by taking on more mortgage debt. During the years of the boom, price levels in the periphery drifted up relative to those in Germany, helping create the trade imbalances that were necessitated by the financing flows.

The collapse of housing bubbles and the global financial crisis pushed the euro area into a recession in which the periphery was hit hardest. Financial market pressures and the fiscal rules of the euro area prevented the periphery from responding aggressively with looser fiscal policy. Monetary policy, which has been too tight for the area as a whole, could not be applied differentially within the union. The result has been a massive and prolonged slowdown in the periphery, which is being forced to adjust through gradual deflation to restore its competitiveness, rather than a sharp depreciation, as in pre-euro days. Of course, preventing such a resort to depreciation was a key motivation for Germany to form a monetary union with its neighbors.

The ongoing recession in the peripheral countries has brought their current account deficits to an end with little effect on Germany's surplus, which has grown entirely from its trade outside the euro area. As a result, the current account balance of the euro area has risen to a large surplus, roughly 80 percent of which is accounted for by Germany.

As a wealthy, aging, and slow-growing economy, the euro area would normally be expected to run a modest current account surplus. But the surplus is also boosted by insufficiently stimulative macroeconomic policy, particularly fiscal policy. A more centralized and activist fiscal policy would be the best option for both euro area citizens and the rest of the world, for which the rising euro area surplus is a drag on aggregate demand at a time of weak economic growth. The euro area has essentially no net official flows, so official exchange rate policy is not a factor in its surplus.

---

1. James Politi, "Jack Lew to Press Germany to Boost Domestic Demand," *Financial Times*, January 5, 2014; and Martin Wolf, "Germany Is the Eurozone's Biggest Problem," *Financial Times*, May 10, 2016.

exchange rate that matters for the current account. Over time the outcome is the same under both fixed and flexible exchange rates. A higher tariff raises the real exchange rate and has no effect on the current account.

The story is somewhat different if the central bank maintains the exchange rate peg by purchasing more foreign assets without lowering interest rates. In this situation the higher current account and higher GDP still exert some upward pressure on prices, but not as much as when the central bank lowers interest rates. Adjustment to a higher real exchange rate takes longer. Indeed, the central bank may delay adjustment considerably by raising interest rates enough to return GDP to its initial level. Higher domestic interest rates attract net private financial inflows and force the central bank to buy even more foreign exchange reserves. At some point, the central bank may find its foreign exchange reserves excessive, although as we show in chapter 4, that point may be a long time in coming.

In the 1950s and 1960s, when exchange rates were fixed and there were barriers to many forms of private financial flows, many analysts believed that a current account deficit was evidence that a country's exporters were not competitive—because, for example, domestic inflation pushed up exporters' costs. In this regime, current account deficits needed to be financed in order to defend the fixed exchange rate. Sometimes governments financed the deficits directly by selling foreign assets or borrowing from foreigners. At other times, they raised barriers to financial outflows or lowered barriers on inflows to induce the necessary financial account surplus. If the current account deficit persisted or grew larger, the government would eventually be forced to devalue its currency, an event that often proved traumatic.[26]

The concept of a "need to finance a current account deficit" still crops up in discussions of modern economies, despite the fact that for countries with truly flexible exchange rates the current account always equals the available financing. The issue becomes whether the exchange rate needed to equate a country's current account with its net financial flows requires an abrupt and excessive depreciation or appreciation, often by more in the short run than in the long run.[27] It is the magnitude and abruptness of the depreciation or appreciation that raises concern. An incipient lack of financing tends to depreciate the currency, whereas an incipient excess of financing tends to appreciate the currency.

---

26. An alternative extreme measure, allowed temporarily under WTO rules in case of balance-of-payments difficulty, is a broad import surcharge.

27. The excess short-run movement is needed to attract or discourage financing in the period it takes the current account to fully adjust.

3

Norms for Current Account Balances

This chapter discusses norms for sustainable trade balances. It shows that large and protracted imbalances are often associated with misallocated investments that lead to disorderly readjustments with occasional financial crises. Both the Mexican crisis of 1994–95 and the Asian financial crisis of 1997–98 were preceded by large and unsustainable trade deficits in the affected countries. The US imbalance of the mid-1980s did not lead to a financial crisis, but its distortion of the US economy led to dangerous protectionist pressures that were assuaged only by the reversal of the dollar's overvaluation and the subsequent narrowing of the US trade deficit. China's huge trade surpluses of 2007–08 were unsustainable both domestically and in terms of the pressure they placed on other countries.

Trade imbalances shift the pattern of employment across industries. When these imbalances are not sustainable, the resulting adjustments impose substantial and long-lasting economic costs. If macroeconomic policy does not respond quickly enough or strongly enough, trade imbalances can lead to prolonged overemployment or underemployment. For example, the incomplete adjustment of the US trade deficit after 2009 contributed to a slower economic recovery and higher unemployment than would have been desirable.

A key condition for a sustainable trade balance is a stable ratio of a country's net international investment position to its GDP. We show that countries with negative net investment positions often face difficulties when this ratio falls below –60 percent of GDP. For the United States, trade deficits have often raised issues of political sustainability long before financing becomes a problem.

The chapter concludes with a discussion of currency policies. Our view, consistent with that enshrined in the IMF's Articles of Agreement, is that exchange rate policy should target stable and sustainable trade balances. Countries should be encouraged to intervene to reduce excessive imbalances in either direction. They should not be allowed to intervene in foreign exchange markets to maintain or increase excessive trade surpluses.

Current Account Imbalances: The Good and the Bad

A key feature of current account balances around the world is that they all add up to zero.[1] For any country to have a current account surplus requires some other country to have a current account deficit. If the economic circumstances of all countries were the same, all would have a current account balance of zero. Analysis of any country's current account balance thus inherently involves a comparison of its circumstances with those of all other countries. Differences across countries—in policies, attitudes, institutions, demographics, and endowments—drive imbalances.

Long-Term Influences on the Current Account

Differences in demographic prospects, the pace of development, and national wealth are some of the most important reasons for lasting current account imbalances. Fast-growing, younger, and poorer countries are expected to borrow from slow-growing, older, and richer countries, because the first group of countries has greater investment opportunities. Imbalances arising from these differences should improve welfare in both borrowing and lending countries, because investment is more productive in the borrowing country. The returns should exceed what lenders would have earned at home but be less than what borrowers would have paid had they had access only to domestic lenders.

An important factor limiting the flow of capital from richer to poorer countries is the quality of institutions and the security of property rights. Institutional quality and property rights are generally stronger in advanced economies. To some extent, these features can attract capital in the reverse direction from poorer countries.

The results in table 2.1 show a significant effect of trend growth on current accounts but only a small effect of per capita income.[2] In countries

---

1. This accounting necessity in no way implies that trade itself is a zero-sum game. Indeed, the evidence abundantly supports the benefits of both exports and imports.

2. The coefficient on per capita income has the wrong sign under high capital mobility, but its size is small. An increase in per capita income equal to 10 percent of the US level

with no restrictions on capital mobility, a 1 percentage point increase in trend growth reduces the current account by about 0.5 percent of GDP. This effect shrinks to zero in countries with the greatest restrictions on capital mobility.

Differences in five-year growth rates are large across countries (the cross-country standard deviation is about 3 percentage points). Differences in trend growth could support differences in persistent current account balances on the order of 2 to 3 percentage points for many countries, especially countries with open capital markets. However, episodes of rapid trend growth with large current account deficits may reflect unsustainable financial flows, as discussed below.

Prospective population aging tends to increase the current account, but not by a statistically significant amount. An annual increase of 1 percentage point in the ratio of the number of people 65 and older to the number of working-age people over the next 10 years increases the current account by about 0.2 percent of GDP. Capital mobility has little effect on the relationship between aging and the current account. As the difference between the most and least rapidly aging countries is only about 1 percentage point per year, aging should not lead to large differences in sustainable current account balances.

The large and persistent imbalances of China and the United States since 2000 have stood out from most other countries in this regard: China has had a persistent surplus despite rapid growth and relative poverty, and the United States has had a persistent deficit despite moderate growth and relative wealth.[3] Currency policy can largely explain why China and the United States defy the general pattern. Fiscal policy has also played a significant role in the United States. In both countries, other factors that are difficult to measure—most likely related to high household saving in China and low household saving in the United States—are playing significant roles. Factors behind low US household saving may include a mortgage system that facilitates the withdrawal of home equity and the easy availability of auto and student loans. In China high saving may reflect a weak social safety net (IMF 2014) or the one-child policy (Wei and Zhang 2011).

---

would reduce the current account by 0.2 percent of GDP under the highest degree of capital mobility. This result may reflect the importance of stronger institutional quality and property rights in countries with higher per capita income.

3. On aging the difference is smaller. China is younger than the United States, but is aging more rapidly. The data suggest that prospective aging is more important that the current age ratio for current account imbalances.

Cyclical Imbalances

The current account is part of the natural equilibrating mechanism of business cycles. When a country's output is above potential, it tends to import more and run a current account deficit. This drains off some of the excess demand to the rest of the world. When output is below potential, a country tends to import less and run a current account surplus, cushioning the effects of weak domestic absorption. This "automatic stabilization" feature is a benefit of open markets in trade and finance.

For a typical country, imports for domestic use are about 25 percent of GDP and the cyclical income elasticity of imports is about 2.[4] Thus about half of any excess demand shock spills over to foreign producers and half to domestic output. This spillover is somewhat less for the United States, where trade is a smaller share of GDP than it is in other countries.

Table 2.1 does not include cyclical effects, because they are endogenous to the current account. It focuses on relatively exogenous longer-term factors.

Costs of Unsustainable Imbalances

An unsustainable imbalance is one that is not justified by long-lasting differences in rates of return on investment or the automatic stabilization of business cycles. If private financial markets were efficient, there would be no unsustainable imbalances.

The history of financial crashes shows that financial markets are not efficient. They are prone to fads, excesses, and waves of greed and myopia followed by panics. Economies are often unable to productively absorb capital that flows too rapidly, sometimes causing it to fund white elephants. Sometimes the financial excess may be contained within one country. More often it seems that booms draw in investors from around the world and are associated with an unsustainable current account deficit in the country experiencing the boom.

In some cases, especially in the United States, political sustainability can be a stronger limiting factor on imbalances than financial sustainability. As current and former IMF chief economists Maurice Obstfeld and Kenneth Rogoff (2007) note, global capital markets appear to be willing to extend credit to the United States even when its trade deficit is clearly unsustainable. But the same large trade deficits may stir up political pressures for protectionism that force adjustment before the markets get around to it.

---

4. We distinguish between imports for domestic use and imports to be used as components of exports, which are not responsive to domestic absorption.

Over the past 50 years, the world has lurched from one international financial crisis to the next. First was the unsustainable fixed exchange rates of the United Kingdom and the United States in the 1960s. Then came the oil-induced deficits in Latin America in the 1970s, which led to the debt crisis of the early 1980s. The US current account deficit of the mid-1980s did not lead to a crisis, but it came close to bringing on a wave of protectionist US trade policies that would have threatened the global trading system, and its resolution occupied much of the attention of international policymakers. Mexico's unsustainable current account deficit led to a crash in 1994, and unsustainable current account deficits in several Asian economies in the mid-1990s preceded the Asian financial crisis of 1997-98. Turkey and Argentina underwent external crises in 2000 and 2001, respectively. The US record current account deficit of the mid-2000s also proved unsustainable. It led to strong political pressures against new trade agreements and ultimately against globalization more broadly; the deficit narrowed significantly following the global financial crisis of 2008.

Goldstein (1998) and Hills, Peterson, and Goldstein (1999) document the tremendous damage caused by excessive international borrowing and the subsequent reversal of that borrowing. Unemployment rates soar, growth rates decline, stock prices crash. The evidence is often as clear as the half-finished skyscrapers that dotted Bangkok's skyline for years after 1997. The sheer waste of abandoned and delayed construction projects is enormous. Lives are disrupted, as many newly urbanized workers are forced to return to a subsistence living in remote villages. Poverty rates and school dropout rates rise, stunting the economic prospects of the next generation.

Current account deficits are always financed by current account surpluses in other countries. Although markets force more of the costs of adjustment onto borrowers than lenders, it is wrong to lay all of the blame for financial excesses at the feet of borrowers. Lenders also bear responsibility for enabling excessive and wasteful borrowing, and surplus countries occasionally have to make painful adjustments, as Japan did when its exports collapsed in the global financial crisis.

Table 3.1 displays economic indicators for three-year periods before and after some prominent international financial crises. As with Tolstoy's unhappy families—each unhappy in its own way—the underlying policies and private behavior that gave rise to each of these crises as well as the policy responses were different. What they had in common was excess financial flows that included an international component. In each case the current account was negative before the crisis and the deficit narrowed or shifted to a surplus after the crisis. In some cases adjustment of the current account

Table 3.1   The costs of financial crises

Variable	Mexico 1994	Thailand 1997	Korea 1998	Turkey 2000	Argentina 2001	United States 2008
Current account, pre	−5.4	−7.2	−2.5	−1.1	−2.5	−5.2
Current account, post	−0.9	6.8	5.7	−0.3	5.3	−2.8
Unemployment rate, pre	3.3	n.a.	2.2	6.1	17.5	5.0
Unemployment rate, post	5.1	n.a.	6.0	8.4	17.8	9.3
GDP growth, pre	3.5	7.3	7.7	2.2	−2.9	1.4
GDP growth, post	2.4	−1.9	4.9	1.9	2.3	0.5
CPI inflation, pre	10.8	5.6	4.6	68.2	−1.1	3.3
CPI inflation, post	30.0	4.6	3.5	41.6	14.6	1.5

CPI = consumer price index; n.a. = not available

Note: Figures are three-year averages before and after crises. Current accounts are percent of GDP; unemployment rates are percent of labor force; growth and inflation are annual rates of change. For crises that occurred early in the year (Thailand and Korea), the year of the crisis is included in the after sample. For crises that occurred late in the year (Mexico, Turkey, Argentina, and the United States), the year of the crisis is included in the before sample.

Sources: IMF, World Economic Outlook database, and authors' calculations.

was an important driver of the crisis. In others domestic factors were primarily responsible.

In every case unemployment rose after the crisis (albeit only slightly in Argentina), and in every case except Argentina the GDP growth rate declined. The US crisis led to a near-doubling of the unemployment rate. In Thailand and Korea, the growth rate was probably unsustainably high before the crisis, but for Thailand, at least, the crash in the growth rate after the crisis was excessive. In Argentina much of the cost of the imbalance was incurred before the crisis, as domestic policies were excessively tight in order to defend the fixed exchange rate. The overvalued exchange rate caused a recession in the late 1990s as Argentina lost exports. After the crisis the economy began to grow, but it took a long time to reemploy the workers who had lost their jobs earlier.

The buildup of current account deficits before each of these crises and the narrowing of deficits (or even rising surpluses) afterward were associated with major shifts across economic sectors. Such shifts are costly, involving laid-off workers and idled plants. The costs are incurred during both the buildup and the drawdown, imposing a huge deadweight loss on society, which is all the greater when the shifts happen so quickly.

Many large imbalances arise from private financial flows. Another source of unsustainable imbalance is government policies, in the form of fiscal balances, official external borrowing, and foreign exchange intervention. Government borrowing in domestic markets tends to increase net financial inflows and reduce the current account balance; this effect is larger when capital markets are more open (see table 2.1). Governments sometimes borrow externally in foreign currencies, as they did in Mexico before 1994 and Argentina before 2001. Such borrowing is a negative net official flow that reduces the current account. Foreign exchange intervention is a form of financial outflow that increases the current account balance. In the pursuit of export-led growth, countries may pile up excessive stocks of foreign exchange reserves. In the pursuit of exchange rate stability, they may run these stocks down to dangerously low levels. In addition, large fiscal deficits and official external borrowing are not sustainable indefinitely. Like imbalances caused by overexuberance in private financial flows, unsustainable imbalances caused by official policies are costly. Indeed, there is a greater presumption that policymakers who do not have to face a market test of profitability may waste taxpayers' resources.

Financial crises provide the most vivid examples of the costs of unsustainable imbalances, but such imbalances have serious economic costs even when they are resolved without a crash. These costs arise from the need to shift economic resources across industries as the imbalances grow and then shift back again as the imbalances shrink. The record global imbalances of the early 2000s had far-reaching costs that go beyond any role they may have played in the global financial crisis, as we discuss in chapter 4.

Norms for Imbalances

Current account deficits become unsustainable when a country's net international investment position (NIIP) becomes negative enough that markets question the country's ability to bear the burden of net debt or the domestic political response to the deficits threatens an outbreak of protectionism. There is often no corresponding pressure on large surplus positions, an asymmetry that has dogged the international system for generations and that is a central theme of this book. Here we focus on financing issues and the NIIP (although for the United States the domestic political response has typically been the more important limiting factor, a fact confirmed by the backlash against globalization, manifested by the opposition to the TPP in Congress and more broadly in the antitrade rhetoric of the 2016 US presidential election).

The IMF began to publish a set of normative current account balances for most large and some medium-size economies in its *External Sector Reports* in 2011. It considers both the secular and the cyclical factors discussed here and applies a common globally consistent framework to obtain a set of current account targets. In principle, the IMF approach should lead to a plausible and consistent set of norms for current accounts. Unfortunately, the IMF often shades its norms to be closer to recently realized current accounts than can be justified by fundamentals. Moreover, the sustainability of NIIPs does not appear prominently in the determination of the IMF norms, a critical drawback.

The 2016 *External Sector Report* calls for a current account deficit of 1 percent of GDP in the United States and current account surpluses of 1 percent in China, 2 percent in Japan, and 4 percent in Germany. These figures compare with actual 2015 figures of a 2.5 percent deficit in the United States and surpluses of 3 percent in China, 3 percent in Japan, and more than 8 percent in Germany. Thus, according to the IMF, the US balance is too low and the Chinese, German, and Japanese balances too high.

In the 2015 *External Sector Report*, the norms for China, Germany, and Japan were all closer to zero (indeed, China's norm was zero). As actual imbalances widened, the IMF moved the goalposts in the same direction for no justifiable reason. As wealthy economies with relatively old populations, Germany and Japan arguably should run modest surpluses, but 4 percent stretches the limit. It is even harder to understand why the United States, even richer and with a population that is almost as old as Germany's, should have a negative norm or China, which is far poorer and still growing rapidly, should have a positive norm (somewhat more rapid population aging in China is one factor in that direction). The real reason behind these changes appears to be pressure inside the IMF not to criticize countries for deviating from a consistent benchmark and rather to ratify the outcomes countries have implicitly chosen.

The IMF norms are even less appealing for some smaller economies with large imbalances. For these economies the IMF includes ad hoc factors and judgmental adjustments that have the effect of ratifying very large imbalances, especially large surpluses. For example, in its 2016 *External Sector Report*, the IMF lists norms for current account surpluses of 14 percent of GDP in Singapore, 12 percent in Switzerland, and 7 percent in the Netherlands. These large surpluses are said to reflect in part the status of these economies as "financial centers," but these countries almost exclusively comprise the dummy variable used to estimate the financial center effect, which does not include the world's largest financial centers (London, New York, and Tokyo).[5] The IMF analysis thus appears to be a case of ex post

---

5. The IMF also points to a measurement issue concerning the reporting of retained earnings on portfolio investment that has a particularly large effect on Swiss data. Adjustment

rationalization of the observed imbalances rather than a serious attempt to assess country circumstances by rigorously imposed common standards.

The IMF norms factor in a cyclical effect on the current account. In the data underlying table 2.1, the standard deviation of the output gap (the difference between actual and potential GDP) is about +/-5 percent of potential GDP. If about half of this gap were to spill over into the current account, cyclical swings in the current account would be on the order of +/-2.5 percent of GDP. For a large country such as the United States, output gaps are typically smaller than +/-5 percent, and spillovers to the current account are proportionally smaller (a typical cyclical swing in the current account would be about +/-1 percent of GDP).

Cyclical differences across major regions are currently fairly small, with the United States in a modestly stronger position than Europe. The IMF estimates output gaps for 2016 of –0.5 percent of potential GDP for the United States, –1.2 percent for the euro area, and –1.5 percent for Japan (IMF 2016). These small cyclical differences should be associated with current account deviations of much less than 1 percent of GDP from any secular norm. The IMF does not publish output gaps for China, but China is widely viewed to be coming out of a modest slump and operating close to potential.

A large body of literature on early warning indicators of crises generally supports the view that large current account deficits are a source of risk for currency or financial crises (Berg et al. 2000; Goldstein, Kaminsky, and Reinhart 2000). Goldstein, Kaminsky, and Reinhart find that a trigger for concern was a current account deficit above the 80th percentile of observations in a panel of countries over time. In the data underlying table 2.1, the 80th percentile would be a current account deficit of 6 percent of GDP. Freund (2000, 2005) finds that a current account deficit of more than 5 percent of GDP has often triggered currency depreciation and an economic slowdown. For large economies, which tend to be less exposed to trade, it is possible that the trigger may be smaller than 5 percent of GDP, because they may have greater difficulty in adjusting (the United States may be a special case, as discussed below).

In principle, long-lived imbalances associated with demographics and development might be expected to be large, given the huge differences in growth rates and wealth across countries. A country with one-tenth of the capital per worker of the United States (Thailand, for example) could in principle borrow in excess of its initial GDP on a path to catching up with

---

for this issue would raise the norm for the Swiss current account by about 2 percent of GDP (Gagnon 2014).

US productivity.[6] Its NIIP would become more negative, but its GDP would grow rapidly, keeping net financing costs at a bearable level. However, domestic saving rates tend to be high in rapidly growing economies, reducing the need to borrow. Rapidly growing economies also face bottlenecks to investment and rapid transformation. Thus, estimated imbalances arising from demographics and development are not likely to exceed 2 to 3 percentage points of GDP.

The ultimate determining factor for sustainable current accounts in most countries is the country's ability to finance them. Financing, in turn, requires that the burden of net investment payments be manageable. Net investment payments reflect a return (interest, dividends, retained earnings) on the NIIP (total domestic holdings of foreign assets minus total foreign holdings of domestic assets). In particular, the ratio of the NIIP to GDP must not decline indefinitely.[7]

The top panel of figure 3.1 displays the distribution of NIIPs (in percent of GDP) of the 65 countries with nominal GDP greater than $100 billion in 2014. The asymmetry of the figure is striking, with a long tail of countries with extremely large positive NIIPs and no countries with NIIPs much less than –100 percent of GDP. All four countries with NIIPs below –70 percent of GDP (Spain, Greece, Portugal, and Ireland) are in the euro area. These countries almost surely would not have been able to borrow so much if they had not been in an economic and currency union. Even within that union, their huge net debts led to a major crisis in 2010–12 that has forced them to maintain fiscal austerity and switch from current account deficits to current account surpluses.

This asymmetry becomes even starker in the bottom panel of figure 3.1, which includes the euro area as a single entity. The country with the largest negative NIIP is Hungary at –66 percent of GDP, followed by Vietnam, Poland, Morocco, New Zealand, and Turkey between –60 and –65 percent. Romania and Australia have NIIPs between –50 and –60 percent. Out of 54 countries, none has a NIIP below –70 percent of GDP, and 11 have NIIPs greater than 70 percent, ranging up to 420 percent of GDP. These results confirm a pattern that many observers have long noticed: Financial markets

---

6. Data on national capital stocks are scarce. According to the World Bank's Atlas measure, Thailand's per capita national income is about 1/10th the US level. Depending on labor force participation, labor quality, and parameters of the production function, capital per worker in Thailand may be about 1/10th the US level.

7. To the extent that holders of foreign assets differ from issuers of liabilities to foreigners, financing could become a problem even with the net position close to balance. What matters in that case is the total debt burden of any given sector, not merely its cross-border debts.

Figure 3.1 Frequency distribution of net international investment position/GDP, 2014

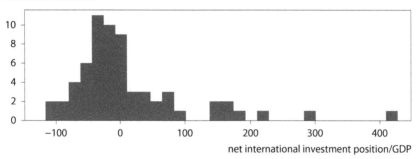

a. Euro area members included individually

number of countries

net international investment position/GDP

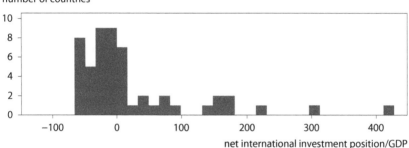

b. Euro area included as single country

number of countries

net international investment position/GDP

Note: Includes only economies with nominal GDP of at least $100 billion.
Source: Authors' calculations based on data from sources listed in appendix A.

limit the ability of countries to incur debts but not the ability of countries to accumulate assets.

Because a country's NIIP is essentially the cumulation of its past current account balances, focus on sustainability typically concerns the size and persistence of a country's current account balance. However, two other factors also enter the analysis. The first is valuation adjustments on the assets a country holds and on the liabilities it owes to foreigners, which may arise from changes in exchange rates or stock prices, for example. The second is the growth rate of the economy, the denominator in the *NIIP/GDP* ratio. At the end of any year, the ratio of the NIIP to GDP is equal to last year's ratio divided by the gross growth rate of this year's GDP plus the ratio of the current account and valuation adjustments to GDP:

$$(NIIP/GDP)_t = (NIIP/GDP)_{t-1}/(GDP_t/GDP_{t-1}) + (CAB_t + NVA_t)/GDP_t$$

where *CAB* is the current account balance and *NVA* the net valuation adjustment. For any fixed ratio of *CAB* + *NVA* to *GDP*, *NIIP/GDP* will stabilize at a constant value as long as GDP is growing steadily.

In their work on sustainable current accounts, Cline and Williamson (2008, 2012) use a range of +/–3 percent for the current account as a ratio to GDP. If one assumes that valuation adjustments are close to zero on average and nominal GDP growth is 5 percent per year (as used to be common), the above equation implies that a 3 percent current account deficit is consistent with a stable NIIP/GDP ratio of –60 percent. With trend nominal GDP growth of 4 percent per year (consistent with the Federal Reserve's long-run forecast for the United States), a stable NIIP/GDP ratio of –60 requires a current account deficit of only 2.4 percent. As can be seen in figure 3.1, a NIIP/GDP ratio of –60 percent appears to be close to the sustainable limit, at least if one excludes countries in the euro area. Thus we find the Cline-Williamson ranges for sustainable current accounts to be reasonable, or perhaps even a bit too wide, under plausible assumptions. For large economies another argument for limits to imbalances less than +/–3 percent of GDP is the larger spillovers of imbalances in these economies to the rest of the world. Clearly, surplus countries have little trouble running even larger surpluses than 3 percent of GDP, but we agree with Cline and Williamson in their normative judgment that a symmetric standard should be applied.

Figure 3.2 displays elements of the equation for four important deficit countries. Australia ran an average current account deficit of 4.4 percent of GDP between 1995 and 2014. Its (volatile) net valuation adjustments (a positive offset to the current account) averaged 0.8 percent of GDP. In addition, it had a relatively high annual growth rate of 7.0 percent in terms of US dollars. Our NIIP arithmetic suggests a steady-state NIIP/GDP of –54 percent. It appears that Australia has been in steady state over this period. However, if Australia's trend growth rate declines or net valuation adjustments do not continue to be positive on average, the steady-state NIIP/GDP would become more negative and raise issues of sustainability. If, for example, future valuation adjustments average close to zero, the steady-state NIIP/GDP ratio would decline to –67 percent of GDP, outside the range of non-euro-area countries in figure 3.1.

Spain presents a more extreme example. Although its average current account deficit was somewhat smaller than Australia's (3.6 percent), it had a slower growth rate (4.8 percent) and suffered negative average valuation adjustments (–1.7 percent). These numbers imply a steady-state NIIP of –116 percent of GDP. Actual NIIP moved down steadily toward this value. Despite Spain's membership in the euro area and European Union, financial markets became unwilling to support its large debt, and Spain was hit by the euro crisis in 2010. Massive fiscal austerity and a grinding recession

Figure 3.2   Sustainability analysis for four debtor countries, 1995–2014 (percent of GDP)

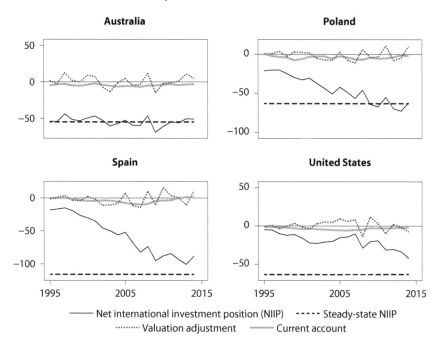

Source: Authors' calculations based on data from sources listed in appendix A.

pushed the current account into balance, which should ultimately raise NIIP/GDP if Spain can resume steady growth.

Poland is a member of the European Union but not the euro area. Its average current account plus valuation adjustments were similar to Spain's, but its GDP grew much faster, leading to a less extreme steady-state NIIP of –63 percent of GDP. Although Poland was not hit by the euro crisis, markets did begin to question the sustainability of its net borrowing, much of which was in foreign currencies, which created risky currency mismatches. The depreciation of the zloty and rapid underlying productivity growth as Poland catches up to its more advanced neighbors have brought the current account back into balance without requiring the massive recession Spain endured.

The United States had an average current account deficit of 3.4 percent of GDP, which was offset to a modest extent by average valuation adjustments of 0.8 percent of GDP. Average nominal GDP growth was 4.3 percent. Together, these data imply a steady-state NIIP of –64 percent of GDP, close to the apparent limit on debtor countries. Assuming 4 percent nominal GDP growth, a 4 percent current account deficit (Cline 2016), and continued average valuation adjustments of 0.8 percent, the United States would reach a NIIP of –60 percent of GDP in roughly 20 years. If the deficit widens to 5 percent of GDP, as may be likely under the Trump administration's policies (Prakken and Varvares 2016), or valuation adjustments average close to zero, the United States would reach a NIIP of –60 percent of GDP in about 10 years.

Is the –60 percent limit on NIIP/GDP relevant for the United States? The main arguments in favor of a potentially larger net debt are the unique role of the US dollar as the world's reserve currency and its dominant share in financial transactions. In addition, US Treasury securities are the world's principal safe asset, and US institutional governance is viewed favorably (though not notably more so than many other advanced economies). The disproportionately large size of the US economy makes it risky for investors to concentrate so much of their holdings in dollars, however, especially as a more negative US NIIP/GDP ratio increases the possibility of a substantial fall in the value of the dollar. The United States has already far exceeded all previous records for the size of any one country's net liabilities to the rest of the world relative to world GDP.

Another concern is that the true NIIP limit for most countries may not extend as far below zero as 60 percent of GDP. Of the eight countries with NIIP/GDP below –50 percent, two (Australia and New Zealand) have large natural resource sectors to service the debt; one (Vietnam) is a rapidly growing developing economy building its export capacity; three (Hungary, Romania, and Turkey) have had recent or ongoing IMF adjustment programs; and two (Morocco and Poland) have already experienced market-driven pressures to narrow the current account deficit. It is not clear that even –50 percent is a safe level for NIIP/GDP in a slow-growing, non-resource-focused economy like the United States.

Much has been made of the fact that the total reported payments on US foreign liabilities are less than the reported earnings on US foreign assets, implying that the negative US NIIP does not impose a net financing burden on the US economy. Much of this outcome reflects measurement error, however, and much of the part that is not measurement error stems from ultralow interest rates on debt, which are not likely to last much longer. The mismeasurement arises from the incentive for US corporations to report profits in their overseas activities, where they are not taxed unless the earnings are repatriated. Because US corporate tax rates are among the highest in the world, US companies and foreign companies operating in the United States have an incentive to book profits outside the United States, in low-tax jurisdictions such as Ireland.

A component that may be persistent arises from the larger proportion of high-grade debt in foreign claims on the United States relative to high-grade debt in US claims on foreigners. To some extent, the United States is a "banker to the world," taking in cheap deposits and lending them out profitably abroad—or more accurately, issuing low-yield bonds and investing the proceeds in foreign equity and foreign direct investment (FDI) (Gourinchas and Rey 2007). This financial arbitrage does not require a negative NIIP, however, as it implies equal claims on, and liabilities to, the rest of the world.

If profits on FDI in the United States had been reported at the same rate (relative to the stock of FDI) as profits on US FDI abroad, and the average interest rates on US debt held by foreigners and foreign debt held by Americans had been higher by 3 percentage points (retaining the same spread), US net investment income in 2015 would have been -$275 billion instead of the reported $182 billion (authors' calculations based on annual data from the US Bureau of Economic Analysis, assuming no change in portfolio equity income or payments).

Rising interest rates increase the current account deficit directly, through higher net interest payments to foreigners. An increase in US and foreign interest rates of 3 percentage points would leave interest rates still somewhat below their average of the past 30 years. Such an increase would widen the US current account deficit by $250 billion. In order to keep the current account at its previous level, the dollar would have to depreciate by roughly 8 percent. If US interest rates were to rise more rapidly or by more than foreign interest rates, as now seems likely, the net effect would be even larger.

Figure 3.3 displays the NIIP sustainability exercise for four surplus economies. Germany ran an average current account surplus of 3.1 percent of GDP between 1995 and 2014, which was offset by average valuation adjustments of -1.5 percent. With moderately slow nominal GDP growth (2.8 percent), the implied steady-state NIIP was 60 percent of GDP. Most of the surpluses occurred in the second half of the sample, and German NIIP is now rising rapidly. Norway had an even larger average current account surplus, of 11.1 percent of GDP, offset modestly by valuation adjustments of -1.0 percent. (The much larger scale on some of these panels makes the current account surpluses look smaller than they are.) Norway had relatively rapid nominal annual GDP growth of 6.9 percent. The implied steady-state NIIP is 157 percent of GDP, and actual NIIP is almost there.

Singapore ran an average current account surplus of 18.4 percent of GDP and had positive average valuation adjustments of 4.3 percent. It had relatively rapid nominal annual GDP growth of 7.1 percent. It made rapid progress toward its steady-state NIIP of 342 percent of GDP in the first half of the period. Average valuation adjustments turned negative in the second

Figure 3.3 Sustainability analysis for four creditor countries, 1995–2014 (percent of GDP)

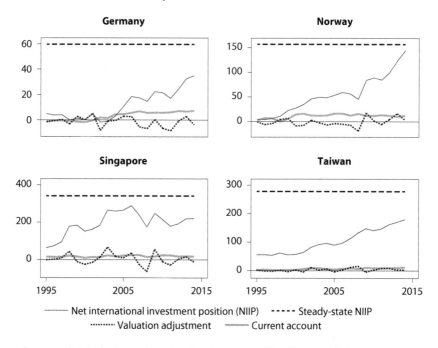

Germany

Norway

Singapore

Taiwan

——— Net international investment position (NIIP)   ---- Steady-state NIIP
·········· Valuation adjustment   ——— Current account

Source: Authors' calculations based on data from sources listed in appendix A.

half, and nominal GDP growth sped up considerably, preventing a further rise in NIIP/GDP.

Taiwan had an average current account surplus of 6.6 percent but large positive valuation adjustments, averaging 3.2 percent of GDP. With modest nominal annual GDP growth of 3.6 percent, its steady-state NIIP was 278 percent of GDP.

A key message from figure 3.3 is that surplus countries do not face external pressure to adjust. Their actual and steady-state NIIP ratios can thus be much larger than those of deficit countries. In three of the four economies, NIIP/GDP rose steadily. In Singapore internal factors halted this rise. Nevertheless, Singapore's NIIP remained an astonishing 200 percent of GDP.

As with current account balances, NIIPs must add up to zero across all countries (in dollar terms); a positive NIIP for one country thus requires a negative NIIP for another. The ability of some surplus countries to pile up massive amounts of net foreign assets raises a key threat to the global economy, because it makes adjustment in deficit countries more difficult to achieve. After all, for debtor countries to reduce their net debts, creditor countries must relinquish their net claims. As currently constituted, the international system does not impose pressures on surplus countries to adjust. Such pressures would be helpful to ease debtor adjustment.

This analysis strongly supports the Cline-Williamson range for sustainable current account imbalances of +/-3 percent of GDP for most countries. Indeed, with prospects for long-run nominal GDP growth in many advanced economies having declined to well below 5 percent, an even narrower range of sustainable imbalances might be indicated. The primary exception is exporters of nonrenewable natural resources, which should be allowed to run larger surpluses in some cases, as discussed in chapter 4.

Currency Policies: Legitimate and Illegitimate

Legitimate Intervention

IMF Article IV encourages countries to intervene in foreign exchange markets to counteract disorderly movements in exchange rates.[8] Such intervention should be symmetric with respect to appreciations and depreciations.[9] Intervention to counter disorderly market conditions should not lead to a trend change in reserve holdings.

For a country with less than adequate foreign exchange reserves, acquiring more reserves is a legitimate ground for intervention in most circumstances. (We discuss how to determine what is adequate in the next chapter.) An adequate level of reserves enables a country to more effectively use intervention to counter disorderly market conditions.

Intervention can be useful for stabilizing current account balances in the face of unsustainable swings in private capital flows or illegitimate intervention by other countries. The IMF Articles of Agreement suggest that countries are allowed, and even encouraged, to use foreign exchange intervention to counteract unsustainable imbalances. The idea of using inter-

---

8. Official statements issued during or after foreign exchange intervention often mention the goal of countering disorderly market conditions. After the Japanese earthquake and tsunami of 2011, for example, the G-7 finance ministers and central bank governors agreed on concerted intervention, stating "As we have long stated, excess volatility and disorderly movements in exchange rates have adverse implications for economic and financial stability. We will monitor exchange markets closely and will cooperate as appropriate" (G7 Statement on Currencies, March 18, 2011, www.smh.com.au/business/markets/g7-statement-on-currencies-20110318-1bzsj.html).

9. Many financial asset prices, such as stock prices, move asymmetrically, tending to fall more rapidly than they rise, which might justify an asymmetric policy response. However, exchange rates are by definition symmetric (they are the price of one currency in terms of another), so that falls are not more rapid than rises.

vention to help correct imbalances was central to the Plaza Accord of 1985, as discussed in chapter 1.

Illegitimate Intervention

Article IV of the IMF Articles of Agreement states that members of the IMF are obliged to "avoid manipulating exchange rates or the international monetary system in order to prevent effective balance-of-payments adjustment or to gain an unfair competitive advantage over other members." Article 15 of the WTO charter states that countries should not "by exchange action, frustrate the intent of the provisions of the Agreement." This article means that countries should not move exchange rates to offset reductions in tariffs and other barriers to trade.

To flesh out the meaning of "manipulating exchange rates," the Integrated Surveillance Decision of 2012 lists "protracted large-scale intervention in one direction in the exchange market," "fundamental exchange rate misalignment," and "large and prolonged current account deficits or surpluses" as three potential developments that might point to a violation of the ban on exchange rate manipulation. International obligations prohibit countries from actively using official financial flows to create or sustain a current account balance higher than its normative or equilibrium value, which, we suggest in the next chapter, should not be greater than 3 percent of a country's GDP.

Capital Flow Measures

Capital controls, also known as capital flow measures (CFMs), are another policy option countries use to minimize spillovers from other countries, including potentially disruptive swings in financial flows. On December 3, 2012, the IMF published a formal statement of its "institutional view" on the management of capital flows (IMF 2012b). This document codified the results of staff papers in recent years that examined the benefits and costs of capital flows and policy measures to control them.

The IMF based its new doctrine primarily on the study of developing economies, but the findings have broad applicability, including to advanced economies. In its advice on managing large capital inflows, the IMF stresses the importance of a sound institutional and regulatory structure that channels inflows toward productive investment. It also recognizes that large capital inflows have macroeconomic consequences. The first line of defense against large capital inflows is appropriate macroeconomic policies—namely, reducing interest rates if there is no risk of inflation or asset bubbles, allowing the currency to appreciate if it is not overvalued, and accumulating more foreign exchange reserves if the level of reserves is not excessive.

When the scope for adjusting macroeconomic policies is limited, the IMF acknowledges that CFMs "can be useful for supporting macroeconomic policy adjustment and safeguarding financial system stability" (IMF 2012b, 18). If accumulation of more reserves is not feasible or does not improve the macroeconomic outlook sufficiently, the IMF doctrine allows for the use of CFMs.

The general principles are that CFMs should be transparent, targeted, temporary, and nondiscriminatory. Well-targeted CFMs are a natural tool to consider in response to destabilizing and volatile financial flows. The IMF notes with tacit approval three specific examples of CFMs that were used in recent years: Brazil's tax on certain types of inflows, Indonesia's holding period on central bank bond purchases, and Korea's leverage caps on banks' derivatives positions.

Domestic Policies

Monetary and fiscal policies affect exchange rates, but these domestic policies are not subject to the limitations written into the IMF Articles of Agreement or other international agreements. They are, however, legitimate topics for surveillance and discussion by, and advice from, the IMF. Expansionary monetary policy has an ambiguous effect on the trade balance, because any boost to exports from a currency depreciation is offset by an increase in domestic demand for imports. In contrast, fiscal policy has a strong effect on the trade balance, especially in economies with open capital markets. For economies with the most open capital markets, the trade balance increases by roughly half of any increase in the fiscal balance (see table 2.1).

The adoption of unconventional monetary policies, in particular quantitative easing—first in the United States and the United Kingdom in 2009 and later in the euro area and Japan—led to charges that the advanced economies were seeking to stimulate their economies by weakening their currencies. Quantitative easing did tend to weaken the exchange rates of countries that implemented it, especially Japan, but it did not cause the current accounts of these countries to rise, as shown in figure 2.2.

Domestic versus External Policies

Some countries have viewed quantitative easing as a new weapon in the global "currency wars." Most of these views have emanated from emerging-market economies, whose currencies have been buffeted by sharp and often sizable shifts in international capital flows in the wake of quantitative easing by rich countries. It was the finance minister of Brazil who popularized the term *currency wars*, in bemoaning the appreciation of his own exchange rate in response to expected quantitative easing by the Federal Reserve in 2010. The former governor of the Reserve Bank of India (and former IMF chief economist) Raghuram Rajan (2014) has echoed this view (although his complaints about quantitative easing in higher-income countries relate as much, or more, to their triggering of volatile capital flows to and from emerging markets as to their impact on exchange rates—a different aspect of "currency wars").

It is understandable that countries like Brazil, which have become highly integrated with global capital markets, do not distinguish between quantitative easing and currency manipulation. Both policies have immediate effects on exchange rates, making other countries' exports less competitive. Their effects on domestic spending, which ultimately boosts other countries' exports, are quite different and not immediately obvious. Quantitative easing increases domestic spending, thus boosting foreign exports; foreign exchange intervention does not.

Central banks in emerging markets may be emulating monetary policy in the advanced economies excessively, in part out of a desire to stabilize their exchange rates (Gagnon et al. 2017). In so doing, they transmit a clear boost from quantitative easing in advanced economies to growth in their own economies (IMF 2011b). This boost may be the right medicine if they had previously kept policy too tight or if quantitative easing in advanced economies is a response to a drop in global demand. But if quantitative easing in advanced economies is responding to a shock that is limited to advanced economies, emerging markets risk overheating their economies if they loosen monetary policy in response.

A fundamental difference between domestic and external policies is that domestic policies operate in domestic markets with domestic instruments (bank reserves, domestic bonds, and credit to domestic banks) whereas external policies operate in foreign markets with foreign instruments (foreign exchange reserves held as foreign bonds and foreign currency deposits in banks, which in turn hold foreign assets). External policy affects the exchange rate directly and as its main intent, whereas domestic policy does so only indirectly and as a byproduct of its basic goal of managing the domestic economy.

If a large purchase of domestic assets is viewed as having harmful spillovers onto foreign economies, it stands to reason that a similarly sized purchase of foreign assets must have even greater spillovers. Currency intervention affects the relative economic conditions of the two countries whose currencies are involved, shifting production and employment from the target country to the intervening country. It is thus a zero-sum game, with no net gain for the world economy as a whole.

Expansionary monetary policy, by contrast, raises economic activity in the country adopting it (if the policy works as intended), with only small spillovers to other countries. It is a positive-sum game from the viewpoint of the world as a whole. Expansionary fiscal policy also raises economic activity in the country adopting it, with unambiguously positive spillovers for the rest of the world.

These conceptual distinctions have a solid grounding in economic theory and evidence. The IMF Articles of Agreement enshrine them, and the G-7 and G-20 countries have implicitly accepted them in repeated statements. Countries agree to adopt domestic policies to achieve strong and sustainable growth with low inflation; they agree on the goal of reducing current account imbalances; and they also agree not to use exchange rate policies for competitive advantage (G-20 2013).

International agreements and institutions support the use of foreign exchange intervention, and net official flows more broadly, to achieve sustainable current account balances. Use of these instruments for competitive advantage, or to prevent balance-of-payments adjustment, contravenes these rules. The problem, as we show, is that there is no effective mechanism to enforce them.

4

The "Decade of Manipulation" (2003–13)

This chapter describes the "decade" (really 11 years) of unprecedented foreign exchange intervention and net official flows that began around 2003. During this period worldwide net official flows averaged $1 trillion per year. More than half of those flows were excessive. Many countries that did not have excessive flows by the criteria presented in this chapter may still have had greater flows than they would have in the absence of currency manipulation by their trading partners. These official flows supported large current account surpluses in the manipulators and caused or widened current account deficits in the nonmanipulators. The US current account was the most negatively affected. The larger US deficit imposed major costs for the US economy through several channels.

First, it added fuel to a housing boom that wasted resources, because it led to uneconomic shifts in employment and activity across sectors, including the construction of housing that was not needed and financially unsustainable, contributing in an important way to the onset of the Great Recession. Second, it accelerated the speed and increased the intensity of the shock caused by China's rapid export growth, which caused lasting unemployment and devastated many communities across America, substantially eroding support for globalization and especially open trade policies across the United States. Indeed, import competition from China was an important factor behind political polarization and the shift toward antitrade candidates on both the right and the left of the political spectrum (Autor et al. 2016). Third, the persistence of the trade deficit increased the severity of the Great Recession and retarded the subsequent recovery, likely holding down US employment by 1 million or more between 2009 and 2014.

Since 2014 net official flows have declined dramatically, reflecting the fall in oil and commodity prices and a shift in financial market sentiment that put downward pressures on the currencies of many of the countries that had been manipulators in the previous decade. This lull in manipulation is likely to persist for commodity exporters as long as commodity prices remain low. However, for many of the other manipulators, the lull may last only as long as the notoriously fickle attitudes of participants in international financial markets.

Currency Aggressors of the Early 21st Century

Foreign exchange intervention and current account imbalances soared to record levels beginning in 2003 and remained high through 2013 (figure 4.1). Most intervention was aimed not at reducing imbalances but at maintaining or increasing surpluses. The timing of the increase in intervention (net official flows) reflects three factors: (1) many emerging markets decided to build up foreign exchange reserves after the Asian financial crisis of 1997–98; (2) the dollar depreciated from 2002 through 2008, and many countries (most notably China, which had pegged its currency to the dollar since 1994) resisted upward pressure on their currencies in dollar terms; and (3) oil prices rose sharply in 2003, and many oil exporters decided to save most of the increase in revenue.

Twenty economies intervened aggressively in at least one of the 11 years from 2003 through 2013 to keep their currencies undervalued and thus to unfairly maintain excessive current account surpluses (table 4.1). To be included in any given year, a country had to meet all of the following criteria:[1]

- The current account surplus exceeded 3 percent of GDP.
- Net official flows exceeded 2 percent of GDP.
- Net official flows exceeded 65 percent of oil exports minus production cost or 50 percent of gross commodity exports for other nonrenewable commodities.[2]

---

1. Denmark and Latvia met these criteria for three years and one year, respectively. We excluded them from the list because they have a mutually agreed currency peg with the euro, all of their intervention is conducted in euros, and the euro area is not a net purchaser of official foreign assets. Denmark and Latvia may be viewed as a part of the euro area currency bloc, which has no net official flows with the rest of the world. Iran, Iraq, and Syria were excluded from the analysis because of missing data for several years each.

2. Botswana (diamonds), Chile (copper), and Suriname (gold) would have met the other criteria in at least one year. In Botswana net official flows were highly volatile, switching from positive to negative, but were never close to 50 percent of diamond exports over any four-year period. We therefore excluded Botswana from table 4.1.

Figure 4.1 External accounts of surplus countries, 1980–2015

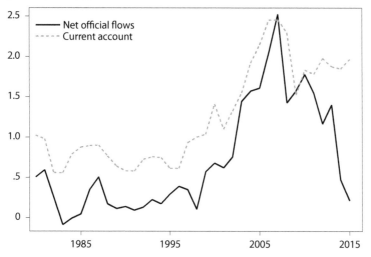

percent of world GDP

Source: Authors' calculations based on data from sources listed in appendix A.

- Foreign exchange reserves and other official foreign assets exceeded the traditional criterion for reserve adequacy of three months of imports (IMF 2011a).
- Foreign exchange reserves and other official foreign assets exceeded the Greenspan-Guidotti rule for reserve adequacy of 100 percent of short-term external debt in foreign currencies, public and private.[3]
- Classification by the World Bank as high-income or upper-middle-income as of 2015.[4]

---

3. The World Bank's external debt data are not reported for advanced economies and certain emerging-market and developing economies (notably the Persian Gulf oil exporters). In most cases missing data reflect a judgment that the country does not have significant foreign currency external debt. We assume that official assets exceed external debt in these countries.

4. Bolivia, Lesotho, Morocco, Myanmar, the Philippines, and Timor-Leste met the first five criteria in at least one year. We excluded these lower-income countries from the list of manipulators for three reasons: (1) institutional shortcomings are often more important than macroeconomic policy mistakes in preventing low-income countries from growing rapidly, (2) there is a longstanding presumption (e.g., in the WTO) that low-income countries should be held to a laxer standard of conduct, and (3) these countries are small in economic terms. Excluding them does not imply an endorsement of currency manipulation as the best development strategy; indeed, currency manipulation runs against standard economic analysis that recommends that low-income countries should borrow from rich countries to invest in productive capital. But undervalued currencies are widely viewed as having "worked" for China and other developing economies (Bhalla 2012), and wealthy countries can afford to give their less wealthy brethren greater scope to pursue policies they deem effective.

Table 4.1 Official assets and net official flows of currency manipulators, 2003–13

Economy	Years of manipulation	2013 official assets Billions of dollars	2013 official assets Percent of GDP	Average net official flows as percent of GDP	Average current account as percent of GDP
Manufacturing exporters					
Taiwan	9	417	81	6	8
China	7	4,023	42	8	5
Korea	4	396	30	3	2
Malaysia	3	82	25	3	12
Thailand	3	190	45	4	2
Israel	3	80	27	2	3
Japan	2	1,204	25	1	3
Sweden	1	68	12	1	7
Financial centers					
Macao	11	16	31	16	30
Singapore	10	603	201	22	21
Hong Kong	6	311	113	7	9
Switzerland	4	522	76	6	11
Resource exporters					
Norway	11	883	169	13	13
Algeria	6	191	91	13	12
United Arab Emirates	5	863	222	24	12
Russia	5	384	17	5	6
Libya	5	179	271	22	23
Kuwait	4	301	173	29	36
Trinidad and Tobago	3	16	60	6	17
Oman	1	41	53	9	9

Note: See text for criteria for currency manipulation. Average net official flows and current account are based on entire 11-year period.

Sources: See appendix A.

Currency manipulators can be divided into three groups: manufacturing exporters (eight economies), financial centers (four economies), and natural resource exporters (eight economies). The largest manipulators by volume are the manufacturing exporters, with a total of $5.4 trillion in net official flows during these 11 years, more than half of the total of all net official flows of the currency manipulators. Appendix table A.1 displays annual data for each of these countries.

Table 4.2   Net official flows of currency manipulators, 2000–15 (billions of dollars)

| Year | World net official flows | Flows of countries in table 4.1 | Of which | | |
			Manufacturing exporters	Financial centers	Resource exporters
2000	188	190	83	23	84
2001	153	184	116	0	68
2002	262	238	181	–3	60
2003	550	509	382	20	106
2004	713	627	456	33	138
2005	794	627	342	16	270
2006	1,129	865	376	77	412
2007	1,660	1,190	733	69	388
2008	927	698	556	–33	176
2009	1,179	914	580	247	86
2010	1,272	1,046	662	219	165
2011	1,210	945	606	129	210
2012	881	623	109	279	236
2013	1,040	944	605	39	300
2014	356	323	172	61	89
2015	–130	73	–315	137	251
Total 2003–13	11,354	8,988	5,407	1,095	2,485
Total 2000–15	12,183	9,996	5,644	1,314	3,038

Note: Flows are summed over all countries listed in table 4.1, regardless of whether they exceeded the criteria for manipulation in any given year.

Sources: See appendix A.

Table 4.2 displays the aggregate net official flows since 2000 of the countries listed in table 4.1. Table 4.3 covers the net official flows of the same countries over the same period but includes only flows that occurred in years in which a country exceeded the criteria for currency manipulation and only the flows that exceeded the criteria. The totals for the financial centers are similar across the tables, because the financial centers typically exceed the criteria by a wide margin. The totals for resource exporters are lower in table 4.3 because of the exclusion of net official flows of up to 65 percent of oil export profits. The totals for manufacturers are lower in table 4.3, because some countries (of which China is by far the most important) fell slightly below the criteria of a 3 percent current account surplus and 2 percent of GDP net official flows in some years. Given the very large

Table 4.3 Excess currency manipulation, 2000–15 (billions of dollars)

Year	Excess currency manipulation	Of which		
		Manufacturing exporters	Financial centers	Resource exporters
2000	67	13	20	34
2001	68	33	1	34
2002	110	80	0	30
2003	286	233	19	34
2004	347	293	28	26
2005	349	247	24	78
2006	480	249	70	161
2007	747	595	59	93
2008	556	498	29	29
2009	656	422	228	6
2010	659	457	197	5
2011	426	314	104	8
2012	284	14	253	16
2013	430	329	13	88
2014	86	19	43	24
2015	347	0	121	225
Total 2003–13	5,219	3,649	1,026	544
Total 2000–15	5,896	3,794	1,210	892

Note: Flows are summed only over countries that exceeded the criteria for manipulation in any given year and only by the amount in excess of 2 percent of GDP or 65 percent of energy export profits for resource exporters.

Sources: See appendix A.

net official assets of most of the countries in table 4.1 as of 2013, it is reasonable to argue that they had excessive net official flows even in years in which they fell slightly short of our criteria. In that sense table 4.2 gives a better sense of total excessive official flows than table 4.3, which provides a conservative estimate of the amount by which official flows might have been reduced by imposing global rules along the lines of the criteria we use.

In absolute terms China was by far the largest intervener over this period, with cumulative net official flows of nearly $4 trillion in 2003–13. The peak year of Chinese intervention was 2007, when China bought an average of nearly $2 billion per business day and its current account surplus reached 10 percent of GDP. By 2012–13 Chinese intervention had dropped to about $1 billion per day, and the current account surplus was

2 percent of GDP. Between the summer of 2005 and its recent peak in the summer of 2015, the renminbi was allowed to appreciate by 35 percent against the US dollar and more than 50 percent on a real trade-weighted basis.[5] China's net official flows turned negative in 2015, a topic discussed toward the end of this chapter.

Taiwan was the most frequent manipulator among the manufacturing exporters, with excessive currency intervention in 9 of 11 years and current account surpluses that averaged 8 percent of GDP over the period as a whole. By 2013 Taiwan had accumulated official assets worth more than 80 percent of its GDP. The remaining manufacturing exporters did not routinely manipulate, but they did have significant net official flows on average over this period.

Japan had the second-largest stock of official assets in 2013, but its intervention was mainly limited to three years (2003, 2004, and 2011) during which there was strong upward pressure on the yen. The government resisted this pressure through massive intervention that averaged about $500 million per day during these years. Japan exceeded all of our criteria in 2003 and 2004. It fell short in 2011, when the current account fell below 3 percent of GDP in the wake of the tsunami that led to a shutdown of nuclear power plants and a large increase in oil imports.

The financial centers are fully open to capital flows and tend to experience capital inflows during times of market turbulence or heightened risk aversion. Switzerland is a favorite destination of non-Swiss investors during troubled times.[6] To some extent, Hong Kong, Macao, and Singapore also experience safe-haven flows. The financial centers as a group had $1.1 trillion in net official flows during these 11 years (see table 4.2).

Hong Kong and Switzerland manipulate only sporadically when financial inflows are high, as seen by the relatively small number of years of manipulation. The level of manipulation in these years is enormous, however.[7]

For Macao and Singapore, the story is different. Currency manipulation is built into the structure of the Singaporean economy. The excess of hefty payroll taxes (roughly 35 percent of wages) over public pension payouts is channeled into foreign official assets through sovereign wealth funds, and the central bank conducts monetary policy mainly by purchasing foreign exchange reserves.

---

5. The real exchange rate is calculated by JPMorgan Chase, based on consumer prices. Data are from Haver Analytics.

6. Japan is similar to Switzerland in that both countries are safe havens for domestic and international investors during turbulent times.

7. The average ratio of net official flows to GDP in table 4.1 refers to all 11 years; it is not limited to the years of active manipulation.

All of these financial centers have consistently run very large current account surpluses. They have thus clearly overcompensated for the upward pressure on their currencies caused by safe-haven inflows, especially considering that other safe havens, such as the United States, have allowed such flows to generate a tendency toward current account deficits.

The resource exporters in table 4.1 jointly purchased almost $2.5 trillion in official assets over this period. Resource exporters not listed in table 4.1, including Qatar and Saudi Arabia, also made routine large official purchases.

The pattern of external savings differs sharply across resource exporters. Australia, Canada, Nigeria, and Venezuela hold relatively low levels of external official assets. Other exporters hold enormous amounts. It is desirable for exporters of nonrenewable resources to save some of the proceeds for future generations, either internally or externally. We explore the issue of optimal external saving by resource exporters below.

What Constitutes Manipulation?

Supporting an Excessive Current Account Imbalance

The essential element of currency manipulation is official action to push or maintain a country's current account balance above a reasonable norm. Ideally, norms should be set within a relatively narrow band around zero based on long-term and cyclical factors that are fundamental to each economy and not reflective of inappropriate policy choices. As discussed in chapter 3, the norms developed by the IMF are not credible; they are tilted toward ratifying existing imbalances. In the absence of globally acceptable norms, the natural benchmark is a current account of zero.

Any criterion for identifying misbehavior must allow for a certain amount of random variation around that benchmark. One could argue that 1 or 2 percent of GDP is a reasonable tolerance level. However, given that some economies might plausibly have norms somewhat above zero, we settled on a criterion of 3 percent of GDP as excessive. Our colleagues William Cline and John Williamson have long used a 3 percent upper limit on equilibrium current account balances in their work on fundamental equilibrium exchange rates (Cline and Williamson 2008).[8] In its new "intensified evaluation of major trading partners," the US Treasury applies an upper bound of 3 percent of GDP for nonmaterial current account surpluses (US Treasury 2016).

---

8. Current account balances of +/-3 percent of GDP stretch the limit for sustainable net international investment positions under reasonable assumptions for advanced economies, as discussed in chapter 3.

The other element of manipulation is policy action. Many policies, including fiscal policy, affect a country's current account. Germany's fiscal surplus and its trading partners' fiscal deficits support its current account surplus, for example. Such policies are fair game for the international policy discussions that take place routinely at the IMF and the Organization for Economic Cooperation and Development (OECD) and in groups such as the G-7 and the G-20. But currency manipulation as commonly understood requires currency policy. We focus on net official flows (official purchases of foreign assets). Verbal policies, such as "talking the yen down," can also be important, but they are difficult to quantify, and much of their effect relies on expectations of future purchases. For these reasons, we limit our analysis to actual purchases.

Any volume of purchases might be viewed as excessive if the purchases occur when the current account is above 3 percent of GDP. However, a certain volume of sales and purchases may occasionally be useful to smooth disorderly market conditions. In addition, net official flows include reinvested earnings on foreign official assets. We do not wish to impose a requirement that such earnings be sold off continuously.[9] Therefore, we adopt a criterion for currency manipulation that requires net official flows of at least 2 percent of GDP—the same criterion used by the US Treasury for estimated net purchases (box 4.1).

Adequate Foreign Official Assets

Countries are of course justified in holding some level of foreign exchange reserves and other official foreign assets to provide a cushion against adverse shocks. A series of IMF papers discusses the legitimate purposes for which countries hold foreign exchange reserves (IMF 2011a, 2013a, 2015a). The overarching purpose is to smooth adjustment to shocks to financial or trade flows. Generally speaking, a country will want to hold more reserves when it has (1) a fixed or tightly managed exchange rate, (2) more volatile markets for its exports (as is the case for primary commodity exporters), (3) more volatile private financial flows (more open financial markets), (4) a larger share of imports in consumption, and (5) a larger amount of debt in foreign currency, especially short-term debt.

Officials in some of the countries listed in table 4.1 argue that they need high levels of official assets to protect against possible future downward pressure on their currencies given the observed volatility in exchange rates and private capital flows. The experience of Asian economies with the

---

9. Net official flows do not include valuation adjustments, such as adjustments from exchange rate movements. Data on actual interventions are available for only a few countries.

Box 4.1   The US Treasury's new criteria for enhanced analysis of exchange rates

The Trade Facilitation and Trade Enforcement Act of 2015 calls on the US Treasury to undertake "enhanced analysis of macroeconomic and exchange rate policies for each country that is a major trading partner of the United States that has a significant bilateral trade surplus with the United States, a material current account surplus, and engaged in persistent one-sided intervention in the foreign exchange market."

In its first report under the act, the Treasury Department interpreted the "major trading partners" of the United States to be the 12 economies with the greatest bilateral trade (exports and imports) with the United States. A significant bilateral trade surplus is at least $20 billion per year. A material current account surplus is 3 percent of GDP over 12 months. Persistent one-sided intervention must cumulate to at least 2 percent of GDP over 12 months. (In its October 2016 report, Treasury noted that an even smaller amount of intervention might be considered excessive "depending on the circumstances.")

We agree with Treasury's guidelines for "material current account surplus" and "persistent one-sided intervention." In addition, we make allowances for minimum adequate net official assets, saving a portion of nonrenewable resource revenues, and minimum per capita income levels. We do not limit our analysis to the 12 largest trading partners of the United States because we want to see how widespread currency manipulation is (although, as described in chapters 5 and 6, we would limit US policy action against manipulation to G-20 countries, on the view that only they are systemically important). We also do not limit our analysis to economies that have a bilateral trade surplus with the United States, because we feel strongly that the bilateral surplus criterion is not appropriate. Currency manipulation affects all economies, particularly those with open financial markets and especially those that issue reserve currencies such as the United States.

The case of Singapore is instructive. Singapore has a bilateral trade deficit with the United States but a large trade surplus with other Asian economies, including China, because it supplies inputs to their manufacturing plants. These economies in turn have trade surpluses with the United States. Many US imports from Asia include parts and service inputs from Singapore. Singapore's large net official flows, many of which are presumed to flow into the United States, put upward pressure on the US dollar and encourage US imports from all economies, not only from Singapore itself or even Asia.

In its April 2016 and October 2016 reports, Treasury found that no economy met all of the criteria for enhanced analysis. Taiwan had an excessive current account balance and persistent one-sided intervention, but its bilateral surplus with the United States, at $15 billion in 2015, was short of the $20 billion criterion. China, Germany, Japan, and Korea met the criteria for excessive current account surplus and bilateral trade surplus but did not have persistent one-sided intervention in 2015. Treasury put these four countries plus Taiwan on a "monitoring list" for future scrutiny.

region's financial crisis in 1997–98—when shortages of liquid assets in the countries most affected (Indonesia, Korea, and Thailand) forced them to borrow from the IMF and thus accept its policy demands, many of which they resented—underscore these concerns. The lesson they learned from that experience was to hold more foreign exchange reserves than recommended by traditional metrics.

We believe that the focus on reserves has been excessive in many cases and that not enough attention has been paid to the issue of currency mismatch that arises from borrowing in foreign currency. Although reserves help ameliorate the risks of currency mismatch, a better solution is to restrict foreign currency borrowing to exporters that can reasonably expect a stream of income in foreign currency to service their debts.

The traditional rule of thumb had been that reserves should equal three months' equivalent of imports. As financial markets have become more integrated, more attention has focused on countries' external liabilities. The Greenspan-Guidotti rule calls for reserves equal to 100 percent of short-term external debt in foreign currency.[10] The countries listed in table 4.1 exceed both of these criteria by wide margins.

The IMF recently proposed a composite reserve metric for emerging markets with deepening financial markets (IMF 2015a). It is based on historical analysis of the factors related to balance-of-payments outflows and exchange rate pressures during periods of turbulence, such as the Asian financial crisis of 1997–98. The composite metric for floating rate economies is 30 percent of short-term external debt in foreign currencies plus 15 percent of other external liabilities plus 5 percent of broad money plus 5 percent of exports.[11] Most of the economies listed in table 4.1 have official foreign assets that exceed the composite metric by a wide margin, although official assets are close to the composite reserve metric for Japan, Macao, Malaysia, and Switzerland. Hong Kong is the only economy listed in table 4.1 for which official assets fall significantly below the composite reserve metric, reflecting the large gross external liabilities of this financial center.

The IMF classifies the economies listed in table 4.1 for which net official assets are not excessive according to its composite metric as having "mature markets."[12] The composite metric is not appropriate for econo-

---

10. It is typically understood, though not always stated, that this criterion refers to external debt denominated in foreign currency. Most advanced economies have little debt denominated in foreign currency.

11. For countries with a fixed exchange rate, the metric is 30 percent of short-term external debt plus 20 percent of other external liabilities plus 10 percent of broad money plus 10 percent of exports.

12. For purposes of assessing reserve adequacy, the IMF divides economies into three categories: mature markets, deepening financial markets, and constrained market access. These

mies with mature markets and large gross external assets and liabilities, and the IMF does not propose using it for them. We return to the question of the appropriate reserve levels for economies with mature markets below.

One problem with the IMF's composite reserve metric is that it does not take sufficient account of the interaction between currency mismatches and currency volatility. Currency movements tend to have a stabilizing effect on economies when there is little or no currency mismatch. It is mainly when domestic borrowers have large amounts of unhedged foreign currency debts that exchange rate volatility is destabilizing. Of course, the external foreign currency debt component of the reserve metric is meant to reflect the risk of such debt. But in our view, the metric understates the harm of currency mismatches and overstates the need for reserves when there is no currency mismatch. We would raise the coefficient on foreign currency debt and lower the other coefficients. The reserve metric also does not take into account the existence of restrictions on capital flows that may reduce a country's vulnerability to harm from market volatility. Finally, the actual reserve holding of emerging markets in recent years influenced the IMF's analysis. The level of reserves is judged too low in economies with below-average reserves and too high in economies with above-average reserves. If emerging markets on average hold more reserves than optimal, as increasingly seems to be the case, the IMF will tend to recommend holding more reserves than optimal.[13]

Another issue is balancing the benefits of reserves with the costs of reserves. For most countries the interest rate earned on foreign exchange reserves is lower than the interest rate paid on domestic government debt. By reducing reserves and paying off debt, governments can reduce their fiscal deficits.

Jeanne and Rancière (2008) conclude that most Asian emerging markets held more than the optimal level as of 2005. The IMF (2015a) applies their model to foreign exchange reserves as of 2014. It finds that optimal reserves are close to, but less than, 100 percent of short-term foreign currency debt for most countries and exceed 100 percent of short-term debt (by a small margin) for only 2 of 34 emerging markets studied. Actual reserves are thus vastly above optimal levels by the Jeanne and Rancière metric in many countries.

An interesting question is whether national security reasons justify some economies holding reserves that exceed the benchmark. Taiwan (which has no recourse to IMF or other international public funding) and

---

classifications line up closely, but not completely, with the traditional division into advanced economies, emerging markets, and low-income countries.

13. This "comparison effect" was more pronounced in the early versions of the IMF analysis (IMF 2011a, 2013a) than in the latest version (IMF 2015a).

Israel (surrounded by potential enemies) are the most obvious cases. Korea, which would need massive financial resources if unification of the peninsula were to happen on short notice (as it did in Germany), may be in this category, too. The Persian Gulf oil exporters might argue that tensions with Iran or Israel justify holding extra reserves. Kuwait's official foreign assets proved to be a godsend in the aftermath of the first Gulf War.

Many countries might plead extenuating circumstances; it is not clear how widely such arguments would be accepted. It is difficult to quantify needs based on political or military considerations. Although we do not wish to downplay issues related to national security, we feel ill-equipped to factor them into our analysis. We therefore make no explicit adjustment for them in our criteria for excessive official flows.

It is possible to quantify the risk Taiwan faces from its lack of access to IMF financing. The largest loan in IMF history relative to a country's quota was the Greek loan of 2010, which was 32 times Greece's quota (IMF 2013b). This loan vastly exceeded normal guidelines and proved controversial for that reason. It is unlikely that any future loan would be as large relative to a country's quota. Taiwan's GDP is 38 percent of Korea's. If Taiwan were to have a quota 38 percent as large as Korea's, a loan in proportion to the Greek loan would equal $145 billion. Taiwan's net official assets in 2015, at $426 billion, were nearly three times larger than this hypothetical maximum IMF loan. Taiwan's lack of access to IMF funding is thus not currently an important consideration.

On balance we believe that for many economies a reasonable benchmark for a target level of foreign official assets is the greater of 100 percent of short-term external debt in foreign currency or three months' equivalent of imports.

Volatile Capital Flows and Mature Market Reserve Needs

The IMF (2015a, 13) argues that mature market economies that either issue a reserve currency or have a standing swap line with a reserve-issuing central bank "are unlikely to need sizable reserves for precautionary purposes, as they can create assets which can be swapped into any other currency at any time." For other mature market economies, the IMF recommends using scenario analysis based on historical episodes, country characteristics, and assumptions on possible adverse shocks.

We think that mature market economies ought to be allowed to buy reserves to counter pronounced inflows of hot money as well as manipulation of their currencies by other countries. They also ought to be allowed to sell reserves to counter pronounced outflows of hot money, as China has recently been doing. Such transactions would help move a country's exchange rate toward a level that stabilizes its current account balance at a sustainable level. This need exists for both reserve-currency issuers and other mature markets. During a transition period, a country would accumulate reserves gradually to reach a reasonable war chest for these purposes.

Hot money tends to flow to developing economies during periods of optimism and to safe havens, such as Japan, Switzerland, and the United States, during periods of market stress. IMF guidelines encourage governments to intervene to counter disorderly market conditions associated with hot money flows, but such intervention should occur in both directions roughly equally. Periodic episodes of hot money flows do not justify protracted large-scale intervention in one direction only, as has been the case for several countries in table 4.1, notably Japan, Korea, and Switzerland, in all of which the government intervened only when money was flowing in, not when it was flowing out.[14]

To respond symmetrically to hot money flows, governments need to compare the medium-term current account outlooks of their economies to reasonable norms for sustainable current account balances. Ideally, such norms should be agreed through the intermediation of the IMF, but the world needs a far more rigorous approach than the IMF has taken on such norms to date. We therefore settle on a maximum surplus (or deficit) of 3 percent of GDP. Governments would be encouraged to counter hot money flows when such flows threaten to push their current accounts away from sustainable norms and discouraged from countering such flows when they move in a stabilizing direction. (Chapter 5 discusses this reference rate strategy.)

For example, Switzerland faced strong upward pressure on its currency in recent years, which threatened to reduce its current account balance. However, the Swiss current account balance was far above a reasonable norm, suggesting that a large appreciation was desirable from the perspective of medium-term sustainability. By preventing market-driven balance-of-payments adjustment, Switzerland was in clear violation of the dictates of IMF Article IV, which states that "members shall...avoid manipulating exchange rates...to prevent effective balance-of-payments adjustment." We propose an alternative policy strategy for Switzerland later in this chapter.

One gauge for the potential size of hot money flows is the size of a country's gross external debt liabilities. The four categories of a country's external liabilities are direct investment, portfolio equity investment, portfolio debt investment, and other investment, which is dominated by bank

---

14. If the flows of hot money persist in the same direction for several years, they may justify persistent one-sided intervention, but only to push the current account toward a sustainable norm.

Table 4.4   Alternative official asset metric for mature market economies, 2014 (billions of dollars)

Economy	Net official foreign assets	Alternative asset metric[a]	Three months' imports
Australia	47	120	76
Canada	93	134	145
Denmark	70	48	41
Euro area[b]	232	1,190	781
Hong Kong	328	111	156
Israel	85	9	23
Japan	1,192	271	248
Malaysia	65	19	55
Norway	928	55	37
Singapore	579	118	128
Sweden	64	82	57
Switzerland	539	122	93
United Kingdom	60	847	230
United States	138	1,557	717
Total	4,420	4,682	2,787

a. 10 percent of the sum of portfolio debt liabilities and other (mainly bank) liabilities.
b. Data exclude intra-area liabilities and imports.

Sources: See appendix A.

loans. It is widely accepted that direct investment liabilities are not volatile. Portfolio equity flows, while volatile, are less disruptive than debt flows, because they lead to self-limiting changes in equity prices (an incipient equity outflow causes a drop in equity prices that deters investors from selling at a loss). Gross external debt liabilities are the sum of the remaining two categories. These liabilities are almost exclusively denominated in local currency in mature markets.

A country with mature markets may wish to hold reserves equal to some fraction of its gross external debt liabilities. Table 4.4 displays actual official assets and a potential reserve metric equal to 10 percent of gross external debt liabilities for the major mature market economies in 2014. For comparison, it also displays the traditional metric of three months of imports. External debt in foreign currencies is not available for these countries; it is believed to be small or hedged via derivatives markets or export revenues.

One interesting feature of table 4.4 is that the total of actual reserves across economies roughly equals the total of the alternative reserve metric.

This equality does not extend to individual economies. Some, such as Japan, Norway, Singapore, and Switzerland, hold far more reserves than suggested by the alternative metric. Others, such as the euro area, the United Kingdom, and the United States, hold far fewer reserves than suggested by the alternative metric.

There may be a strong case for higher foreign exchange reserves in the United States, the euro area, and the United Kingdom. In 2014 the United States had foreign exchange reserves and other official foreign assets of $138 billion. With the alternative criterion used in table 4.4, the benchmark for US foreign exchange reserves would have been almost $1.6 trillion. The euro area would have had a benchmark of almost $1.2 trillion (compared with actual holdings of $232 billion), and the United Kingdom would have had a benchmark of $847 billion (compared with actual holdings of just $60 billion).

We do not propose that the United States immediately start to build up reserves. Rather, the buildup should be an outgrowth of countervailing currency intervention (discussed in chapters 5 and 6), which would have the United States buying assets of countries that manipulate their currencies. US foreign exchange reserves should be invested in a range of safe government bonds. Although generating profits would not be the main goal of this portfolio, it would probably be profitable because (1) an excessive deficit means the US dollar is likely to depreciate over time; (2) countries with excess current account surpluses should experience exchange rate appreciations over time; and (3) with the notable exceptions of Germany and Japan, the interest rates on most foreign government bonds are higher than the rates on US government bonds.

Nonrenewable Resource Exporters

Officials in many resource-exporting countries argue that they are morally obligated to set aside a substantial share of the profits from resource extraction for future generations. These national savings could be invested internally or externally. In some cases, the savings are almost entirely invested externally, typically through sovereign wealth funds.

Officials in these countries might respond to limits on external saving by reducing production and exports (and, in the critical case of Saudi Arabia, the surge capacity that is essential to maintaining global supply in the face of interruptions elsewhere).[15] Recent papers by IMF staff highlight

---

15. The prospect of ever stronger policies to discourage carbon emissions around the world suggests that oil prices are likely to fall in the long run, making a strategy of leaving the oil in the ground less appealing.

the issues involved (Berg et al. 2012, Cherif and Hasanov 2012, Primus 2016). Resource exporters differ considerably in terms of the years of oil production remaining, the cost of production, the capacity to absorb domestic investment, the rate of return on domestic investment, demographic trends, and the quality of institutions and governance, making it impossible to set a one-size-fits-all standard. Assessing the desired levels of foreign investment, domestic investment, and domestic consumption for each resource-exporting country is beyond the scope of this book. However, appendix 4A illustrates the issues, using data on Angola, Norway, and Saudi Arabia.

Based on the analysis in appendix 4A, a conservative policy for oil exporters with 25 years of production remaining is to save 48 percent of oil revenues net of production cost. To be even more conservative in the face of uncertainty about both future oil revenues and returns on saving, a country might choose to save 75 percent of net oil revenues, the prescribed amount assuming only 10 years of production remain. The split between domestic and foreign saving depends on many factors, which differ widely across countries. To be conservative, we assume that only 10 percent of oil revenues are saved domestically and the rest (65 percent) is saved abroad.

We applied the criterion of net official flows greater than 65 percent of the net profits of petroleum exports in selecting countries for table 4.1.[16] This criterion is almost surely excessively conservative, allowing more saving than is optimal, but it is a reasonable starting point. For nonoil resource exporters, we did not have estimates of production cost. None of them had net official flows in excess of 50 percent of gross resource exports (see footnotes 2 and 4).

Many economies that specialize in exporting a nonrenewable resource have fixed exchange rates. But the effects on the rest of the world of saving oil revenues in foreign assets with a fixed exchange rate are essentially the same as the effects of foreign exchange intervention in a country with a flexible exchange rate (or the effects of intervention to prevent an appreciation of a fixed exchange rate). Because petroleum products are virtually the only tradable good they produce, spending in these economies has a very direct and strong effect on imports. Buying foreign assets instead of spending on goods and services reduces imports and increases the country's current account balance, even without any change in the exchange rate.

---

16. Net profits are defined as total petroleum exports minus estimated production costs by country in 2016, as reported by Rystad Energy UCube (*Wall Street Journal*, April 15, 2016). We extrapolated per barrel costs for previous years based on US consumer prices. For a few countries not included in the Rystad data, we used costs for the geographically nearest available producer.

Impacts of Manipulation

Current Account Balances

The cross-country regression results presented in table 2.1 can be used to estimate how much currency manipulation distorted current account balances over the period 2003–13. In light of the very high ratios of net official assets to GDP of all of the manufacturing and financial centers in table 4.1 except Sweden, we assume that all net official foreign flows by these economies were excessive. For Sweden and the oil exporters, we considered excessive only flows in excess of 2 percent of GDP (Sweden) or 65 percent of net energy profits (oil exporters) in years with a current account surplus above 3 percent of GDP. We use the coefficients in table 2.1 to calculate how much the current accounts of the manipulators would have declined had all excessive official flows been eliminated. We also include the effects operating through smaller official stocks, which grow more slowly over time in the alternative scenario than they do in the actual data. We assume that other variables in the model are unchanged.

The model explains changes in the current account minus net investment income. The counterfactual analysis thus understates the effect of manipulation on current accounts, because smaller cumulative current accounts imply lower net investment income for manipulators and higher net income for nonmanipulators. Investment income differs across countries and over time in ways that are difficult to model. We choose to be conservative in our approach and to avoid getting involved in the thorny problem of modeling net investment income.

We also calculate how much the current account balances of the nonmanipulators would have increased in the absence of manipulation under four alternative sets of assumptions. The first alternative allocates the increased current account balances to individual countries in proportion to their size (as measured by nominal GDP). Note that when multiple countries reduce their currency manipulation, the effects spill over to the current accounts of both nonmanipulators and manipulators.

It is possible that the spillovers of currency intervention do not flow to other countries in proportion to their GDPs. For example, spillovers may go disproportionately to the countries whose assets are being bought. We do not have complete data on which assets are being bought, but the IMF's Currency Composition of Official Foreign Exchange Reserves (COFER) data break down a large subset of official asset purchases. The United States issues the largest share of assets held as reserves (about 60 percent); the euro area is the second-largest reserve issuer (about 25 percent). The second alternative allocates the increased current account balances exclusively to reserve-issuing countries based on the COFER shares in 2010.

Spillovers could also be related to measures of capital mobility or financial integration. We reran the regressions of table 2.1 inserting a variable equal to global net official flows times the capital mobility variable or, separately, global official flows times the financial integration variable. Both coefficients have the expected signs. Only the financial integration variable has a statistically significant coefficient, but it turns out to be too large to be plausible, so we reduced it to a value with reasonable properties.[17] Each of these alternative hypotheses also included an adjustment to ensure that changes in current accounts balanced out across countries; we added up the implied changes in current accounts and subtracted any overall change from each country in proportion to its GDP. There are thus four alternative allocations of the effects of eliminating excessive intervention on current account balances of individual countries.

We believe that allocation by GDP share understates the increase in current accounts of the major advanced economies and that allocation by COFER share overstates the increase. However, the latter alternative may provide a good estimate of the effects of eliminating excessive net official flows if one assumes that many emerging-market and developing economies with significant net official flows but small or negative current account balances reduce their net official flows in response to the elimination of excessive net official flows by other countries. For example, Brazil and India typically run current account deficits but sometimes have significant positive net official flows, which are aimed at preventing even larger deficits. If elimination of currency manipulation elsewhere reduced the upward pressure on their currencies, they might reduce their own currency purchases, which would increase the current accounts of the major advanced economies even more. The COFER allocation alternative effectively fixes the current accounts of emerging-market and developing nonmanipulators at their historical values and assigns all of the increases to the major advanced economies.

The volume of official flows considered excessive averaged $638 billion per year over the "decade of manipulation." Depending on the alternative assumptions used for the spillovers of these purchases, eliminating excessive official flows would have reduced the current accounts of the manipulators by $250 billion to $350 billion. The current accounts of the nonmanipulators would have increased by a corresponding amount.

---

17. The problem is that too much of the reduction in net official flows is allocated to highly integrated economies, so that enforcement of no change in the sum of all current account balances forces economies with low integration to have declining current account balances even if they were not manipulators. We reduce the estimated coefficient by an amount sufficient to ensure that no current account of a nonmanipulator declines.

Panel A of figure 4.2 compares the average current account balances of the major economies over 2003–13 with the estimated current account balances in the absence of manipulation. The dark bars are the historical averages. The lighter bars display the maximum and minimum outcomes associated with the four alternative assumptions regarding spillovers of the effects of manipulation. The effects of these alternatives differ across the manipulating countries because countries' manipulation affects other countries in different ways.

The figure shows that China's average current account surplus of $205 billion would have been nearly or entirely eliminated. The other large manipulator, Japan, would have experienced little net effect, because the reduction from less manipulation in Japan would have been offset by positive spillovers from reduced manipulation elsewhere. The United States would have experienced the largest increase in its current account, ranging from $90 billion to $230 billion, depending on the assumed allocation of spillovers. The euro area would have had the second largest positive effects, with gains of between $60 billion and $95 billion. The United Kingdom would have had an increased balance of between $15 billion and $30 billion.

Panel B of figure 4.2 displays the effects on the current accounts of selected other manipulators. All except Norway's are estimated to decline in response to the elimination of excessive net official flows. The effects on Norway are small, reflecting the modest extent to which its net official flows exceeded 65 percent of energy export profits plus some positive spillovers to its current account from the ending of manipulation in other countries.

Panel C of figure 4.2 displays the effects on the current accounts of selected other nonmanipulators. For all of these countries, some of the alternative spillover assumptions yield significant increases in balances. But for the emerging-market and developing economies, the alternative allocation of all of the spillovers to the reserve-issuing advanced economies leaves current accounts unchanged.

The peak year of excessive net official flows was 2007, at $891 billion. China was responsible for more than $600 billion of these flows. Eliminating excessive net official flows in 2007 would have reduced China's current account surplus by about $370 billion to $400 billion, essentially eliminating the surplus in the latter case. The US deficit would have decreased by $140 billion to $340 billion. Goldstein and Lardy (2008) estimate that the hypothetical elimination of currency undervaluation in all Asian economies in 2007 would have reduced the US current account deficit by $100 billion to $140 billion. As Asian economies contribute the lion's share of, but by no means all, excess net official flows, the Goldstein-Lardy range comfortably overlaps our range after taking account of non-Asian manipulators.

**Figure 4.2   Effect of ending currency manipulation on
current accounts of selected economies, 2003–13**

a. Major economies

average current account (billions of dollars)

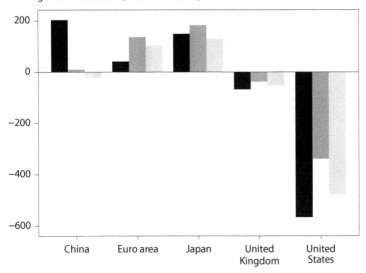

b. Selected other manipulators

average current account (billions of dollars)

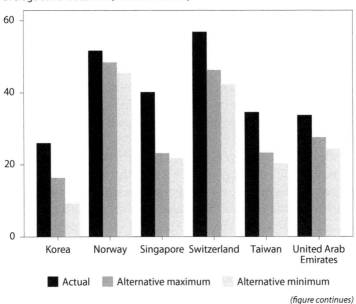

■ Actual   ■ Alternative maximum   Alternative minimum

(figure continues)

Figure 4.2   Effect of ending currency manipulation on current accounts of selected economies, 2003–13 *(continued)*

c. Selected other nonmanipulators

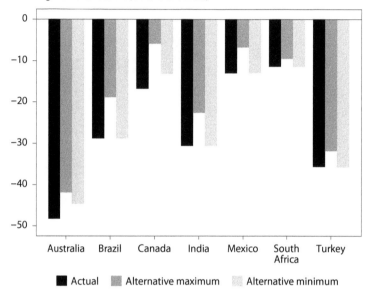

Source: Authors' calculations based on data from sources listed in appendix A.

Employment and Economic Activity

Discussions of trade policy and currency manipulation invariably turn to the vexing issue of the effect of trade balances on jobs. When one country loses exports to another or its domestic producers lose sales to imports, it loses jobs. But the effect on overall employment depends on what is driving the trade deficit.

A trade deficit is often caused by an overheating economy that is importing more. The economy may be above the level of full employment and the loss of jobs in import-competing industries may be a partial safety valve for letting off some of the excess pressure. In this case the level of employment is not sustainable, and the jobs lost to imports are part of the necessary adjustment process.

Alternatively, a trade deficit may be caused by an economic slowdown in the rest of the world. If this is the case, the trade deficit tends to leave the economy below the level of full employment. But it is the responsibility of macroeconomic policy to maintain full employment; monetary or fiscal policy should ease to create jobs in other sectors and maintain full employment.

Thus in the traditional view trade deficits, including those caused by currency manipulation, have no more than an ephemeral effect on total employment. Indeed, for much of modern US history, fluctuations in employment were transitory and, if anything, periods of low employment were associated with increases rather than decreases in the trade balance.

In contrast, the Great Recession of 2008-09 led to a prolonged period of underemployment that many feel is still not over. The US trade balance did rise significantly in 2009, as the deficit was cut roughly in half from its record level in 2006. But adjustment stalled after 2009, as many partner countries continued massive purchases of foreign exchange to maintain their current account surpluses. During this period Federal Reserve Chair Ben Bernanke testified before Congress that Chinese currency manipulation in particular was slowing the US recovery and delaying a return to full employment.[18] Many observers, including us, believe that the Fed should have eased more aggressively during this period and that fiscal policy should have been more expansionary. For whatever reason, US macroeconomic policy was not as responsive as it should have been to underemployment. Given that fact, a reduction of foreign currency manipulation in the years following the Great Recession would have boosted US growth and employment.

How much extra employment might the United States have gained from the elimination of excess currency intervention in 2009-13? Average excess intervention in these years was $720 billion per year, somewhat above the average over the entire 11-year "decade of manipulation" of $638 billion. The average effect on the US current account balance was thus likely to have been a bit above the range shown in figure 4.2. If we take $100 billion to $250 billion as a plausible range for the effect of foreign currency manipulation on the US current account balance in 2009-13, the effect is roughly ¾ percent to 1½ percent of US GDP.

Research by staff at the US Commerce Department suggests that $100 billion to $250 billion in additional net exports would create 600,000 to 1.5 million jobs (Rasmussen 2016). Exchange rate shocks in the Federal Reserve's FRB/US model that generate increases in the current account balance of $100 billion to $250 billion after two years (as of 2013) imply

---

18. In response to a question from Senator Bob Casey (D-PA) on October 4, 2011, Bernanke said, "I think right now a concern is that the Chinese currency policy is blocking what might be a more normal recovery process in the global economy." Bernanke revisited the issue of reserve accumulation by oil exporters and Asian economies as a factor behind weak recoveries and low interest rates in his blog, "Why Are Interest Rates So Low, Part 3: The Global Savings Glut," Brookings Institution, April 1, 2015, www.brookings.edu/blog/ben-bernanke/2015/04/01/why-are-interest-rates-so-low-part-3-the-global-savings-glut.

increases in employment of roughly 1 million to 2 million jobs.[19] These estimates are based on the key assumption—which we believe is reasonable for 2009-13—that the Federal Reserve and Congress would not have tightened monetary and fiscal policies in response to dollar depreciation and stronger economic growth.

Even if US macroeconomic policy had succeeded in maintaining full employment after the Great Recession, there is another cost of unsustainable current account imbalances arising from shifts in activity and jobs across sectors of the economy. The growing US trade deficit caused the manufacturing sector to shrink. Stimulative macroeconomic policies encouraged other sectors, most notably the housing sector, to grow more rapidly to take up the slack. Shifting activity across sectors is a time-consuming and expensive undertaking, the costs of which are borne disproportionately by lower-income people. Many people who lose their jobs suffer permanent declines in lifetime earnings, and some never work again. The workers usually affected have few financial resources to cushion the adjustment. These transition costs raise the economy's natural rate of unemployment, at least temporarily, and represent a loss of economic output that can never be fully recovered.

At some point an unsustainable trade imbalance must be reversed. The economy must undergo a protracted and costly rebalancing. If the imbalance lasts for more than a year or two, the readjustment is not likely to be a simple matter of reopening shuttered factories and rehiring laid-off workers. When companies go out of business and workers move away, the reverse adjustment is just as costly as the initial stage. The potential level of output and employment declines for a while, and the lost output is never fully recovered. These costs are not limited to countries with unsustainable deficits. China's unsustainable surplus led to massive overinvestment in the steel industry (half of global steel capacity is estimated to be in China). Rising exports from this sector are causing trade frictions around the world and a major headache for the Chinese government as it seeks to reduce excess capacity in the sector.

In the case of the record US trade deficit of 2006, there was an additional cost beyond that of shifting resources across sectors. Much of the output produced during this period reflected a waste of economic re-

---

19. Bergsten and Gagnon (2012) estimate a total employment effect of currency manipulation of 1 million to 5 million jobs. These estimated ranges are lower than the range in our previous work because (1) our latest estimates of the effect of net official flows on current accounts (table 2.1) are lower than our earlier estimates and (2) our previous work focused on total net official flows at the peak and assumed a reduction in net official flows of $1 trillion, as opposed to $720 billion here.

sources—the building of too many houses in the desert of Nevada that have stood empty for a decade or more, for example. Although foreign currency manipulation was not the primary cause of the US housing bubble, large inflows of foreign official capital supported more housing construction than could otherwise have occurred.[20]

New research shows that even during the apparently healthy US labor market of 2005–07, millions of people were suffering lost employment opportunities. Several studies document the tremendous damage to US employment from the "China shock" during this period (Autor et al. 2014; Pierce and Schott 2016; Acemoglu et al. 2016; Autor, Dorn, and Hanson 2016). They claim that as a result of Chinese imports, at least 2 million Americans lost their jobs and had not found alternative employment as of 2007. The job loss arises from changes in the skills needed for workers to take on new jobs and from costs of moving to new locations where jobs are growing, representing a massive waste of human potential and economic output. The cost of this displacement is particularly painful because it falls so heavily on poorer and older workers, who have the least ability to adapt, retrain, and relocate.

These studies provide an upper bound on net job losses, because they probably understate job gains from additional exports generated by Chinese demand, including through components and services that are inputs to Chinese exports.[21] However, the large US trade deficit, especially with China, and the lower labor intensity of US exports relative to US imports from China, argue for much smaller gains on the export side than losses on the import side. Indeed, analysis of US imports from China net of US exports to China results in estimated effects that are only modestly smaller than those based on imports alone (Autor et al. 2014). One of the largest expanding sectors at the time was housing construction; employment in this industry expanded by much less than average in areas with industries that were more exposed to Chinese imports (Acemoglu et al. 2016).

The studies document a surprising lack of mobility of displaced workers. The 1.1 percentage point overall decline in the male employment rate between 2001 and 2007 (and a smaller decline in the female employment rate) despite a continuous economic recovery strongly suggests that the employment losses from the China shock far outweighed any gains.

---

20. Private foreign inflows might have offset some of any reduction in official inflows, but the evidence strongly shows that any private offset is far from complete.

21. The phaseout of the Multi-Fibre Arrangement in 2005 shifted apparel exports from countries that had had special quotas to China, but it should not have had a net effect on US workers. Autor et al. (2014) obtain similar results when they focus on imports from all developing countries instead of only China, suggesting that any bias from this source is small.

Not all of the job losses documented by these studies can be attributed to Chinese currency policy, however, as China likely would have had rapidly growing exports even in the absence of currency manipulation. US industries would have had to adjust to a China shock even if there had been no decline in the US trade balance. But if China had allowed its currency to appreciate more than it did, its export growth would have been reduced and its imports would have increased further, keeping the current account balance closer to zero in both China and the United States. The jobs effect would have been significantly muted. Between 2000 and 2007, for example, Chinese exports increased by more than $1 trillion and the Chinese current account surplus increased by $330 billion. If China's surplus had not increased, the increase in China's exports and the cost to US import-competing industries would have been as much as one-third smaller. If some of the adjustment had come in the form of higher Chinese imports instead of entirely through lower Chinese exports, the losses to US import-competing industries would have been reduced by less than one-third but there would have been some corresponding gains for US exporters. To the extent that the public conflates the China shock with the US trade deficit, public perceptions of the cost of trade deficits may be exaggerated. Nevertheless, the true cost remains economically important.

It seems likely that adjusting to a shock like the China shock is more costly the more rapidly the shock unfolds. Slow adjustment can be accomplished through natural attrition of workers and depreciation of fixed capital; rapid adjustment requires laying off workers and scrapping plant and equipment prematurely. Indeed, the unprecedented speed with which China ramped up exports—compared with other development bursts in Europe, Japan, and the Asian tigers—probably accounts for much of the disruption documented by Autor, Dorn, and Hanson. In this regard China's currency manipulation was especially costly, as it boosted China's exports precisely when they were already set to grow rapidly.

The focus on China reflects the unprecedented size and speed of its emergence as a global exporter. However, other emerging markets were also expanding their exports during this period, and some of them also supported their exports through currency manipulation. There is an ongoing debate as to the importance of various factors in explaining the export boom in China and other countries. Whether it was economic reforms in the 1990s, China's accession to the WTO in 2001, or the phaseout of the Multi-Fibre Arrangement in 2005, all that matters for our analysis is that currency manipulation accommodated these export booms and enabled them to be larger and more rapid than they would otherwise have been. The point is not that the United States could have avoided painful adjustments if only there had been no currency manipulation but that the necessary adjustments were larger, more rapid, and thus more costly than they would have been.

Currency manipulation contributed significantly to the political backlash against globalization in general and to trade in particular that has been rising in the United States over the past two decades. This backlash culminated in the bipartisan opposition to new trade agreements, especially the TPP, in the electoral campaigns of 2016. Autor et al. (2017) conclude that if the China shock had been half as large as it was, a sufficient number of votes would have been changed in the key states of Michigan, Pennsylvania, and Wisconsin to have elected Hillary Clinton. The halting of further trade liberalization, as seems likely for at least a while, or its possible reversal pose a significant risk to the entire global trading system and thus the stability of the world economy.

Partially Offsetting Gains

Not all of the effects of currency manipulation on trade partners are negative. An important beneficial effect is the provision of cheaper imports, which raises consumer welfare. This benefit is typically greatest for low-income households. Cheap Chinese imports at WalMart are the most widely cited example.

One study finds that higher Chinese exports held down import price inflation around the world by as much as 0.25 percentage points per year from 1993 through 2004 (Kamin, Marazzi, and Schindler 2006). If that pattern continued for the next 10 years, consistent with the rapid growth of Chinese exports, it would have reduced import prices by 5 percent compared to where they would otherwise have been. The effects on overall consumer prices would be considerably smaller.[22] Moreover, it is not clear how much of this effect would have occurred even in the absence of currency manipulation; China's entry into global markets would have had a profound effect on prices and quantities of traded goods even if China had maintained balanced trade.

Another benefit from currency manipulation is the provision of cheaper credit to the rest of the world. Most of the official financial inflows to the United States take the form of high-grade debt. The United States is borrowing from the rest of the world at record-low interest rates. This benefit is not unalloyed—because it reduces the incomes of US savers at the same time that it reduces the costs for US borrowers—but the net effect for

---

22. In some historical periods, the dampening effect on inflation would have been viewed as a benefit. However, with US inflation generally below target over the past decade, the effect on overall consumer prices was not a benefit from the perspective of price stability.

the United States is positive, because the United States is a net debtor to the rest of the world. A harmful side effect, however, is that currency manipulation hampered the ability of the Federal Reserve to respond forcefully to the Great Recession, because it helped push interest rates so close to zero.

Necessary Policy Adjustments

Currency manipulation shifts aggregate demand away from other economies toward the manipulating economies. A cessation of manipulation would thus have shifted demand in the opposite direction. Early in the "decade of manipulation," as monetary and fiscal policies were tightening somewhat in the United States and the euro area, the increased aggregate demand from a cessation of currency manipulation would have called for an acceleration of this tightening. However, in the aftermath of the Great Recession, from 2009 through 2013, most advanced (and some developing) economies were operating far below potential output. We believe a more reasonable assumption for the second half of the manipulation period is that monetary policy would not have tightened in response to depreciating currencies and higher trade balances.

What policies should manipulators have adopted in the absence of manipulation? The answer depends critically on whether they were overheating. The guiding principles for policy adjustments are that domestic economic policies should be used to achieve domestic objectives (mainly full employment with low and stable inflation) and external policies should be used to achieve external objectives (mainly small and sustainable current account imbalances). These principles are enshrined in the IMF surveillance decisions of 2007 and 2012. They have been adopted by the leaders of the G-7 and G-20 nations. Ever since their London summit of 2009, G-20 leaders have repeatedly pledged to use monetary and fiscal policy to foster sustainable growth while maintaining low inflation and to refrain from competitive devaluation or targeting exchange rates for competitive purposes.

The rest of this section examines alternative policies in three of the manufacturing exporters (China, Japan, and Korea) and two of the financial centers (Switzerland and Singapore) with some of the largest stocks of official assets.[23]

---

23. For a more detailed discussion of policies in Hong Kong, Singapore, and Switzerland, see Gagnon (2014).

Figure 4.3   China's external accounts and real effective exchange rate, 2000–16

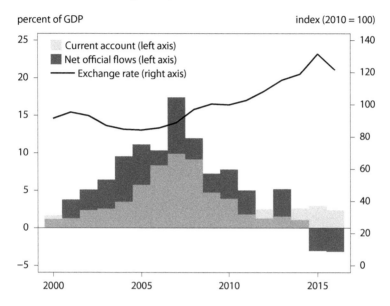

Note: Light gray denotes current account; dark gray denotes net official flows; and medium gray denotes overlap between the two variables.
Source: Authors' calculations based on data from sources listed in appendix A.

China

From January 1994 until July 2005, China pegged its currency tightly to the US dollar. It followed the depreciation of the dollar in real effective terms between 2001 and 2005 (figure 4.3). Beginning in 2005 China allowed its currency to appreciate against the dollar gradually but not continuously. It took four years to undo the real effective depreciation of 2001–05. This period was one of rapid development of export industries in China, which caused the equilibrium real effective exchange rate to increase steadily (Goldstein and Lardy 2008). For at least 10 years (2003–13), China's currency was undervalued by as much as 30 percent against the dollar (20 percent on a trade-weighted basis) (Cline and Williamson 2008, 2012). Even larger estimates of Chinese undervaluation are possible if one assumes that China's equilibrium current account is close to zero instead of 3 percent of GDP, as Cline and Williamson posit.

In order to maintain its undervalued currency, China purchased massive amounts of foreign exchange reserves. Its current account surplus grew strongly, peaking at 10 percent of GDP in 2007. The current account began to narrow in 2008 with the Great Recession in the advanced econo-

**Figure 4.4   GDP growth and consumer price inflation rates in
China, 1995–2016**

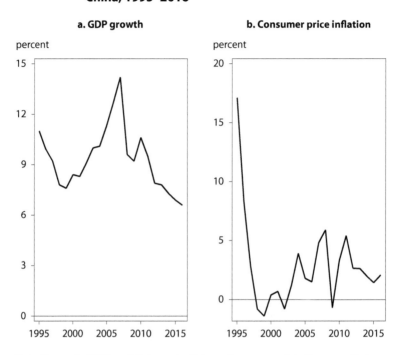

a. GDP growth

b. Consumer price inflation

Note: Figures for 2016 are IMF forecasts. Data are from sources listed in appendix A.

mies; the continuing real effective appreciation kept the surplus below 3
percent of GDP from 2011 onward.

China's economy was overheating at the peak of its manipulation
in 2007, with GDP growth of an astonishing 14 percent and inflation of
nearly 5 percent (figure 4.4). A cessation of manipulation and appreciation of its currency would have helped cool off the Chinese economy at
an opportune moment. It was at this point that international pressure on
China's currency policy peaked, including within the executive board of the
IMF (Blustein 2012). Frankel (2008) argues that a currency appreciation in
or before 2007 is the only policy change that was needed, because it would
have slowed growth to an appropriate rate. However, China had plenty of
scope to use monetary and fiscal policy to achieve domestic balance at the
same time it achieved external balance through appreciation. In the end
the global financial crisis of 2008 took some of the international political
pressure off China, and the lagged effects of earlier renminbi appreciation
began to reduce China's trade surplus.

From 2009 onward Chinese growth slowed and inflation approached its
target of about 3 percent. Further appreciation to push the current account

Figure 4.5   General government budget balance in China as percent of GDP, 1995–2016

percent of GDP

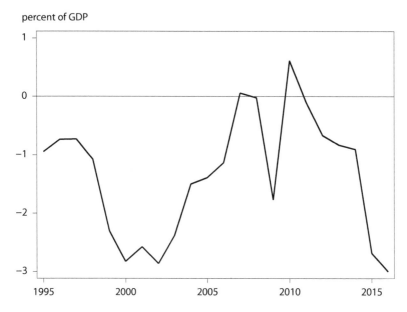

Note: Figure for 2016 is IMF forecast. Data are from sources listed in appendix A.

toward balance would have called for more stimulative policies than adopted in these years. China had plenty of space for additional monetary and fiscal policy stimulus after 2009 (figure 4.5).[24] The fiscal deficit has not exceeded 3 percent of GDP during the past 20 years, and general government gross debt was estimated to be only 46 percent of GDP in 2016.[25] Data on net debt are not available, but net debt was surely much lower than gross debt, as a result of the government's equity stakes in many state-owned enterprises. At about 3 percent, short-term interest rates were considerably higher than in most advanced economies, for example, the United States (figure 4.6).

China's high private saving rate has prompted many observers to conclude that China would run a current account surplus even in the absence of official outflows if it were to remove restrictions on private financial flows. Bayoumi and Ohnsorge (2013) suggest that China would be expected to have net private outflows if capital controls were removed but that the cumulative net private flows would be considerably smaller than the existing stock of net official assets. China's government could thus

---

24. It could be argued that the increase in corporate and household leverage in China is sowing the seeds of future crisis, pointing to the importance of sound financial supervisory and regulatory policies.

25. Debt data are from the *IMF Fiscal Monitor*, October 2016.

Figure 4.6 Three-month interbank rates in China and the United States, 1995–2016

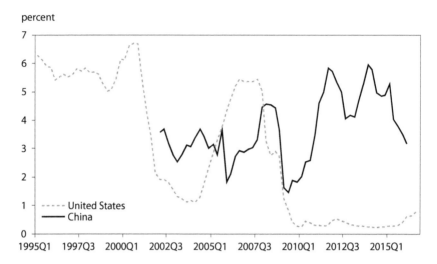

percent

Note: For the United States, three-month interbank rates refer to the three-month London Interbank Offered Rate (LIBOR) based on the US dollar; for China, it is the 90-day interbank rate, which is not available before 2002.

Source: Haver.

easily fund these private outflows by selling foreign official assets.[26] Given China's high domestic investment rate and relatively high interest rates, it is not at all clear that the equilibrium outcome would be a large current account surplus. Moreover, research suggests that extending the social safety net, especially in health care, would have a very strong positive effect on consumption, even if it were fully financed by tax increases. Two cross-country studies find that consumption increases by more than 50 percent of any balanced-budget increase in healthcare spending (IMF 2012a, Gagnon 2013). China faces a difficult problem of rebalancing its economy toward household consumption and away from business investment (Hellebrandt et al. 2015). However, the world cannot allow China to remedy any deficiency in domestic demand by relying on net external demand.

Japan

Japan ran a current account surplus of 2 to 5 percent of GDP for most of the past 16 years (figure 4.7). Net official flows were concentrated in three

---

26. Indeed, to the extent that China's current account already exceeds its long-run equilibrium, selling foreign official assets to prevent a currency depreciation is the preferred policy under a reference rate regime, as discussed in chapter 5.

Figure 4.7   Japan's external accounts and real effective exchange rate, 2000–16

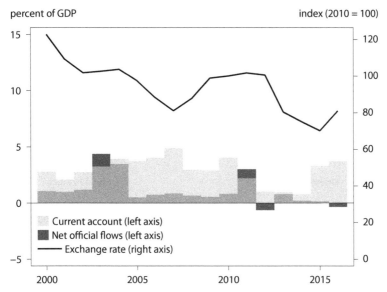

Note: Light gray denotes current account; dark gray denotes net official flows; and medium gray denotes overlap between the two variables.

Source: Authors' calculations based on data from sources listed in appendix A.

years: 2003, 2004, and 2011, when Japan used them to prevent any significant increase in the value of the yen despite pressure on it. Japan did not resist downward pressures on the yen, except in 2012, when net official flows briefly turned negative. The overall result was to maintain a tendency to run a current account surplus.

The trend decline in the real effective exchange rate is consistent with Japan's declining labor force and shrinking share of global economic activity. Many of Japan's key trading partners in Asia still have rapid growth rates as they catch up to incomes and productivity in the advanced economies. The net effect of Japanese currency policy has not been to put the exchange rate on a steeper downward trend but rather to keep the exchange rate somewhat below its equilibrium level (which does have a downward trend).

Japan's surplus declined after 2011 because of the combination of high oil prices and the shutdown of the nuclear power plants, which forced Japan to increase its oil imports to produce electricity. With the drop in oil prices since 2014, Japan's surplus has returned to its historic range.

The Japanese economy was not overheating during this period (figure 4.8). Indeed, Japan has long struggled with deflation and high unemployment (relative to its historical experience). If it had not manipulated its

Figure 4.8   Macroeconomic indicators in Japan, 1995–2016

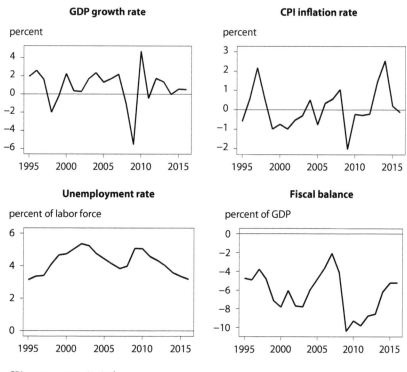

GDP growth rate

CPI inflation rate

Unemployment rate

Fiscal balance

CPI = consumer price index
Note: Figures for 2016 are IMF forecasts. Data are from sources listed in appendix A.

currency to maintain a current account surplus, it would have required further stimulus from domestic policies. With the already large fiscal deficits in Japan implying a growing national debt, monetary policy was the preferred instrument.

Short-term interest rates in Japan have been stuck at zero for two decades (figure 4.9). But monetary policy was too tight throughout this period, as reflected in the very low and often negative rate of inflation. Had Japan adopted easier monetary policy in the early 1990s and maintained inflation at or above 2 percent, it would be in a much better position today (Ahearne et al. 2002). By allowing inflation expectations to become entrenched near zero, Japan tightened the constraint imposed by the zero lower bound on nominal interest rates.[27]

In April 2013 Japan embarked on a major program of quantitative

---

27. It is now apparent that the lower bound may be below zero, albeit not by a lot (Ball et al. 2016).

Figure 4.9 Financial indicators in Japan, 1995–2016

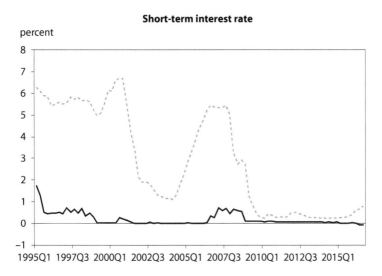

Short-term interest rate

percent

1995Q1 1997Q3 2000Q1 2002Q3 2005Q1 2007Q3 2010Q1 2012Q3 2015Q1

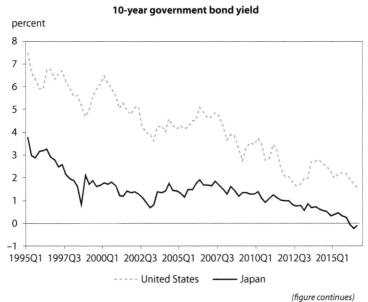

10-year government bond yield

percent

1995Q1 1997Q3 2000Q1 2002Q3 2005Q1 2007Q3 2010Q1 2012Q3 2015Q1

----- United States   —— Japan

(figure continues)

easing to achieve a new inflation target of 2 percent. The program contributed to a decline in the unemployment rate to a 20-year low and a modest rise in inflation, despite fiscal contraction.[28] Since late 2015 core inflation

---

28. Part of the rise in inflation in 2014 reflects the hike in the consumption tax, but measures of core inflation that exclude the effects of the consumption tax also increased after 2012.

Figure 4.9   Financial indicators in Japan, 1995–2016
(continued)

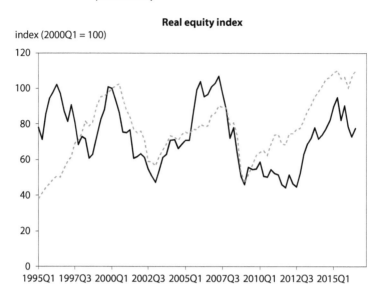

Real equity index

index (2000Q1 = 100)

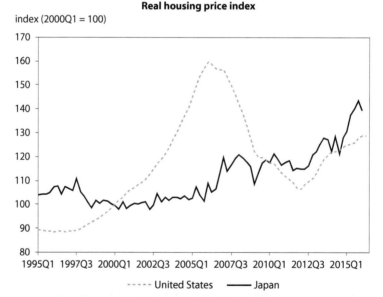

Real housing price index

index (2000Q1 = 100)

- - - - United States   ———— Japan

Note: For Japan, variables refer to the overnight call rate, the Japanese 10-year bond yield, the Tokyo Stock Price Index (TOPIX), and the Residential Property Price Index. For the United States, variables refer to the three-month London Interbank Offered Rate (LIBOR) based on the US dollar, the 10-year Treasury yield, the S&P 500 index, and the Case-Shiller Home Price Index. Real equity and housing price indices are divided by the consumer price index.

Source: Haver.

Figure 4.10 Korea's external accounts and real effective exchange rate, 2000–16

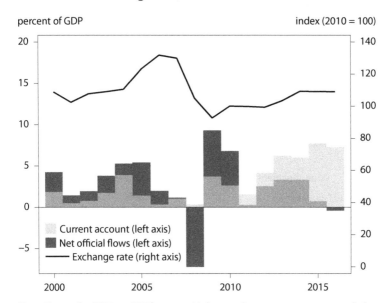

Note: Figures for 2016 are IMF forecasts. Light gray denotes current account; dark gray denotes net official flows; and medium gray denotes overlap between the two variables.

Source: Authors' calculations based on data from sources listed in appendix A.

and inflation expectations in Japan have drifted down as the Bank of Japan has disappointed markets by not taking steps to achieve its 2 percent inflation goal (Ball et al. 2016). Given that long-term bond yields are now at zero, additional monetary stimulus should take the form of large-scale purchases of equity. It may be necessary to temporarily use fiscal policy, including through higher government and minimum wages and other labor market reforms, to jumpstart inflation expectations.[29]

Korea

Korea piled up foreign exchange reserves rapidly in the years after the Asian financial crisis of 1997–98 (figure 4.10). By 2005 net official flows began to subside as the government judged it had sufficient reserves. The global financial crisis exposed lingering weaknesses in Korea's financial sector, including a maturity mismatch between dollar assets and liabilities. Reserves

---

29. Olivier J. Blanchard and Adam Posen, "Japan's Solution Is to Raise Wages by 10 Percent," *Financial Times,* December 2, 2015; Adam S. Posen, "Shinzo Abe's Stimulus Is a Lesson for the World," *Financial Times,* August 3, 2016.

Figure 4.11   Macroeconomic indicators in Korea, 1995–2016

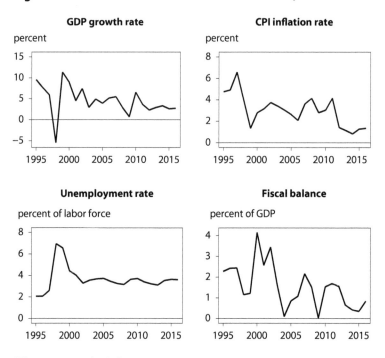

GDP growth rate

CPI inflation rate

Unemployment rate

Fiscal balance

CPI = consumer price index

Note: Figures for 2016 are IMF forecasts. Data are from sources listed in appendix A.

were drawn down to a significant extent in 2008 but were quickly rebuilt in 2009. Reserve accumulation occurred at a steady pace of about 3 percent of GDP in 2012–14. These net official flows contributed to a large and growing current account surplus. In 2015 and 2016, reserve accumulation was negligible on balance, yet the current account continued to register a large surplus, as net private financial outflows rose.

Korea's GDP growth has trended downward over time, but the unemployment rate has remained stable around its historic norm, suggesting that Korea is close to potential output (figure 4.11). Inflation dropped below target in 2012, in part reflecting the decline in energy prices, but began to rebound in 2015.

Overall, Korea's macroeconomic policy stance appears appropriate (figure 4.12). If net private outflows decline and upward pressure on the Korean won resumes, the appropriate response would be an easing of monetary policy rather than a resumption of reserve accumulation. In the current global environment of flat or rising interest rates, the zero lower bound is not likely to be a concern in Korea. However, in the event the

Figure 4.12 Financial indicators in Korea, 1995–2016

Short-term interest rate

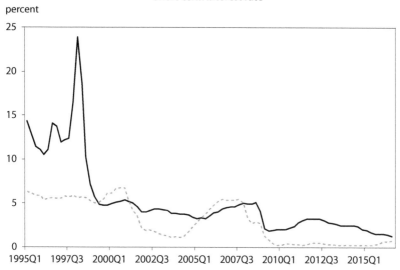

10-year government bond yield

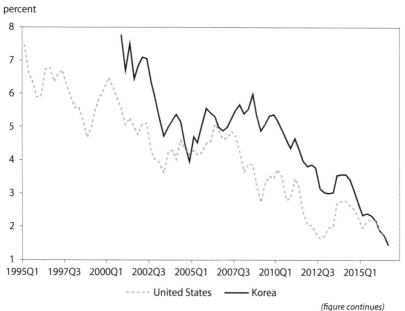

(figure continues)

policy rate reaches zero, the Bank of Korea would have the option of pursuing a modestly negative interest rate, as in some European economies, or making large-scale asset purchases, as in Japan and the euro area.

Figure 4.12   Financial indicators in Korea, 1995–2016 *(continued)*

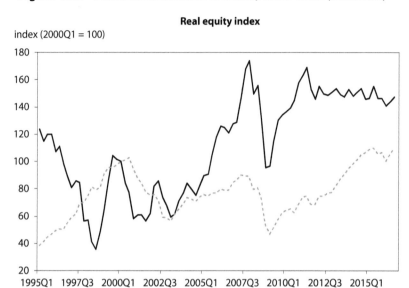

Real equity index

index (2000Q1 = 100)

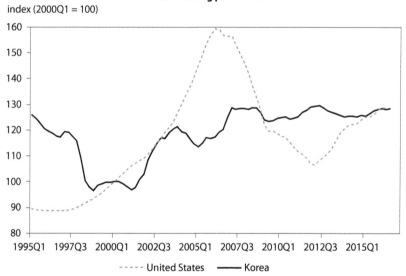

Real housing price index

index (2000Q1 = 100)

----- United States   —— Korea

Note: For Korea, variables refer to the call money rate, the Korean 10-year treasury bond, the Korea Composite Stock Price Index (KOSPI), and the House Purchase Price Index. For variables for the United States, see figure 4.9. Real equity and housing price indices are divided by the consumer price index.

Source: Haver.

Figure 4.13   Switzerland's external accounts and real effective exchange rate, 2000–16

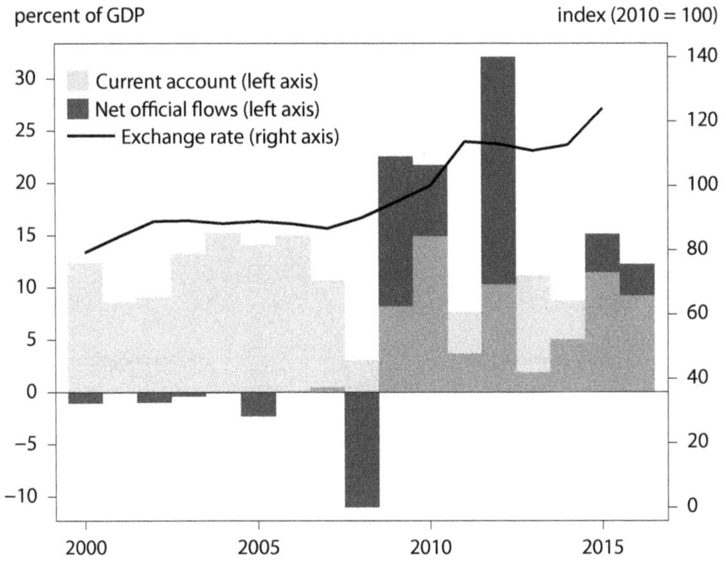

percent of GDP   index (2010 = 100)

Note: Light gray denotes current account; dark gray denotes net official flows; and medium gray denotes overlap between the two variables.
Source: Authors' calculations based on data from sources listed in appendix A.

Switzerland

Switzerland's large current account surplus before the Great Recession reflected private investor behavior, not official financial flows (figure 4.13). However, some observers argued that it was harmful and unsustainable and that policymakers should have taken steps to reduce it, including through negative net official flows (Williamson 2007, Cline and Williamson 2008).

Since the global financial crisis of 2007–09, Switzerland has faced intermittent waves of financial inflows as both domestic and foreign investors were attracted by the relative safety of Swiss assets. The Swiss exchange rate soared, although it did not significantly exceed its previous peak in 1995 in real effective terms. The appreciation plus the slowdowns in Switzerland's trading partners put downward pressure on the Swiss current account. To limit the size of this downward adjustment and the associated negative shock to Swiss aggregate demand and inflation, the Swiss National Bank (SNB) conducted large-scale interventions in the foreign exchange market almost every year since 2009. These interventions succeeded in stabilizing the Swiss current account at about 10 percent of GDP.

Figure 4.14   Macroeconomic indicators in Switzerland, 1995–2016

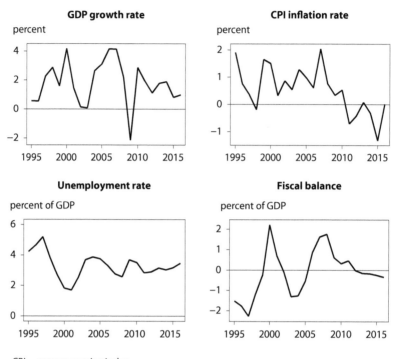

CPI = consumer price index
Note: Figures for 2016 are IMF forecasts. Data are from sources listed in appendix A.

The SNB's currency intervention is a striking example of manipulating a currency to prevent balance-of-payments adjustment and a clear violation of Switzerland's obligations under IMF Article IV. Its actions had harmful effects on the rest of the world, because they came at a time of deficient global aggregate demand and sharp recessions in several of Switzerland's European neighbors, which were denied the ability to increase net exports to Switzerland. Nevertheless, Swiss intervention was not generally viewed as controversial in international economic policy circles. The IMF in particular has not objected to Switzerland's apparent contravention of Article IV (IMF 2015b) and in fact argues that the Swiss franc is overvalued.

With the unemployment rate close to its average of the past 25 years (figure 4.14), the Swiss economy may be operating near its potential. However, inflation is considerably lower than the advanced-economy norm of 2 percent. If Switzerland were to cease manipulating its currency and allow the franc to rise, there would be further downward pressure on inflation and economic activity. With short-term interest rates already below zero, there is little room for conventional monetary stimulus. Long-term interest rates also are below zero, limiting the usefulness of unconventional monetary stimulus in the form of purchases of government bonds. However, Switzerland could conduct unconventional monetary policy by purchasing equity and other private financial assets or subsidizing lending to the banking system (Ball et al. 2016). In addition, Switzerland has low government debt and plenty of space to use fiscal stimulus to keep the economy operating at potential.[30] Swiss purchases of foreign currency assets should be the last line of defense against deflation; in practice, they have been the only tool the Swiss have used.[31]

The authorities have expressed concern about equity and real estate prices being excessively high in Switzerland, but neither has exceeded its previous peak (figure 4.15). Moreover, some long-run growth in real equity and house prices is to be expected in economies with trend increases in real GDP. Posen (2011) shows that many historical instances of large increases in asset prices are not harmful and that the connection between monetary policy and harmful bubbles is very weak. Even if asset prices were exceeding long-run appropriate levels, the correct policy response would be to make sure that holders of these assets are not excessively leveraged.

There is no fundamental reason that assets should always have positive expected rates of return; the possibility or even the expectation of falling asset prices is not necessarily a sign of an undesirable bubble. The job of monetary policy is to set the overall rates of return in the economy where they need to be to keep inflation at its target and output at potential.[32] Meeting this objective may require negative expected real rates of return on some assets.

---

30. According to the October 2016 *IMF Fiscal Monitor*, Switzerland's general government net debt stood at 24 percent of GDP in 2016, considerably lower than the G-20 advanced-economy average of 80 percent.

31. Because Swiss purchases of foreign assets have been largely unsterilized, they can be viewed as a combination of easy monetary policy and sterilized intervention (see box 2.2). The easy monetary policy is appropriate, but it would be better achieved through purchases of domestic assets, which would spur more domestic demand, than through net exports.

32. Conventional monetary policy, operating through the risk-free short-term interest rate, also has important influences on rates of return on other real and financial assets. Unconventional monetary policy operates more directly on these other rates of return.

Figure 4.15   Financial indicators in Switzerland, 1995–2016

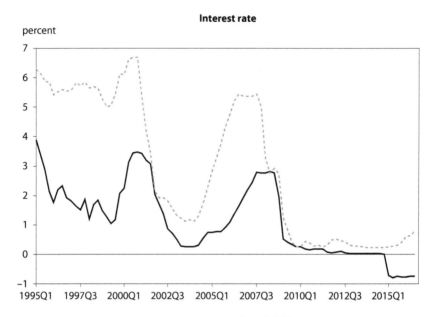

Interest rate

percent

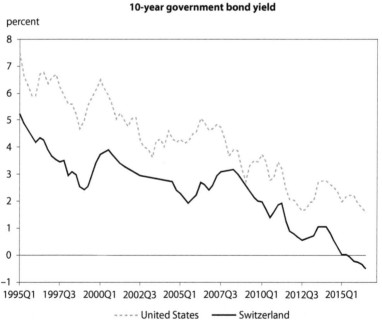

10-year government bond yield

percent

- - - - United States ——— Switzerland

Figure 4.15   Financial indicators in Switzerland, 1995–2016
         (continued)

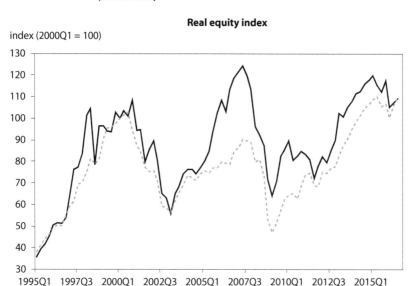

Real equity index

index (2000Q1 = 100)

Real housing price index

index (2000Q1 = 100)

----- United States   ——— Switzerland

Note: For Switzerland, variables refer to the three-month interbank offered rate, the Swiss 10-year government bond yield, the MSCI share price index excluding dividends, and the Swiss House Price Index for single family homes. For variables for the United States, see figure 4.9. Real equity and housing price indices are divided by the consumer price index.
Source: Haver.

**Figure 4.16   Singapore's external accounts and real
effective exchange rate, 2000–16**

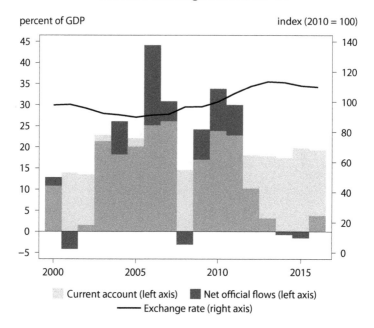

percent of GDP   index (2010 = 100)

Current account (left axis)   Net official flows (left axis)
Exchange rate (right axis)

Note: Light gray denotes current account; dark gray denotes net official flows; and medium gray denotes overlap between the two variables.
Source: Authors' calculations based on data from sources listed in appendix A.

Singapore

Singapore requires very large compulsory pension contributions (combined employer and employee contributions of 36 percent of gross salary). The government invests the vast majority of these contributions in foreign assets through a large sovereign wealth fund (the Government Investment Corporation). In addition, the country's central bank backs the monetary base almost entirely (97 percent) with foreign currency assets, and another sovereign wealth fund (Temasek) manages a portfolio of domestic and foreign assets that is left over from an earlier period of Singapore's development. Together these policies have delivered a current account surplus that did not fall below 10 percent of GDP, and often exceeded 20 percent, for more than 20 years (figure 4.16).

Singapore has long had volatile real GDP and inflation, in part owing to the unique properties of its large bioengineering sector (figure 4.17). Inflation has averaged about 2 percent over the past 30 years but is currently below its target of 2 percent, largely because of the decline in energy prices. After a brief tick upward in 2009, the unemployment rate fell back toward the level maintained before the Asian financial crisis of 1997–98.

Figure 4.17   Macroeconomic indicators in Singapore, 1995–2016

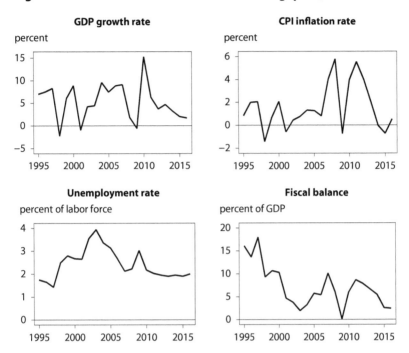

GDP growth rate

percent

CPI inflation rate

percent

Unemployment rate

percent of labor force

Fiscal balance

percent of GDP

CPI = consumer price index
Note: Figures for 2016 are IMF forecasts. Data are from sources listed in appendix A.

On balance Singapore is in a good macroeconomic position and does not need to either loosen or tighten its overall policy stance. However, the central bank should significantly rebalance toward domestic assets in order to eliminate the policy distortion that encourages excessive net foreign saving out of Singapore and shifts net aggregate demand away from foreign trade partners to Singapore.

The government of Singapore shields pension savers from the volatility of foreign investments, offering guaranteed rates of return in domestic currency. The policy distorts market outcomes. If the government would stop taking on the enormous exchange rate and market risk of foreign investments and force those risks onto private investors, Singapore would hold far fewer foreign assets. Home bias in investment is well documented. In Japan, with about 9 percent of global GDP, the private sector holds 80 percent of its financial assets domestically.[33] In Korea, with about 2 percent of global GDP, the private sector holds 87 percent of its financial assets domestically.

---

33. Private foreign assets equal total foreign assets minus official foreign assets. Total private financial assets equal the sum of domestic stock market capitalization, bond market capital-

The government should allow workers to direct the allocation of their pension investments, through private fund managers or a menu of government-run options that include equities, fixed income instruments, and real estate in Singapore and abroad. Savers who want guaranteed rates of return should be required to buy government of Singapore bonds or government-guaranteed bank deposits. The government should convert the Government Investment Corporation into a fund manager for workers or a pool of foreign assets from which workers can choose to invest.

These changes would almost surely require an easing of Singapore's monetary policy, which would imply lower interest rates on a range of bonds and deposits (figure 4.18). Lower interest rates would probably lead to higher equity and property prices. But as discussed in the case of Switzerland, higher asset prices and lower expected future rates of return are not necessarily signs of a bubble. The job of monetary policy is to set the spectrum of returns on domestic assets to the level that is appropriate for price stability and full employment. Concerns about asset price bubbles should be dealt with through limits on leverage, such as loan-to-value and debt-to-income ratios. The central bank has been proactive in combatting excessive leverage in finance and real estate (Menon 2014). Singapore's success in avoiding most of the damage of both the Asian financial crisis of 1997–98 and the global financial crisis of 2008–09 speaks well of its ability to prevent harmful fallout from an asset price bubble.

Recent Developments and Outlook

A Lull in Manipulation

Currency intervention dropped sharply in 2014, though it remained important, at about $350 billion for the year on a global basis (table 4.2). In 2015 global net official flows turned slightly negative for the first time in nearly two decades, as many emerging-market and developing economies resisted downward pressure on their currencies. Official flows also dropped dramatically for the countries that had manipulated over the "decade of manipulation" (table 4.1). The manufacturing exporters, led by China, are responsible for this drop; the financial centers and oil exporters continued to experience significant net official outflows.

Table 4.5 lists countries that met our criteria for currency manipulation in 2015 and 2016.[34] It shows that the collapse in the prices of oil and

---

ization, bank deposits, and net private foreign assets. Data are for 2010 and come from the IMF's Balance of Payments Statistics and the World Bank's World Development Indicators.

34. Except for Norway, 2016 data are limited to changes in foreign exchange reserves, as other official financial flows were not available yet. Data on Norway are from the Norwegian

Figure 4.18   Financial indicators in Singapore, 1995–2016

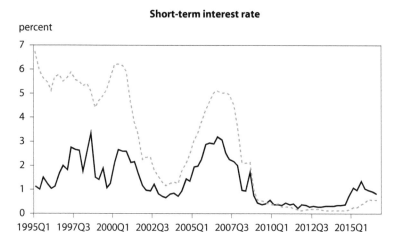

Short-term interest rate

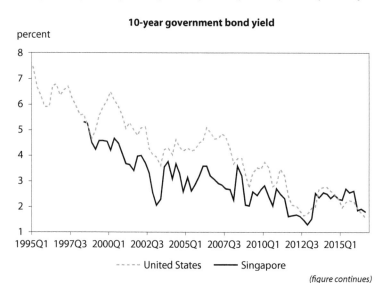

10-year government bond yield

- - - - - United States　　——— Singapore

(figure continues)

other primary commodities reduced surpluses and official outflows in most resource exporters, including countries that were not identified as manipulators in table 4.1. The main beneficiaries have been advanced and emerging-market economies in Europe and Asia that are net commodity importers.

Finance Ministry budget for 2016. The large official flows in the United Arab Emirates primarily reflect estimated earnings on official foreign assets.

Figure 4.18   Financial indicators in Singapore, 1995–2016
(*continued*)

Real equity index

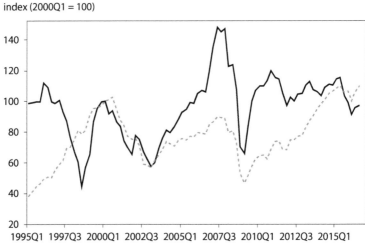

index (2000Q1 = 100)

Real housing price index

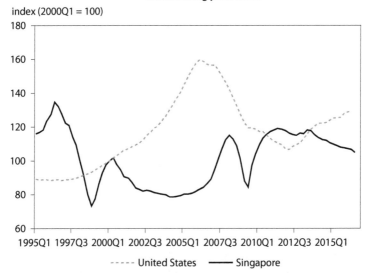

index (2000Q1 = 100)

----- United States   ——— Singapore

Note: For Singapore, variables refer to one-year government bond yield, the 10-year government bond yield, the *Straits Times* stock price index, and the Singapore Property Price Index. For variables for the United States, see figure 4.9. Real equity and housing price indices are divided by the consumer price index.

Source: Haver.

Table 4.5   Currency manipulators, 2015–16

| Economy | Years of manipulation | 2016 official assets | | 2015–16 net official flows (percent of GDP) | 2015–16 current account (percent of GDP) |
		Billions of dollars	Percent of GDP		
Financial centers					
Switzerland	2	699	106	14	10
Hong Kong	1	381	121	9	3
Macao	1	27	62	5	28
Singapore	1	582	196	1	20
Manufacturing exporters					
Israel	1	98	31	2	4
Thailand	1	199	51	4	9
Taiwan	1	440	85	2	15
Resource exporters					
United Arab Emirates	1	1,213	323	34	2
Norway	1	902	240	5	8

Note: 2016 estimates are based on 2015 totals and the change in foreign exchange reserves in 2016. Nonreserve data were not available for 2016, except for Norway, for which nonreserve flows in 2016 were taken from the Finance Ministry's 2016 budget. Net official flows of the United Arab Emirates largely reflect estimated earnings on its foreign assets. Iceland exceeded the criteria in 2016 but is not included because its net official flows are related to the settlement of outstanding liabilities to foreign creditors related to the collapse of Icelandic banks in the global financial crisis.

Sources: See appendix A.

A related development is the slowdown in China and other emerging-market and developing economies, which has sparked a net outflow of private capital from these economies. This net outflow supports China's current account surplus without currency manipulation. Indeed, China has been selling foreign exchange reserves on net since the middle of 2015.

The current set of exchange rate pressures may prove temporary. Net private outflows from emerging markets may subside, and China may settle into a slower, but still rapid, rate of growth. At some point over the next few years, private capital will likely flow into emerging markets again, putting upward pressure on their currencies. At that point many governments in emerging-market and developing economies will be tempted to manipulate their currencies again to maintain current account surpluses. As long as the economies of Europe and Japan remain weak, the bulk of the corresponding deficit is likely to be lodged in the United States. In many ways, the situation would be a return to the pattern that prevailed before and immediately after the Great Recession of 2008–09.

A separate development is the monetary policy divergence between the United States on the one hand and Europe and Japan on the other, which has encouraged private financial flows out of Europe and Japan and into the United States, pushing the dollar up against the euro and the yen. Given the strength of the US economy relative to most of the rest of the world, some increase in the US current account deficit would be justified. The problem is that the United States already has a current account deficit equal to nearly 3 percent of GDP, and its external net investment position is on an unsustainable downward path, as discussed in chapter 3. A further decline in the US current account seems inevitable. It would not take much more dollar appreciation to return to the record imbalances of 2006.

In its 2016 *External Sector Report*, the IMF stated that the US current account deficit of 2.6 percent of GDP was considerably larger than its midpoint deficit norm of 0.9 percent of GDP.[35] A further increase in the US current account deficit is likely because of the lagged effects of the dollar appreciation that started in late 2014. The UK cyclically adjusted current account deficit is also moderately above its norm. The Chinese adjusted current account surplus of 3 percent of GDP is significantly above its midpoint norm of 0.7 percent of GDP. The euro area and Japanese cyclically adjusted current account surpluses are within the IMF ranges for their norms, albeit at the high end.

The large official outflow from oil exporters is not likely to return quickly. At current and projected oil prices, most oil exporters are likely to have only small (or even negative) net official outflows. Only Norway and the United Arab Emirates are likely to have excessive net official outflows, which arise mainly from earnings on their large stocks of net official assets.

Medium-Term Prospects for Imbalances

The appreciation of the US dollar since late 2014 is likely to increase the US current account deficit over the next two years. Because its currency moved up with the dollar to a large, but not complete, extent, China also may face downward pressure on its current account balance (reducing its surplus). Indeed, data released just before this book went to press show that China's surplus dropped to around 2 percent of GDP in 2016.[36] Table 4.6 displays projected current account balances of selected countries in 2021, based

---

35. Because the US economy is close to potential, the IMF judges the cyclically adjusted current account to be almost the same as the actual current account.

36. Data are from Haver Analytics.

Table 4.6 Recent and projected current account imbalances in selected economies

Economy	2015 (percent of GDP)	2021 (percent of GDP)	2021 (billions of US dollars)
United States	−2.7	−3.9	−888
China	2.7	1.0	180
Euro area	3.9	3.0	425
Japan	3.3	3.6	202
United Kingdom	−4.3	−2.9	−88
Saudi Arabia	−6.3	−0.8	−7

Sources: Cline (2016) and IMF, *World Economic Outlook,* October 2016.

on constant exchange rates in real terms until then. These projections are from Cline (2016), who bases his projections largely on the IMF's April 2016 forecast.

Imbalances are projected to narrow for all economies except the United States and Japan. Japan's surplus is projected to widen slightly. Only for the United States is the imbalance projected to widen significantly. Saudi Arabia's narrowing deficit reflects an assumption of fiscal consolidation over the next five years. Most of the 2015 currency manipulators (table 4.5) are projected to continue to have large current account surpluses in 2021.

One problem with these forecasts (and those of the underlying IMF forecasts) is that the widening of the US current account deficit is not accompanied by a commensurate widening of surpluses (or narrowing of deficits) in other countries. A longstanding concern with the IMF's forecasts is that they tend to project narrowing imbalances even when recent exchange rate movements would suggest otherwise. We find the projected narrowing of the euro area and other surpluses in table 4.6 to be implausible in light of dollar appreciation over the past two years.

In the IMF's April 2016 projections for 2021, global current account deficits exceed surpluses by $350 billion, which violates the adding-up constraint. In the IMF's October 2016 projections, this discrepancy was largely eliminated by dramatically reducing the projected US deficit to 2.7 percent of GDP. We find it implausible that the US deficit would remain unchanged as a share of GDP after the substantial appreciation of the dollar in 2014–16. We find the April 2016 projection for the United States to be more reasonable and argue that the global current account discrepancy in that forecast called for a widening in other countries' projected surpluses rather than a narrowing of the US deficit. As with its current account norms (discussed in chapter 3), the IMF is too prone to make judgments that will please its constituent members, in this case by showing the desired narrowing of imbalances going forward. We believe this is wishful thinking.

Between October 2016, when Cline prepared his forecast, and February 2017, the US dollar rose another 2 percent on a broad trade-weighted basis (Federal Reserve index). This further appreciation of the dollar suggests that the US current account deficit is likely to increase even more than shown in table 4.6.

These considerations suggest that overvaluation of the US dollar against almost all currencies is the primary currency misalignment in the world today. A small portion of this overvaluation is being supported by lingering currency manipulation, but the main driver has been private financial flows. However, if private flows reverse in the next few years, many countries will be tempted to resume large-scale manipulation in order to hang on to their current account surpluses. The next chapter identifies policy options for deterring a return to widespread manipulation and the increased imbalances that would result.

Appendix 4A

Public Saving of Nonrenewable Resource Revenues

It is generally accepted that at least some of the net revenues from exploiting a nonrenewable resource should be saved for future generations. However, it is possible to save too much as well as too little.

Figure 4A.1 displays four options for a country that begins to export a nonrenewable resource. In the absence of resource exports, consumption is assumed to grow at a rate of 1 percent per year, reflecting productivity increases (the heavy solid line). (For simplicity, we assume no population growth.) Resource production is assumed to last 25 years and equals 25 percent of initial consumption. The thin solid line shows the "no saving" scenario, in which all resource revenues are consumed as soon as they are produced. This path leads to a very sharp drop in consumption in year 26; consumption does not regain its peak value until year 44.

One goal of policy may be to avoid any declines in consumption. Economic theories of habit formation or loss aversion suggest that the damage to welfare from such declines may far exceed the benefits of an equal rise in consumption. With even a small positive trend in productivity, however, future generations may reliably expect to consume more per capita than past generations. Society may thus wish to bestow more of the benefits of resource extraction on the relatively poorer current generation than on richer future generations.

One strategy (the "no drop in consumption" scenario), shown by the thick gray line, is to let the current generation consume most of the revenues but to save enough to avoid a drop in consumption when the resource runs out. We assume a real rate of return on saving of 3 percent. However, given the uncertainty surrounding the amount of resources that will ultimately prove exploitable, the price they will command, and the rate of return on saving, it may be desirable to save even more of the resource, in order to avoid any future drop in consumption.

A more conservative strategy, shown by the dashed line, is to save enough to raise the consumption path of all generations equally. This strategy builds a larger stock of savings, which can also be used to smooth out any unexpected decline in resource revenues or asset returns. We refer to this as the "shared benefits" strategy.

The dotted line displays an extremely conservative strategy of saving all of the resource revenues and increasing consumption only in the future and only by the amount of the expected average real per capita return to the saving. The government of Norway has adopted this "ultrafrugal" strategy. It essentially guarantees that consumption will never fall in any year—but it

Figure 4A.1 Alternative scenarios for allocating resource wealth over time

index of per capita consumption

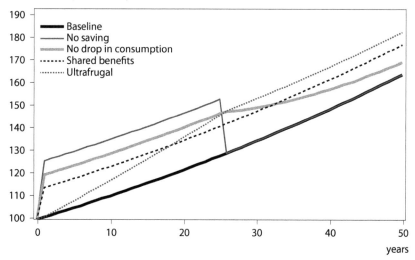

Source: Authors' calculations.

does so by giving all of the windfall to future generations, which are already expected to be richer than the current generation.[37]

Table 4A.1 displays the fraction of resource production that is saved under the shared benefits strategy for certain parameters. When resource production ends in period T, assets will have reached a level sufficient to support the higher consumption permanently. This condition is defined by the equation

$$(r - n) * \text{Assets} = (1 - s) * \text{Resource Production},$$

---

37. A different framework within which to examine the issue is that of Dutch disease, named after the stagnation of certain economic sectors in the Netherlands after the discovery of offshore gas in 1959. When resource revenues are spent instead of saved abroad, the exchange rate rises, nonresource imports increase, competing industries at home decline, and nontradable industries at home grow. If resource production could last forever, there would be no fundamental problem. However, when the resource runs out, the economy must shift back. The costs of adjusting in both directions may be large. The shared benefits scenario in figure 4A.1 represents the optimal response to Dutch disease. Higher consumption pushes up the exchange rate, but by less than in the no saving case, engendering a smaller shift from tradables to nontradables. Moreover, because this consumption path is sustainable permanently, there is no need to shift back when the resource runs out. The country can pay for higher imports from the earnings on foreign assets. The ultrafrugal scenario represents an excessive response to the Dutch disease. Unchanged current consumption means there is no initial pressure on the exchange rate and thus no initial shifting across sectors. The shift must come eventually; in this scenario it ends up being even larger than in the consumption-equalizing scenario.

Table 4A.1 Fraction of resource production to save (s) with shared benefits strategy

r − n (percent)	T=10	T=25	T=50
1	0.90	0.78	0.61
3	0.75	0.48	0.23
5	0.61	0.30	0.09

r = real return on assets, n = population growth rate,
T = years of resource production

where r is the real return on assets, n is the population growth rate, and s is saving out of resource production (implying that $1 - s$ is the share of resource production that adds to consumption each year). (For simplicity, we assume that production grows with population until resources run out.)

We consider table 4A.1 for the case of Norway. The government of Norway assumes a long-run real return on its foreign assets of 4 percent.[38] The average real return on foreign assets since the founding of its sovereign wealth fund is 3.6 percent.[39] Population growth in Norway is expected to average about 0.8 percent between 1985 and 2035. Thus a reasonable estimate of $r - n$ for Norway is 3 percent.

Norway began contributing to its sovereign wealth fund in 1996. At current production rates, proved reserves would last only about 10 years. The Norwegian Petroleum Directorate believes that future discoveries and technologies are likely to extend current production for at least another 15 years.[40] A very conservative estimate for the number of years of resource production at the start of Norway's sovereign wealth fund is thus 25.[41] According to table 4A.1, under the shared benefits strategy, Norway should have saved about half of its net oil revenues. In addition, it should save all of the earnings on its savings during the 25 years of production.

As the resource fund grows, total public sector saving increases to reflect reinvestment of earnings on assets. When the resource runs out, earnings must equal the amount of resource revenue being consumed, in order to stabilize consumption. Because the resource revenue saved plus

---

38. See appendix 1 in the National Budget 2016, Norwegian Ministry of Finance.

39. The home page of Norges Bank Investment Management, www.nbim.no (accessed on October 5, 2016) lists an average nominal return of 5.6 percent. Inflation averaged about 2 percent over the same period.

40. See *Petroleum Resources on the Norwegian Continental Shelf 2016*, www.npd.no/en/Publications/Resource-Reports/2016/.

41. Using a conservative estimate of total resources is one way to hedge against the risk of a future decline in the resource price.

the resource revenue consumed equals 100 percent of revenue, total public saving should rise toward 100 percent of net resource revenue as the depletion date nears.

The table can be used to show how total saving evolves. Suppose, for example, that Norway started with 25 years of production and saved 48 percent of its net oil revenues. After 15 years, with only 10 years of production left, total saving (including earnings on assets) should have risen to 75 percent of net oil revenues.

An important question is how much of the saving should be invested at home versus abroad. Many resource exporters are poor and could benefit enormously from greater investment in infrastructure, housing, factories, and offices. But economies can effectively absorb only so much investment at a time. In countries with poor institutions and governance, waste and corruption are problems. Nevertheless, Berg et al. (2012) argue that roughly half of net oil revenue in Angola and western Africa could be usefully invested at home. In economies that are richer (more capital abundant) or more dominated by oil production (and hence have smaller nonoil sectors), the share that should be invested at home is smaller.

There are two components of domestic public sector saving: financial and physical. Financial saving is used to pay down government debt, lend to the private sector, or buy private sector assets. Physical saving is used to make public investments, mainly in infrastructure. Most countries measure public investment only in gross terms and do not calculate an estimate of depreciation of the capital stock. Norway is one of the few countries that reports depreciation of public sector capital and thus allows net public investment (the basis for the analysis above) to be calculated. At the peak of oil prices (2012–13), Norway invested about 10 percent of its oil revenues at home (this figure refers to net investment: public investment in excess of public consumption of fixed capital [depreciation]). IMF staff project that Norway will invest about 20 percent of the projected lower future oil revenues at home.

Saving that is not directed domestically must flow abroad in the form of increased foreign exchange reserves, additional sovereign wealth fund assets, or reduced external public debt. These are net official flows. Table 4A.2 displays net official flows of three major oil exporters with projections through 2020 based on IMF staff reports (the definition of net official flows differs somewhat from that used in tables 4.1 to 4.3, which are based on data from the IMF's Balance of Payments database). Official flows are expressed as a percent of net oil revenues to the government. To estimate total public sector saving, one would need to add in net domestic saving, which averages 10 to 20 percent of net oil revenues for Norway and is not available for the other countries.

Table 4A.2 Net official flows in Angola, Norway, and Saudi Arabia, 2012–20 (percent of net oil revenue)

Year	Angola	Norway	Saudi Arabia
2012	7	124	37
2013	–20	108	25
2014	–25	58	3
2015	–57	82	–97
2016	–9	176	–94
2017	–43	77	–56
2018	n.a.	70	–44
2019	n.a.	63	–38
2020	n.a.	66	–31

n.a. = not available

Sources: IMF 2015 and 2016 Article IV Staff Reports for Angola, Norway, and Saudi Arabia, the Norwegian Finance Ministry's 2016 budget, and authors' calculations.

In the years of high oil prices (2012–13), Angola appears to have saved too little, Norway too much, and Saudi Arabia arguably about the right amount, after making some allowance for domestic saving, which Saudi Arabia was ramping up at the time. Going forward, Angola and Saudi Arabia are projected to save too little, although the projection for Angola extends only one year. The high ratio of net official flows to net oil revenues for Norway in 2016 reflects a combination of unusually low oil revenues and high projected earnings on its sovereign wealth assets. Although Norway is projected to have positive net official flows in 2016, the partial transfer of fund earnings to the fiscal budget exceeded the inflow of oil revenues to the fund for the first time. Considering that Norway is projected to have domestic net government saving of about 20 percent of oil revenues, which must be added to the numbers in the table to get total saving, it is projected to continue to save too much, albeit by less than previously.

5

Policy Options

A wide array of policy options is available to respond to currency manipulation and thus to seek to deter currency conflict. The choices among them rest on several key conceptual distinctions. This chapter briefly addresses them and then turns to an appraisal of the specific alternatives.

Macroeconomic/Monetary versus Trade Policy

The first key distinction is whether such responses should be conducted through measures that affect all of an affected country's transactions with a manipulating country, or through trade policy and other steps that apply only to imports or a subset thereof from such a country. The former could include at least four types of measures: fiscal policy, aggregate monetary policy, intervention in the foreign exchange markets, and capital controls to limit or tax a manipulator's access to domestic currency or investments in domestic markets. The latter could include import surcharges, countervailing duties, antidumping duties, and the inclusion of currency provisions in multilateral, regional or bilateral free trade agreements (FTAs). Export subsidies are also a theoretical possibility but generally require budget outlays and have very little practical appeal.

Different authorities manage different policies. In the United States, the administration and Congress handle fiscal policy, the Federal Reserve handles monetary policy, the Treasury and the Fed handle currency intervention, and the Treasury handles capital controls.

Macroeconomic policy measures are useful to stabilize domestic output and employment. They are unlikely to target foreign currency manipulators, especially in a large and relatively closed economy like the United States. Financial measures are much more likely than trade measures to be effective in countering the impact of, and thus deterring, currency manipulation, as they affect all trade flows between manipulating and affected countries, both exports and imports, whereas most trade policy measures address only imports. Currency intervention operates directly and very precisely via the exchange markets themselves. Capital controls operate indirectly but precisely via the financial flows generated by intervention. Hence financial measures are to be preferred.

Multilateral versus Unilateral Action

A second key distinction is whether the policy response would be multilateral, unilateral, or somewhere in between (plurilateral, including regional). Multilateral approaches involve invoking the rules, procedures, and mechanisms of the relevant international institutions, primarily the International Monetary Fund (IMF) and the World Trade Organization (WTO). Under the unilateral option, the aggrieved country adopts macroeconomic/monetary and/or trade policy measures on its own. An intermediate strategy would be plurilateral, using groups such as the G-7, the G-20, or an FTA or creating new groups specifically to deal with the currency question (such as the stillborn Trans-Pacific Partnership (TPP) Macroeconomic Group or any new coalition that might be formed on manipulation itself).

There is probably a rough correlation between the degree of international participation in a policy to counter currency manipulation and the extent of cooperation, as opposed to coercion, among countries embedded in it, suggesting that multilateral or plurilateral options are preferable to unilateral steps in foreign policy terms. That correlation is by no means perfect, however. The Plaza Accord, which achieved a dramatic realignment of exchange rates and a successful adjustment of current account balances in the second half of the 1980s, was probably the high-water mark of postwar international cooperation on these issues. It was implemented collegially by the G-5, but it originated as a unilateral US initiative, under the acute threat of congressional protectionism, that was not based on any agreed upon rules or institutional arrangements (Bergsten and Green 2016). At the other extreme, US efforts to foster implementation of the IMF rules on manipulation in the mid-2000s left bruised feelings in China, and perhaps elsewhere; any initiative to take it to the WTO would undoubtedly have had similar effects (Blustein 2012).

Table 5.1 shows a matrix of policy options. Countervailing currency intervention is an across-the-board measure implemented unilaterally (though perhaps with plurilateral or multilateral approval, as discussed

Table 5.1   The policy matrix

Approach	Macro/monetary policy	Trade policy	
Multilateral	Invocation of IMF rules Reform of international monetary system (e.g., reference rates)	Imposition of import surcharges (WTO Article XV (4)) Imposition of countervailing duties (WTO Subsidy Code)	
Plurilateral	Use of G-7 or G-20 (e.g., in the Plaza Accord)	Currency provisions in free trade agreements (e.g., TPP Macroeconomic Group)	
Unilateral	Use of fiscal policy Use of monetary policy Defensive intervention Countervailing currency intervention Imposition of capital controls	Import surcharges Countervailing duties	[Subject to retaliation if not ultimately approved by WTO]

IMF = International Monetary Fund; WTO = World Trade Organization; TPP = Trans-Pacific Partnership

below). Import surcharges and countervailing duties are trade policy measures that could be applied either multilaterally, under the aegis of the WTO, or unilaterally (though they would then be subject to retaliation if not ultimately approved by the WTO). Inevitable tradeoffs will affect the choices of specific measures.

Markets to the Rescue?

Could markets drive correction of currency misalignments caused by official manipulation, obviating the need for a policy response by governments? They might do so by triggering economic forces that offset the impact of the manipulation itself or compel the manipulator to cease manipulating. Either is conceptually possible, and each has occurred to a degree.

A country that suppresses its exchange rate for a prolonged period will suffer inflationary pressures from the resultant currency undervaluation unless it takes steps to contract macroeconomic policy. Any increased inflation that results will lead to an appreciation of the country's real exchange rate, thus reversing to some extent the initial competitive nonappreciation of the nominal rate.

Currency manipulation also encourages an inflow of private capital to the undervalued currency. The inflow may become immense for countries that permit free capital movements, forcing the authorities to engage in even more intervention, particularly when macroeconomic policies succeed in holding down inflationary pressure. Huge reserve buildups from manipulation can also trigger extensive domestic criticism as a misallocation of national resources, especially for developing countries with large alternative investment opportunities.

The largest manipulators in recent years, China and Switzerland, have experienced these effects to some degree. China limits capital inflows (and outflows), so it has been able to keep macro policy sufficiently restrictive to avoid price inflation even with a large buildup of reserves. Nevertheless, the reserve buildup was large enough to engender domestic opposition that presumably contributed to the decisions over the course of the decade to let the renminbi appreciate substantially in both trade-weighted and dollar terms (see the discussion of China in chapter 4). By contrast, Switzerland, with its smaller economy and near absence of capital controls, was swamped with safe-haven inflows and had to abandon the ceiling it had maintained for the Swiss franc for three years, despite the renewed appreciation that resulted (see the section on Switzerland in chapter 4). Nevertheless, Swiss intervention continues to support a very large current account surplus, with foreign exchange reserves roughly equal to its total GDP (and still rising).

Three lessons might be drawn from these episodes for the efficacy of the "market option" to remedy currency manipulation. First, small and relatively open economies are more susceptible to market pressures; large, relatively closed economies—which are more likely to have systemically important effects—can resist them longer. Second, resistance can be sustained especially by countries that are prepared to deploy extensive capital controls. Third, at best this option will play out over an extended period of time, with a great deal of economic impact taking place in the meanwhile.

Market pressures usually help push in the direction of the needed outcome, as they have in the cases of both China and Switzerland. However, they cannot be counted on to achieve a definitive resolution—certainly not in a timely and low-cost manner (for either the manipulator or the affected countries). The uncertain prospect of a market-based correction would not deter manipulation, the objective in seeking a comprehensive and effective resolution of this practice. Other policy alternatives therefore need to be explored.

Specific Alternatives

This section describes and analyzes 10 potential policy responses to manipulation, primarily for the United States:

1. private diplomacy,
2. mobilization of the IMF,
3. reform of the IMF,
4. mobilization of the WTO,
5. inclusion of currency issues in FTAs,
6. changes in fiscal policy,
7. changes in monetary policy,
8. use of countervailing currency intervention,
9. imposition of capital controls, and
10. imposition of unilateral import controls (countervailing duties and surcharges).

The first alternative describes recent US policy. The next four options would be conducted through multilateral channels. The last five are unilateral.

Private Diplomacy

Private diplomacy has been the preferred US currency policy. It has encompassed (1) a steady drumbeat of pressure on China throughout the "decade of manipulation"; (2) occasional entreaties to other countries, especially Japan in late 2012 and early 2013 and Korea when its surpluses rose sharply in recent years; and (3) consistent efforts to produce statements by the major international consultative groups, especially the G-7 and G-20, to reiterate and strengthen where possible the commitments of their members to avoid manipulation after a futile effort to mobilize the IMF in 2006–08.

In 2015 the strategy added the issuance of a Joint Declaration of the Macroeconomic Policy Authorities of Trans-Pacific Partnership Countries, a currency side agreement to the TPP, and through it the creation of a TPP Macroeconomic Group that was to meet at least annually once the TPP came into effect. All these efforts were most vigorous when the Obama administration wanted to demonstrate to Congress that it was addressing the currency issue seriously, especially as the trade policy debate heated up and headed toward floor votes in 2015–16. The Obama administration ultimately embraced cooperation with Congress to craft new and modestly tougher currency legislation that was included in the Trade Facilitation and Trade Enforcement Act of 2015.

The most contentious issue throughout the decade was whether the secretary of the Treasury should publicly designate China a currency manipulator, as called for under the Trade Act of 1988. Many private studies (e.g., Goldstein 2004, Goldstein and Lardy 2008) and Treasury's own analyses in its semiannual foreign exchange reports clearly showed that China was manipulating. Treasury argued, however, that it would have to demonstrate that China *intended* its actions to achieve competitive gains and that it could not do so. Even with such a designation, in any event, the secretary of the Treasury would have been required by law only to enter into negotiations to correct the problem, which successive administrations were pursuing anyway.

Both the Bush 43 and Obama administrations chose private diplomacy over tougher options, even during the period of maximum intervention by China and others. They argued that diplomacy was more likely than public confrontation to induce China to cease or at least reduce its manipulation because of Chinese aversion to any appearance of capitulation to foreign pressure. With the onset of the financial crisis and Great Recession in 2008, they also needed Chinese cooperation to rescue the world economy and gave lower priority to the currency issue. These tactical views were reinforced by broader US strategic considerations, which sought to avoid escalating the currency conflict and thereby risking needed Chinese cooperation with respect to North Korea, Iran, and other priority geopolitical issues. The administrations also argued that designation of China as a manipulator, by acknowledging the problem but probably doing little about it, could stimulate rather than quiet protectionism in Congress. They feared that taking tangible steps to weaken the dollar, by strengthening the renminbi, could lead to excessive and uncomfortable dollar depreciation and even undermine the currency's international role, which they viewed as a major benefit to the United States.

The approach was partly successful. China began to let the renminbi appreciate gradually in 2005 and, after halting its appreciation during the Great Recession, again in 2010. The cumulative appreciation reached 35 percent against the dollar at its recent peak in 2015, and China's current account surplus dropped sharply from its record high of 10 percent of GDP in 2007 to less than 3 percent in 2014–15 (see figure 4.3). Other potential major manipulators, notably Japan and Korea, know that the United States is watching them closely and may have been deterred from new intervention as a result.

The other possible payoff from recent policy, about which one can only speculate, is that it may have succeeded in spawning new behavioral norms to reject manipulation in at least some major economies. Manipulation has largely gone into remission over the past couple of years, as described in chapter 4, primarily because of changes in the direction of market pressures as the dollar has strengthened against virtually all currencies. China has totally reversed its intervention policy. It has experienced large capital outflows and depreciation of the renminbi, defending its currency against even more sizable declines by selling dollars. Other economies have not experienced such abrupt turnarounds, but only a few, relatively smaller, ones have continued to intervene (as indicated in table 4.5).

It is thus conceivable, though by no means certain, that the cumulative impact of US pressure and repeated statements from the G-7, G-20, and other international groups has sufficiently discredited manipulation that the practice will not be resumed widely even when market pressures shift again, as they surely will. The circumstantial evidence is stronger for the G-7 than for the G-20, because the Japanese government has resisted intervening even when it was under strong domestic pressure to do so in 2013 and 2016. The jury remains out on this crucial question, but it should be noted as a possible payoff from the policy responses, mainly by the United States, during the "decade of manipulation."

The only major deviation from private diplomacy was the periodic public congressional criticism of China (and to a much lesser extent Japan and still less so Korea). Treasury relied on Congressional participation in the traditional "good cop, bad cop" routine for what little leverage it had with China; that pressure appears to have had a greater impact than the administration's negotiating efforts per se. The initiations of renminbi appreciation in 2005 and 2010, and especially the acceleration in the pace of those appreciations in 2007–08 and 2011–12, correlate closely with the likelihood of congressional action; Congress seriously considered currency bills for the first time during 2007–08 and each house of Congress passed such a bill in 2011–12.[1]

Chinese actions, in contrast to Chinese rhetoric, thus seemed to be responsive to rather than resistant to meaningful external pressure. Previous manipulators also clearly responded to indications of congressional concern (sometimes reinforced by administration threats, mainly regarding trade policy). Japanese governments, for example, even sought "foreign pressure" (*gaiatsu*) to promote their own policy reforms. European governments, which were not actively manipulating, were acutely aware of the protectionist tendencies in Congress when they agreed to let their exchange rates appreciate in the wake of the Plaza Accord.

---

1. Possible IMF action was also a factor in 2007–08, as described in the next section.

The United States probably does not have as much international clout now as it had in those earlier periods, and China is a very different partner. But the pattern also seems to conform to contemporary Chinese behavior on other issues. For example, there is some evidence that China curtailed its commercial cyberespionage activities in 2015–16 after the Obama administration threatened to adopt sanctions against China.

The chief advantage of the private diplomacy option is its minimization of political conflicts with the manipulators themselves, with other countries whose support the United States would want to seek to help counter manipulation, and especially with domestic interest groups that oppose tougher action. Most of the US business community, including virtually all of the large multinational firms engaged in China, for example, steadily and strongly opposed the public designation of China as a manipulator under US law, let alone anything tougher; they clearly did not want to roil the Chinese government and risk retaliation against their own operations. This approach also permits the United States to continue reaping the benefits of an overvalued dollar, including cheaper imports and lower interest rates, as outlined in chapter 4.

The chief disadvantage of private diplomacy is that it enabled China and other manipulators, many of which were explicitly mirroring China's behavior, to get away with massive manipulation for a decade, shifting several hundreds of billions of dollars' worth of annual production away from the United States and other affected countries. During the Great Recession, when unemployment was very high, it contributed to the loss of millions of jobs. It accelerated and intensified the "China shock" to the US economy that Autor, Dorn, and Hanson (2016) analyzed years later (but that was not widely understood when it was occurring).[2] Most of the huge Chinese reserve buildup that resulted from the intervention was invested in dollar assets, easing US debt service but flooding the economy with liquidity that contributed to the financial conditions and housing bubble that brought on the financial crisis and the Great Recession, substantially compounding the direct impact of the imbalances on production and jobs.

The more subtle, but perhaps most costly, disadvantage of this option has been its role in the erosion of domestic political support for globalization and open trade policies in general, and new trade agreements (most notably the TPP) in particular, in the United States. Much of Congress lost confidence in the administration's ability and willingness to defend US eco-

---

2. Goldstein and Lardy (2008) identified the renminbi as undervalued by about 30 percent at the time and calculated that elimination of its misalignment, along with parallel adjustments by other Asian manipulators, would reduce the US current account deficit by $100 billion to $200 billion per year.

nomic interests in the face of massive, prolonged, and blatant violation of those interests and of accepted international norms. They therefore linked their requested approval of both Trade Promotion Authority in 2015 and the TPP to more forceful action on currency and threatened to derail both initiatives unless such action was taken. (Collateral damage was done as well to congressional confidence in economic institutions, especially the IMF, which also failed in this case.) The political campaigns of 2015–16 indicated that this erosion of support had spread to both major parties and the public; the election of Donald Trump at least partly reflected his ability to cite currency manipulation as a failure of previous policy—and, much more broadly, the wide acceptance of the notion of a "China shock."

This congressional backlash produced three tangible results. First, the negotiating objectives of the Trade Promotion Authority bill required members of the TPP and future US trade agreements to "avoid manipulating exchange rates" (though not necessarily through those agreements themselves). Second, in partial response, in late 2015 the administration negotiated the Joint Declaration of the Macroeconomic Policy Authorities of Trans-Pacific Partnership Countries, which reaffirmed their policy commitments under the IMF Articles to avoid competitive devaluation and manipulation, committed them to increased transparency and disclosure of their reserves and intervention data, and scheduled annual meetings to discuss and report publicly on those issues.[3] Third, Congress passed the Trade Facilitation and Trade Enforcement Act of 2015. It requires the administration to undertake "enhanced engagement" on the currency issue with "major trading partners" that meet a set of objective criteria: a significant bilateral trade surplus with the United States, a material global current account surplus, and persistent one-sided intervention in the currency markets. It supplements the traditional focus on publicly designating "manipulators" (and thus obviates the need to judge the intent of the countries involved). The law requires the administration to take at least one of a set of specified (though quite modest) remedial actions against countries that fail to correct their situation in a year: (1) denial of Overseas Private Investment Corporation (OPIC) programs and US government procurement (except for members of the Government Procurement Agreement in the WTO), (2) an effort to stimulate special IMF consultations with the country, and (3) the "taking into account" of its currency policy in deciding whether to include it in a future US trade agreement. Recent US currency policy might

---

3. A major gap in disclosure was the lack of specific mention of official foreign currency assets not designated as reserves, such as sovereign wealth funds and public pension assets. In any event, the Declaration became null and void with the demise of the TPP itself due to the US withdrawal declared by President Trump in early 2017.

thus be described as "private diplomacy with a few teeth," but unless the hypothesized possible shift in cultural norms on the issue is much stronger than can yet be reliably counted on, it remains wholly inadequate to deter future resumption of widespread manipulation if major countries decide they want to resume that practice.

Donald Trump's repeated campaign pledges "to label China as a currency manipulator on day one of his administration" implied a sharp reversal of the private diplomacy of the past, though they had not been realized as of March 2017. But this hawkish stance on trade policy and globalization more broadly, especially with respect to China, could still herald a much stronger line on currency as well as other international economic issues. His focus on unilateral and bilateral approaches also probably reduces the prospect for new multilateral initiatives, including the initiatives listed below.

The election of Donald Trump was at least partially the result of his strong and skeptical views on trade and globalization. Currency issues are, of course, only a part of that picture, but it is noteworthy that of all the criticisms launched at the TPP and other FTAs by their critics, including private sector groups such as labor unions and Democratic candidates Hillary Clinton and Bernie Sanders, none was more prominent than currency manipulation. Currency manipulation was also the main target of congressional opponents of the TPP from both parties, some of whom asserted that they had "killed the TPP" even before the election. Past policy on currency manipulation had thus apparently become unsustainable in domestic political terms, even while it remained wholly sustainable in external financial terms. This opposition—along with other objections to traditional international economic policies—threatens to trigger a sea change in US engagement with the rest of the world.[4]

Mobilization of the International Monetary Fund

The one recent departure from the policy of relying on private diplomacy was the Bush administration's effort in 2006–08 to "take China to court" under the rules and procedures of the IMF. China was clearly violating its IMF commitments to avoid competitive devaluation and currency manipulation. But the IMF is a highly political body, so the United States had to persuade both its executive board (representing its member countries and thus subject to strong pressures from a powerful member like China) and

---

4. In the annual Stavros Niarchos Foundation Lecture at the Peterson Institute for International Economics in May 2013, C. Fred Bergsten warned that failure to resolve these issues preemptively could lead to a repetition of the unilateral and protectionist currency and trade initiatives of President Nixon and Secretary of the Treasury John Connally in 1971. That scenario may now be unfolding.

its management (which was reluctant to proceed for similar reasons). After intense effort over a prolonged period, by mid- 2008 the United States succeeded in indicting China. The Lehman crisis and the onset of the Great Recession then completely changed the focus of US and IMF policy, however, which suddenly emphasized the need for cooperation from China to prevent a new global depression. The currency issue was dropped and never picked up again (Blustein 2012).

Even had the United States succeeded in its effort, however, the IMF has no policy instruments to enforce its rules. The outcome that was sought, with prolonged and strenuous effort, was simply a "special consultation" with China by the Fund's managing director to discuss the problem and seek possible solutions. To be sure, the "naming and shaming" of China would have escalated, and it is possible that an official Fund declaration of renminbi undervaluation might have paved the way for trade sanctions in the WTO (see below) if the United States had pursued that additional step and been able to win widespread support in Geneva. China hence strongly opposed the US initiative. But the impact would have been uncertain, and probably limited, even if the initiative had succeeded.[5]

The direct advantage of mobilizing the IMF is, of course, that the multilateral nature of the institution and its rules would confer global legitimacy on any effort to indict a currency manipulator and go far to justify it in terms of public as well as official opinion around the world. Moreover, an IMF determination of undervaluation is an essential step en route to multilateral trade actions, so this option would have to be included in any serious new initiative in that direction.

It would be highly desirable for the Fund to work closely with the WTO to link the Fund's expertise and authority in identifying currency problems with the WTO's ability to impose sanctions to promote enforcement of its (and the Fund's) rules. The WTO must rely on IMF guidance on the existence and extent of currency manipulation as a basis for any actions it might take, under its own rules, against manipulators. If they worked actively and constructively together, the two institutions would constitute a powerful force in implementing the rules of both. But they have resisted minimal cooperation, let alone proactive collaboration, and the WTO has deferred totally to the IMF on these issues. We turn shortly to an assessment of the WTO policy options as a basis for considering a new IMF-WTO alliance.

---

5. Morris Goldstein (2006) took a more optimistic view of the effectiveness of IMF special consultations when he urged the IMF to embrace its role as umpire of the exchange rate system.

There are several disadvantages to the IMF system, however, starting with the lack of teeth in the IMF itself and thus the need for complementary actions, in the WTO and/or unilaterally, if tangible results are to be achieved. In addition, any serious effort in the IMF is bound to take considerable time, as demonstrated in 2006-08. Hence any strategy that relied on the IMF would take significantly longer to implement than most unilateral actions. Failure at the Fund would tend to discredit the entire effort and make it more difficult to pursue other options. In addition, failure on this issue would discredit the Fund more broadly (as it has already done), weakening its ability to continue to conduct policies in other issue areas where it can be much more effective.

Reform of the International Monetary Fund

Currency manipulation, especially by China, has become a leading threat to the world trading system because of the large imbalances it has spawned and (especially) the backlash against open trade it has generated in the United States and elsewhere. To address the problem, there is a glaring need to shore up the basic rules of the international monetary system, especially the IMF itself as the guardian and manager of an open and cooperative global economic order.

The Fund was created largely to prevent a replication of the currency wars of the 1930s, which could easily recur today, especially in light of the unilateral tendencies of the Trump administration. It has failed to do so. Reform of the IMF is needed to fill the gaps left by the architects of the postwar period. The United States should make a renewed push for such reform, whether or not the current remission of manipulation turns out to be lasting or temporary.

Three actions would give the IMF meaningful powers on this issue. First, the United States and other countries that have been injured by currency manipulation, or are simply displeased with such a huge systemic gap, could withhold their support from future candidates for managing director who did not pledge to make a major effort to remedy this shortcoming in Fund policy (countries that oppose such changes in policy could, of course, support other candidates, leading to a stalemate). It is stunning that the United States has apparently never raised such a key issue in this context. It should do so in the future.

Second, the Fund should be able to counteract currency manipulation in the same way that the WTO can counteract unfair trade practices, through direct retaliation by its members. We propose below the institution of countervailing currency intervention, under which affected countries would offset the intervention of manipulators by buying equal amounts

Table 5.2   A reference rate system

Stock of official assets	Current account above norm	Current account below norm
More than adequate	Foreign exchange purchases not allowed	No restrictions
	Foreign exchange sales encouraged	
Less than adequate	No restrictions	Foreign exchange sales not allowed
		Foreign exchange purchases encouraged

of the currencies the manipulators are selling, thereby neutralizing the manipulation and presumably deterring the practice. Such a policy could be implemented unilaterally, mainly by the United States, as will almost certainly be necessary to get it launched. The IMF could eventually authorize the practice, however, bestowing on it all the advantages (though also the disadvantages) of multilateral determination and implementation. Such a step would restore a central role for the Fund on this major issue, on which it has been largely bypassed since the breakdown of "fixed" exchange rates in the early 1970s because of its revealed impotence.

Third, the IMF could authorize (or, in its strongest form, instruct) member countries to push their currencies toward equilibrium levels and to retaliate (inter alia via countervailing currency intervention) against efforts by other countries to push (or keep) their currencies away from such levels. Building on the guidelines for reserve holdings and current account norms developed in chapters 3 and 4, the reference rate matrix shown in table 5.2 governing purchases and sales of foreign exchange reserves could provide the foundation for a new international monetary regime.

The minimum principle would be that countries be banned from conducting currency policies that maintain or increase a deviation of the current account balance from its norm. Surplus countries whose reserves are already adequate, for example, would be forbidden from opposing appreciation of their exchange rates by buying foreign currencies, and other countries could directly counter any such actions. Countries would be encouraged—but at least at first not required—to adopt currency policies that actively push the current account toward its norm; surplus countries would be encouraged to buy their own currencies by selling excess reserves (as Japan and several European countries did to implement the Plaza Accord and as China has been doing since 2015).

The norms for current accounts should be established and regularly reviewed by the IMF in consultation with member countries, as discussed in chapter 3. In setting these norms, the IMF should not simply ratify existing levels of imbalances without strong justification, as its efforts to date have frequently tended to do. The spirit of this policy matrix can be traced back to Ethier and Bloomfield (1975), who proposed that countries not be allowed to intervene in foreign exchange markets to push their currencies away from agreed reference rates. In our matrix, the reference rates would be expected to deliver the targeted current account norms over the medium term.

The policy matrix has a long historical pedigree. Bergsten and Williamson (1983) and Williamson and Miller (1987) developed proposals for target zones that embodied a commitment to maintain specific ranges for exchange rates. This line of research influenced the Plaza Accord (1985) and the Louvre Accord (1987) (Bergsten 2016). The Plaza Accord included a joint agreement that it was appropriate to sell official US dollar assets to bring down the dollar's exchange value and thus move the US current account toward balance. The Louvre Accord effectively declared that the dollar had fallen far enough and that the United States and others should purchase dollar assets to counter further depreciation.

However, the fear that any commitment on exchange rates would eventually force policymakers to choose between moving the focus of monetary and fiscal policy away from stabilizing employment and inflation, and abandoning the agreed commitment and causing financial turbulence, prevented the target zone idea from lasting very long or being adopted more generally. Moreover, despite the relative success of both Plaza and Louvre, there was widespread skepticism about both the ability to agree on desirable exchange rates and the potency of sterilized intervention as a tool to achieve target rates. The major economies were not willing to commit to even a broad and adjustable range for exchange rates, let alone a narrow and permanent band.

Faced with these powerful objections, Williamson (2007, updated 2016) retreated to Ethier and Bloomfield's original reference rate proposal, except that he made explicit the link between reference rates and sustainable current account balances. The key difference between the reference rate and target zone approaches is that under the reference rate approach, countries would not be required to defend any limits on the exchange rate; the reference rates would merely indicate levels or ranges for the exchange rate beyond which foreign exchange intervention in a certain direction would be prohibited and intervention in the opposite direction encouraged. Gagnon (2011) endorsed this version of the reference rate proposal in a study that otherwise extolled the benefits of flexible exchange rates.

Mobilization of the World Trade Organization

A second set of multilateral options would entail taking manipulators to the trade "court" of the WTO. Doing so would necessitate engaging the IMF, because the charter of the WTO requires it to seek guidance from the Fund as to whether the currency of an accused member is undervalued. An approach to the Fund need not involve a parallel, or subsequent, approach to the WTO, but an appeal to the WTO does require a parallel, or prior, entreaty to the Fund.

There are two potential components of the WTO for addressing currency manipulation. The more sweeping is Article XV (4), which bans member countries from taking "exchange action" to "frustrate the intent of the provisions of the Agreement." The United States, and perhaps other affected members, could charge that manipulators were doing so through their currency practices. The provision has never been implemented, but its invocation would presumably lead to WTO authorization for members to apply across-the-board import controls, most likely surcharges, in whatever amounts were determined to be needed to offset the indicated undervaluation. The indictment itself would probably persuade the manipulator(s) in question to cease intervening. If it did not, the United States and others could follow through by applying surcharges to implement the remedy.

The other, much narrower WTO option is to start bringing specific cases against currency manipulation as a "prohibited export subsidy" under Article 3 of its Agreement on Subsidies and Countervailing Measures (ASCM) and then apply countervailing duties if the cases prevailed. A variant on this theme, addressed below, is for the United States to simply start unilaterally applying countervailing duties against manipulation in domestic cases, recognizing that the target countries might argue that the United States itself was violating the ASCM and then take it to the WTO. The difference between the two approaches is the sequencing between the unilateral and multilateral phases of the cases, perhaps along with some claim to "moral high ground" for whichever country (or group of countries) instituted the multilateral phase to emphasize its desire to play by agreed international rules.

Economic logic supports both WTO options, although they would not offset the effects of manipulation as effectively and efficiently as would financial policy measures that would apply much more broadly. The WTO was given powers of enforcement on currency issues that were denied to the Fund (but were to be invoked on those issues only with the explicit guidance of the Fund). Article XV (4) should thus be usable against manipulation. Deliberate currency undervaluation as a result of manipulation has a similar impact in reducing the price of exports as taxes, credits, or other subsidies that are routinely addressed as unfair trade practices in countervailing duty cases.

Unfortunately, the legal framework of the WTO is full of arcane technicalities that do not always reflect economic verities.[6] Neither of the relevant articles has ever been tested, and the US government has hesitated to bring a case under either, fearing that a loss would undermine its case against manipulation (and might well provoke an anti-WTO backlash, including in Congress). For example, Article XV (4) requires the "exchange action" in question to "frustrate the intent of provisions of the Agreement," but it lists no specific measures of frustration. Prohibited subsidies must entail a "financial contribution" and support for "specific" industries or enterprises rather than the economy as a whole, so even invocation of the ASCM could be difficult.[7]

In addition, as noted above, the highly political executive board of the IMF might be unwilling to indict a member country, especially a powerful one like China, for manipulation and for "frustrating the intent." It might, however, be possible for the WTO to seek the required "IMF guidance" from the IMF's management and staff rather than its executive board. Management and staff cannot be oblivious to political considerations, but their judgments would presumably be more technocratic and based on empirical evidence than the judgments of the executive board (as they were when they publicly announced in 2007 that the renminbi was "fundamentally undervalued"). The Fund followed this route in 1997 when it informed the WTO that India could no longer justify its widespread import quotas on balance-of-payments grounds (WTO 1999).[8]

The multilateral trade route is desirable in principle but likely to be difficult in practice. It is unavoidable, however, if the United States (or any other country) adopts trade policy measures against manipulators that expose it to international challenge by the targeted countries. The question thus becomes whether the United States would want to preempt the likely challenge by initiating an appeal to the international institution itself, as the Bush administration did in the IMF against China in 2006–08 and as Brazil tried to do by raising the issue of the trade impact of manipulation in the WTO in 2010.

---

6. In a conversation with C. Fred Bergsten, a top EU trade official warned: "Do not try to bring economics into the GATT [now the WTO]. You will kill it."

7. See de Lima-Campos and Gaviria (2012) for a contrary interpretation.

8. This decision helped the government of India overcome domestic opposition to the economic reforms that it wanted to carry out at that time.

For precisely these reasons, the United States should make a major effort to multilateralize any initiative it takes on these issues, as we argue in the next chapter. Such an effort would be greatly facilitated if the managements of the IMF and WTO, with at least the tacit support of other key members as well as the United States, were willing to forge an alliance to provide effective multilateral machinery to address the issue of manipulation. Such an alliance would enable them to complete the Bretton Woods framework by creating, for the first time, a credible systemic response to the risk of currency conflict.

Inclusion of Currency Issues in Future Trade Agreements

The other main multilateral option is the inclusion of currency issues in future trade agreements.[9] Most such agreements are bilateral or megaregional, but new topics that are initially addressed in bilateral or regional contexts frequently find their way into subsequent global accords (labor and environmental issues are a case in point over the past two decades) (box 5.1).

Such inclusion was the main goal of advocates of stronger US action on currency during the very active trade policy debate in Congress in 2015–16. Unusual bicameral and bipartisan majorities wrote to President Obama and his top officials as early as 2013 to urge the inclusion of enforceable currency disciplines in the TPP and all future US trade agreements. The basic objective was to deter manipulation by partner countries and ensure a level playing field by committing all partners to accept retaliation if they resorted to the practice.

The Obama administration rejected the proposal by arguing that the TPP negotiations had advanced too far to add another major issue and that in any event their consultations indicated that other participating countries opposed the idea and that even raising it could blow up the negotiations.[10] The Senate Finance Committee and the full Senate narrowly defeated proposed amendments to the Trade Promotion Authority bill that would have forced the administration to accept the proposal. The issue was continually raised during the political campaigns in 2016, however, and the election of

---

9. This section draws extensively on Bergsten (2014).

10. It is impossible to assess the validity of this contention, because the TPP partner countries knew that the US administration, especially the Treasury Department, which was handling this issue, did not want to include currency in the trade agreements. They may well have simply been telling US officials what they knew they wanted to hear. The administration also argued that any such disciplines could be turned against the use of quantitative easing by the Federal Reserve, a contention we reject in chapter 2.

Box 5.1 Adding currency to trade agreements

There are striking parallels between the current proposals to add the currency issue to trade agreements and efforts, over the past two decades or so, to add labor and environmental issues to such agreements (and perhaps the protection of intellectual property rights even earlier). These "trade and" debates have been at the forefront of much of the controversy over trade and globalization more broadly, in both the United States and around the world, dating back at least to the congressional battle over NAFTA in the early 1990s. They have become a central part of the discussion of trade policy at all levels: unilateral, regional, and bilateral.

The objectives of the exercises have been very similar, based on commitments that FTA participants had already made in the respective issue areas. Advocates of imbedding labor rights in FTAs have sought the adoption of enforcement provisions to ensure that participants in those agreements fully apply the standards already agreed to in the International Labour Organization. Environmentalists want commitments to faithful implementation of multilateral environmental agreements.

Contemporary currency proposals would aim to discipline countries that failed to uphold their IMF and other obligations to avoid manipulation and competitive depreciation (or nonappreciation). In each of these cases, the key action proposal is to include the "new" issue within the coverage of the dispute settlement mechanism of the FTA to enhance the prospect that its agreed norms will be implemented in practice—though with continuing debates over what trade, or other, remedies are most appropriate to address violations if and when they occur.

The obstacles to action in different issue areas have also been similar. Some actors, especially in the trade policy community, have questioned the appropriateness or even the feasibility of linking labor, the environment, and now currency to trade, despite the obvious relationships that have become clear as the respective debates have proceeded. The United States has to give up some of its other goals for the agreement in question, or accept additional demands from others, in order to win acceptance of chapters on the new issue. Different government agencies and officials, at both the national and international level, are responsible for the different topics. New types of linkages, both substantive and institutional, have been required to implement these relationships.

Inclusion of labor and environmental standards in FTAs has occurred in an evolutionary manner over the past two decades. Each was initially proposed and promoted by the United States, with respective administrations responding with more (generally Democratic) or less (generally Republican) enthusiasm to political (notably congressional) pressures that threatened to derail their overall trade policy strategies in the absence of successful negotiations but against a gradually evolving consensus that has now become widespread. Most other countries, especially poorer countries fearing attacks on their development strategies, tended to resist the US entreaties at first but, over time, not only came to terms with the United States but began to include similar (if usually weaker) provisions in their own trade agreements (e.g., see Bergsten, Hufbauer, and Miner 2014 on China's FTAs). Labor and environment provisions, or even full chapters, have now become standard components of most of the plethora of trade agreements being negotiated around the world by countries of every region and at all levels of development.

Currency issues are likely to undergo a similar evolution. The substantive cost, and therefore political backlash, of currency manipulation during the recent past is probably far greater than the parallel impact of labor and environmental problems in earlier periods, so it can be both hoped and expected that the "trade and currency" linkage will move more quickly than its predecessors. The comprehensive blueprint for such linkage outlined in this chapter will nevertheless probably find its way into trade agreements incrementally rather than all at once.

Donald Trump strongly suggests that it is likely to reappear whenever the United States pursues new trade agreements.

In response to continuing pressure on the issue, the Obama administration negotiated a Joint Declaration of the Macroeconomic Policy Authorities of Trans-Pacific Partnership Countries that was separate from the TPP but announced at the same time as the TPP in November 2015. It also worked with Congress to pass new legislation, the Bennet Amendment to the Trade Facilitation and Trade Enforcement Act of 2015, which strengthened US currency policy. The commitments under the declaration were not legally binding and there was no dispute settlement mechanism. If member countries had wanted to strengthen the compact, perhaps in response to renewed entreaties from the United States had the TPP come up for Congressional approval, they could have done so either by folding the side agreement into the TPP and thus subjecting it to the basic dispute settlement mechanism or converting the side agreement into a binding contract with its own dispute settlement mechanism. The latter would probably have been more feasible, because the arrangement could then have been managed by the parties' monetary authorities rather than their trade officials. (The side agreement died when President Trump abandoned the TPP in January 2017.)

Trade agreements have avoided the currency issue for two reasons. First, trade agreements aim primarily at expanding the level of trade, whereas exchange rates aim at trade balances. Most economists see trade balances as primarily a reflection of savings-investment differences and broader economic fundamentals that are best addressed through monetary, fiscal, and other macroeconomic policies. By contrast, the level and composition of trade are seen as structural and microeconomic, reflecting the resource endowments and comparative advantages of national economies. Tariffs, quotas, and other trade policy measures are thus seen as appropriate tools for addressing the level and composition of trade flows. Trade agreements are explicitly or implicitly premised on the principle of reciprocity in reducing tariffs, subsidies, and other distortions and are not intended to adjust trade imbalances.

Timing has also played a major role in this traditional differentiation. Trade imbalances, and the currency misalignments that can produce them, have been seen as transitory developments that will self-correct (by markets under flexible exchange rates) or be corrected (by governmental policies under fixed exchange rates) within relatively short periods. Trade agreements, by contrast, are intended to permanently alter economic relations between participating countries.

Problems can arise when trade imbalances persist, however. The United States, for example, has run sizable current account deficits for almost all of the past 35 years, and China has run sizable surpluses since the early 2000s. The guidelines for IMF surveillance of countries' exchange rate policies inveigh against "protracted" intervention in the currency markets, because it can prolong imbalances beyond their normal short-run horizons.

The second, institutional, issue is that currency and trade policy are generally managed by different authorities. Finance ministries and central banks (which are often independent from governments) are usually responsible for exchange rates, and trade or commerce or foreign ministries handle trade policy. At the international level, the IMF is responsible for exchange rates, and the WTO covers trade. Turf conflicts between these actors have frequently prevented a coordinated response to issues that link currency and trade, both within and among countries.

The United States has tried to coordinate trade policy and international monetary policy on occasion over the years. In 1971 President Nixon imposed a temporary import surcharge to help negotiate devaluation of the overvalued dollar, a step taken under pressure from Congress (Destler 2005). In 1985 Secretary of the Treasury James A. Baker III, also responding to congressional anxieties about trade deficits, negotiated the Plaza Accord to weaken the overvalued dollar and strengthen the European currencies and Japanese yen.

Lack of coordination is much more common, however. The IMF and GATT/WTO have frequently discussed better coordination and set up mechanisms to promote it but without much effect. The IMF staff vetoed inclusion of currency considerations in China's protocol of accession to the WTO on the grounds that such a provision was within the jurisdiction of the Fund rather than the WTO (IMF 2009), an under-the-radar decision that had profound effects in light of the major role that currency manipulation played in the subsequent explosion of Chinese exports and trade surpluses.

These substantive and institutional considerations have traditionally led the manipulation issue to be addressed by monetary officials and the IMF rather than by trade officials and trade agreements, including the WTO. The United States pursued this approach, primarily with respect to China, for most of the past decade. However, monetary efforts lost much of their credibility, and Treasury Secretary Jacob Lew acknowledged in 2015 that a trade agreement has to be built on firm commitment to market-determined exchange rates. This "monetary issue" played a major role in the widespread rejection of the TPP and opposition to trade agreements more broadly. There is thus a strong case for incorporating manipulation in future trade agreements, as advocated widely in Congress.

Most FTAs, including those negotiated by the United States, include chapters on specific topics. The TPP, which the United States hoped would become the template for future agreements, had 30 chapters. A currency chapter or parallel side agreement could include three components: a statement of objectives, criteria for defining and pursuing those objectives, and policy responses to foster their implementation. These elements should, where possible, conform to existing international agreements, notably the Articles of Agreement of the IMF and the charter of the WTO.

The objectives of the currency chapter could be drawn from the IMF Articles, as are the objectives of both the currency chapter of the Trade Facilitation and Trade Enforcement Act of 2015 and the Joint Declaration of the TPP Monetary Authorities. IMF members have accepted obligations to "avoid manipulating the exchange rate or the international monetary system in order to prevent effective balance-of-payments adjustment or to gain unfair competitive advantage over other members" (Article IV, Section 1 (iii)). The Fund is supposed to maintain surveillance over exchange rate policies and discuss "protracted large-scale intervention in one direction in the exchange markets" with errant members. The Articles also call on member countries to "take into account in their intervention policies the interests of other members, including those of the countries in whose currencies they intervene." These precepts could provide the foundation for specifying the goals of a currency component of an FTA and could even be incorporated by reference, although they embody the vexing issue of intent by conditioning their proscriptions on the purposes for which the manipulation is alleged to have been undertaken.

The G-7 (Canada, France, Germany, Italy, Japan, the United Kingdom, and the United States) has also adopted a commitment to consult within the group before undertaking intervention activities, and members have largely adhered to that agreement. G-20 communiques have pledged that members "will not target our exchange rates for competitive purposes," though some of them have ignored that stricture (while denying that their targeting is done for competitive purposes). Such nonbinding pledges could be incorporated into trade agreements, if binding commitments are not possible, but would fall far short of what is needed.

The methodology for pursuing the agreed objectives should start with commitments to provide data on the relevant variables, per agreed IMF conventions in most cases, as in the TPP Declaration. These commitments should cover reserve levels, including those outside official monetary reserves (notably in sovereign wealth funds); intervention; the currency composition of official reserves; and currencies of intervention.

Determining the existence and extent of currency misalignment, especially as a possible trigger for remedial action, has proven enormously difficult intellectually and politically. Numerous conceptual approaches to defining and measuring currency "misalignment" have been attempted. The IMF uses three different measures, which often produce very different results. Most official discussions, and even many academic efforts, have foundered at this initial level.

FTAs should thus ignore the determination of "misalignment" per se in favor of objective indicators, as the Trade Facilitation and Trade Enforcement Act of 2015 does. The goal would be to prevent a country from running large and persistent external surpluses that result from efforts to depress the value of its exchange rate in the currency markets. Only three variables need to be identified: the levels of reserves (to determine if they are "excessive"), the size of the current account surpluses, and the extent of intervention (or changes in reserve levels as a proxy, if actual intervention figures are not available on a timely basis) (see chapter 4).

A key concept is "intervention." Substantial direct purchases of foreign exchange with domestic currency should be a central criterion for triggering a currency provision in an FTA. Participating countries should fully disclose their intervention activities, though some reporting could remain confidential if necessary during a transition period.

More complex questions surround "oral" and indirect intervention. Oral intervention—that is, calls for market exchange rates to be adjusted unaccompanied by any new policy—can be obvious or extremely subtle. It can have powerful effects, at least in the short run. If the new rules limiting direct intervention are credible, however, oral intervention would be less effective, because no policy follow-up would be permissible.

Indirect intervention could include a wide range of policies, such as capital controls on inflows and/or outflows and macroprudential financial regulations (and particularly the timing of their installation and removal). It would be extremely difficult to define such measures with sufficient precision, however, because many steps seen as indirect intervention could be defended as having much broader purposes. Macroeconomic policies, including quantitative easing and fiscal policies, for example, should not be included, as discussed in chapter 2. All international rules and norms, including those of the IMF, the G-7, and the G-20, explicitly recognize this distinction and exonerate quantitative easing policies from any responsibility for currency manipulation. Some countries may keep raising the issue, but their objections should not deter these new policy initiatives.

Particularly in the case of measures with indirect effects on exchange rates, intent can be an important consideration. Were the steps undertaken to influence exchange rates, or were such influences solely a byproduct of some other primary purpose (as in the case of quantitative easing)? The requirement to demonstrate intent to devalue competitively under current IMF doctrine has enabled countries to defend clearly manipulative actions in the knowledge that no mechanisms exist to override their assertions. This problem underscores the need for objective indicators, such as reserve increases and direct intervention, along with current account surpluses, as triggers for action.

As for the decision-making process through which these concepts would be implemented, traditional practice in both the WTO and existing FTAs provides clear guideposts:

- An aggrieved country requests consultation with the alleged violator of the rules, and a major effort is made to reach a mutually satisfactory voluntary solution.

- Failing agreement in the consultations within 90 days (or some other tight time limit), a panel with the relevant expertise is chosen (from a contingent list) to recommend a solution within another tight time limit (another 90 days).

- A country found to have violated the rules and failed to accept the recommended solution within another tight time limit is subject to the penalty phase, in which a separate compliance panel (perhaps comprising the same experts) authorizes countermeasures.

- That panel monitors the situation, taking into account the expected lagged effects of previous exchange rate changes in eliminating the excessive current account surpluses, and calls for termination of retaliation when the cause of the problem (those surpluses or the manipulation) ceases.

The final question is what enforcement mechanisms could be included to make the agreement work and ensure its credibility; the absence of such mechanisms has been a cardinal flaw of the IMF system throughout its existence and a chief source of congressional criticism. Five types of measures are possible: withdrawal of concessions made in the FTA itself, imposition of import surcharges, imposition of countervailing duties, monetary penalties (fines), and countervailing currency intervention. Gradation of each measure is possible, with modest penalties subsequently adjusted in accordance with the seriousness or extent of the violation.

The usual technique for withdrawing concessions in an FTA is the "snapback clause," under which tariffs are returned to the pre-FTA level (usually the most favored nation [MFN] rate) for "breach of the agreement." Snapbacks are typically applied on a product-specific basis, to counter violations in a particular sector, but they could be installed across the board in the case of currency violations. It would also be possible to apply the snapback concept to concessions other than tariffs, as in a current WTO case in which Brazil has been authorized to withdraw some of its commitments regarding intellectual property rights if the United States continues to violate the dispute settlement panel's ruling on its cotton subsidies. The original concessions would be restored when the problem was corrected.

More extensive retaliation can be envisaged, including the imposition of countervailing duties if currency manipulation is deemed a countervailing subsidy like any other. Given the modest level of most MFN tariffs in both the United States and many potential FTA partners, import surcharges could be authorized as well. Monetary penalties—like the ones NAFTA imposes for violation of its labor and environmental disciplines and through which the United States has compensated Brazil for US violation of WTO agricultural agreements in the cotton sector—could be added to the arsenal of potential measures.

A key problem with each of these options is the difficulty of calculating the amount of the currency undervaluation to provide a basis for determining the magnitude of the permitted retaliation. Because such calculations are fraught with both intellectual uncertainty and political sensitivity, they should be avoided if possible. The snapback approach should be used as the chief trade policy response to manipulation under an FTA.

This also means, however, that it would be highly desirable to add a monetary policy tool that would fight fire with fire. Such an approach would also overcome the problem that trade policy remedies like snapbacks curb only imports whereas currency manipulation also suppresses the aggrieved country's exports (to global markets as well as to the manipulating country itself). An aggrieved country should be authorized to purchase the currency of the manipulating country in order to neutralize the impact of that country's own intervention in the foreign exchange markets upon a finding by the dispute settlement panel that manipulation was taking place. A clear indication by the United States that it was prepared to act on such authorizations should deter most if not all future manipulation efforts.

The US Treasury and the Federal Reserve could carry out such countervailing currency intervention (described in detail below) under current legislative authorities. Specific authorization for such a policy was also included (as "remedial currency intervention") in the currency bill passed by the Senate (but not taken up by the House) in 2011. Including such a provision in FTAs would be a straightforward and effective response to currency manipulation by parties to the FTAs. Lodging implementation of this key sanction in finance ministries and central banks should assuage most of the institutional concerns that normally make it difficult to address the problem through trade agreements.

We recommend that, as the centerpiece of its new currency policy, the United States announce that it will henceforth apply countervailing currency intervention unilaterally against any systemically important (i.e., G-20) country that violates the three criteria just indicated: excessive reserves, excessive current account surpluses, and persistent one-sided intervention in the foreign exchange markets. Such a threat should deter all, or virtually all, major manipulation in the future.

The United States should also seek to include countervailing currency intervention in its future FTAs, for three reasons:

- It could then use the instrument against countries that are outside the G-20 and thus of less systemic importance, as part of the quid pro quo for granting them additional access to the US market via the FTA.
- Including them would put the US administration in a much stronger position with Congress in seeking its approval for any new agreement, which may be necessary to restore an active US trade policy.
- As parties to both the initial agreement to authorize countervailing currency intervention and the dispute settlement mechanism under which it would be implemented, the partners in the FTA would be given significant voice in determining US currency policy, which would otherwise be carried out on a purely unilateral basis.

This part of the argument deserves elaboration. Our FTA proposal is premised on a new US readiness to apply countervailing currency intervention unilaterally when necessary to counter foreign manipulation by other major world economies (including China, Japan, and Korea). This readiness would have the consequence, however, of leaving uncovered smaller countries—some of which, such as Malaysia and Singapore, are not so small and have been active manipulators in the past. It would be hard to justify not covering countries that were about to receive new access to the US market, such as partners in pending FTAs. But they should have a role in determining both the list of remedies that would be applied to future cases of manipulation and the decision-making process that would apply those remedies in specific cases.

It might prove impossible to agree on binding and comprehensive rules subject to an effective dispute settlement mechanism and consequent sanctions. Compromises might be needed on such matters as the ambition of the rules, the degree to which they become legal commitments, the rigor of the dispute settlement mechanism, and the severity of the sanctions against offenders. Tradeoffs among such variables are likely in any FTA negotiations.

The most plausible wiggle room lies in the ambitiousness of the criteria that would trigger action. The term *excessive*, as applied to levels of reserves and intervention as well as current account surpluses, could be set high enough that only the most egregious violators would be caught.

Another possible avenue of compromise relates to the interaction of the obligations binding the participants and the methodology through which they are implemented. Countries wishing to limit their risk of exposure will want to trade off "soft" obligations against "hard" dispute settlement provisions or vice versa. For example, the indicators of violations of the agreed currency obligations could become "presumptions" or even "illustrations," including in side agreements, rather than legally binding commitments. The adjudicatory panels could be limited to recommendations to a politically constructed final arbiter rather than binding protocols, as is the case with dispute settlement mechanisms in some existing FTAs. It is perfectly plausible to set up and finely tune a separate dispute settlement mechanism for the currency chapter (or side agreement) as part of the overall negotiation of the issue.

Trade policy responses to the currency problem are decidedly inferior to monetary policy responses. Inclusion of currency issues in FTAs could not be the centerpiece of a new US currency policy, if only because even the broadest possible US trade agreements include only a subset of US trading partners and exclude some of the most important previous manipulators. Including them could, however, bring a degree of international participation into the policy framework, and might be essential to winning domestic political support for any future FTAs that include the United States.

Changes in Fiscal Policy

Fiscal policy has a large impact on current account positions when financial markets are fully open (see table 2.1). It is properly targeted at much broader economic objectives than countering currency manipulation (growth, full employment, intergenerational equity), however. If the US current account deficit again became a major concern in the context of an overheating economy, there would be a case for considering fiscal tightening. But the US economy is not likely to reach such a position in the next few years, unless the Trump administration goes overboard with its plans for large tax cuts, infrastructure investment, and increases in defense spending.

Changes in Monetary Policy

Monetary policy is usually the main driver of exchange rates in the short run. Some countries deploy it at least occasionally for that purpose. However, changes in monetary policy do not have much net impact on current account balances (the target variable), because their effects on domestic spending and imports largely or even fully offset their currency impact. Monetary policy is therefore not an efficient tool for achieving external adjustment. Moreover, at least in the large industrial countries, monetary policy predominantly targets aggregate economic objectives, notably price stability but also (in some countries) full employment and growth.

The exchange rate is a channel of monetary policy impact; indeed, the Federal Reserve held back its intended normalization of US monetary policy throughout much of 2016 in large part because of the strength of the dollar. In the United States and other large, relatively closed economies (including the euro area, Japan, and probably China), however, the exchange rate is secondary to normal domestic channels. Moreover, the independence of the Fed means that monetary policy could not be part of any US administration's effort to wage or respond to currency conflict and should not be viewed as such around the world.

Monetary policy should not seek to achieve current account or exchange rate objectives.[11] It would not be desirable for it to do so, even if the administration could persuade the Federal Reserve to join a comprehensive currency strategy. Using monetary policy in this way would almost certainly spawn enormous criticism of the United States and trigger or escalate, rather than help counter, concerns about "currency wars."[12]

---

11. The Federal Reserve is traditionally an equal partner with the Treasury Department in providing resources for the conduct of foreign exchange intervention by the United States and is the operating agent in carrying out such intervention. As indicated in the next section, however, US intervention is always sterilized, so this function in no way compromises the independence of the Federal Reserve in conducting monetary policy.

12. The Federal Reserve raised its discount rate by a full percentage point, which was unprecedented at the time, as part of the dollar defense program unveiled by the Carter administra-

Use of Countervailing Currency Intervention

Countervailing currency intervention is a simple concept. The European Central Bank, for example, could buy as many Swiss francs against euros as the Swiss National Bank sold against euros. Doing so would neutralize any impact of the Swiss intervention on the exchange rate between the two currencies. Execution of such a policy, or probably even an indication that it would be executed, should deter the Swiss National Bank from attempting to influence the rate. Any countervailing intervention that had to be carried out would be sterilized by the countervailing central bank to avoid disrupting its monetary policy.

Retaliation against currency manipulation would be based on the criteria outlined above or the slightly modified set of criteria contained in the Trade Facilitation and Trade Enforcement Act of 2015. Such retaliation would be far superior to the usual alternative of emulation. Countries in Asia, such as Malaysia and Thailand, frequently felt compelled to intervene against the dollar along with China to avoid losing competitive position to it. Countries elsewhere that were adversely affected by China's competitive undervaluation, such as Brazil, felt compelled to buy dollars to keep their currencies from rising (and to take other defensive actions, including imposing capital inflow controls and new import restrictions). One result was further appreciation (or nondepreciation) of the dollar and thus additional adverse effects on the competitive position of the United States. It would be far better for these countries, and for the system as a whole, if the initial currency manipulation were instead countered directly. Instead of emulating China by buying dollars to hold their currencies down, Brazil and Malaysia would be better advised to counter China's policy of holding the renminbi down by buying renminbi to push it up.

Most of China's own intervention takes place against the dollar, however. Moreover, the cross-currency real-renminbi and ringgit-renminbi markets are thin, and smaller countries would be hesitant to respond to China in this manner in any event. It would be far more efficient systemically, and far more realistic in both market and political terms, for the United States to carry out the bulk of the countervailing currency intervention, ideally with some parallel efforts by the European Central Bank and perhaps Japan.

Countervailing import duties are a standard tool of trade policy for countering export subsidies. Countervailing currency intervention would be a parallel instrument on the monetary side. During the Tokyo Round

---

tion in late 1978. Other countries universally applauded the move, which many of them had called for to fight inflation in the United States.

of the GATT, an Agreement on Subsidies and Countervailing Measures (ASCM) was negotiated to provide multilateral rules for the implementation of countervailing duties. The IMF should encourage countries to carry out countervailing currency intervention under clear procedural safeguards like the WTO rules on countervailing duties. Even without agreed IMF action, countervailing currency intervention by the United States would be multilateralized de facto, because countries against which it counterintervened could charge it with competitive undervaluation under the existing IMF Articles if they thought they could make that case (the charge would be very difficult to sustain as long as the US intervention was countervailing against a country that violated the objective criteria).

Countervailing currency intervention raises five practical questions. First, are there enough assets denominated in the currency of the manipulating country to enable the aggrieved country to fully offset the manipulation? The answer is unambiguously positive in the case of manipulators that have large and open financial markets of their own, which excludes a few smaller economies but now includes all the major manipulators.

Until recently, China forbade foreign purchases of its bonds and foreign deposits in its banks except by special arrangements. It now allows the issuance of renminbi bonds in Hong Kong and has fully opened its domestic bond market. The obligations accepted by China to win inclusion of the renminbi in the Special Drawing Rights (SDR) basket at the IMF strongly suggest that this liberalization will continue. Countervailing currency intervention thus can now have the full desired impact in directly influencing any resumption of China's currency manipulation.[13]

Second, would the aggrieved countries be taking an unacceptable financial risk by buying currencies of the manipulators? By definition they would be buying currencies they thought were substantially undervalued, so they should make a hefty profit (as the United States would have had it bought renminbi in line with our recommendation at the peak of its undervaluation in the mid-2000s, as described in box 5.2). In addition, the securities of most manipulator economies pay higher interest rates than those in the United States now and for the foreseeable future. The currency countervailers could, of course, miscalculate, or the situation of the current manipulator could change over time. Moreover, one cannot rule out the

---

13. Substantial countervailing currency intervention against China might provoke China to reimpose restrictions on bond purchases. Capital controls are available to all countries, and there is evidence that China tightened its limits on outflows during 2016 to counter capital flight and downward pressure on the renminbi, as discussed in the next section. But such a step would be awkward, to say the least, given China's strong push to make the renminbi an international reserve currency.

Box 5.2   Would countervailing currency intervention by the United States against China in 2005 have made sense?

Suppose that the United States had announced—and, if necessary, implemented—a credible policy of countervailing currency intervention in 2005, when China announced that it would let the renminbi appreciate gradually but simultaneously intensified its heavy intervention to keep the renminbi from rising very much. Would China have been deterred, in whole or in part? What would have happened to the renminbi? Would the operation have been profitable for the United States?

A credible US announcement of countervailing currency intervention would probably have deterred China from seeking to maintain its substantial undervaluation, which contemporary estimates placed at 30 to 40 percent (Goldstein 2004, Goldstein and Lardy 2008). Those estimates are validated by the actual appreciation of 35 percent that took the renminbi to its recent peak in mid-2015. The Chinese might have argued, however, that a rapid one-time appreciation of 30 to 40 percent would have been too disruptive for their economy and might even have thrown it into recession; it is thus plausible that they would have been "permitted" to "lean against the wind" to pro-rate the actual correction to something like 10 percent annually for three years.

Figure B5.2.1   Historical and hypothetical Chinese exchange rates, 2000–16

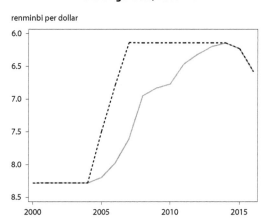

Note: The solid line is actual exchange rate and dotted line is hypothetical exchange rate.

Sources: IMF, *World Economic Outlook* database; and authors' calculations.

Alternatively, suppose that China had proceeded undeterred and intervened in the amounts actually recorded for at least two or three years. Had the United States undertaken countervailing currency intervention equal to half of China's historical intervention for three years, the renminbi would have appreciated smoothly, reaching its 2014 peak in 2007 and remaining at that level through 2014 (figure B5.2.1). This policy would have prevented the large increase in

China's current account surplus in 2006 and 2007, accelerated its decline there-after, and reduced the US current account deficit by a substantial fraction of the change in China's surplus.

Over the three years from 2005 through 2007, the United States would have purchased $582 billion worth of renminbi, financed by Treasury issuance of short-term debt at the US money market interest rate, with the proceeds invested in short-term Chinese government debt at the Chinese money market interest rate. By the end of 2016, the accumulated principal and interest on the countervailing currency intervention assets would have equaled $864 billion at the November 2016 renminbi exchange rate and the accumulated principal and interest on the associated liabilities would have equaled $636 billion, for a net profit of $227 billion.

possibility that China would regard countervailing currency intervention by the United States as a provocative act against which it would retaliate financially (or even default), although such a possibility is unlikely.[14]

Third, would the use of dollars to buy the foreign currencies targeted by the countervailing currency intervention have any adverse impact on the US budget? The purchases would presumably be shared by the Treasury and the Federal Reserve, as has traditionally been the case with currency intervention. The Treasury would use the Exchange Stabilization Fund (ESF), whose authority would clearly permit it to conduct such intervention. ESF expenditures would not be treated as a budget outlay, because they would be matched by an equal volume of new assets (the foreign currencies that would be purchased). Although the higher interest rate earned on most foreign assets relative to Treasury's cost of borrowing might seem to make a positive contribution to the budget, established rules apply a zero budgetary effect to any exchange rate exposure associated with an asset swap.[15] The Fed itself is not subject to budget limits.

---

14. The history of the United States on this issue is instructive. During the 1960s, when the United States was desperately trying to allay foreign fears of dollar devaluation, it offered large volumes of Roosa bonds (named after the undersecretary of the Treasury at that time), through which it tried to convince surplus countries not to convert their dollars into gold by guaranteeing the value of those dollars in terms of the holders' own currencies. After the substantial dollar devaluations of the 1970s, the United States eventually took large losses on the redemption of those bonds. Had it instead sought dollar depreciation by buying those currencies, it would have made large profits.

15. See, for example, the Congressional Budget Office's treatment of US holdings of SDRs at the IMF (CBO 2016).

Countervailing currency intervention could proceed with the existing ESF of about $100 billion and presumably a matching $100 billion from the Fed.[16] It would be desirable to augment these amounts to ensure the credibility of the new policy, however, and any larger operation would require congressional action to authorize additional ESF borrowing. Market sources should be consulted to assess the level of resources that should be obtained by the authorities for these purposes. We suspect that it would it run on the order of $1 trillion, so the ESF should seek borrowing authority of $500 billion and the Fed should be asked to provide an equal amount. Any borrowing actually required by the ESF to conduct large-scale intervention would count against the debt ceiling but not against budget authority; hence it would not add to the budget deficit.

Fourth, against whom might countervailing currency intervention be deployed? The analysis in chapter 4 shows that 20 surplus economies intervened to limit the appreciation of their currencies during the "decade of manipulation." Should the United States seek to counter all economies that might implement such policies in the future?

The goal of US currency policy in general, and countervailing currency intervention in particular, should be to deter manipulation by systemically important countries. Smaller economies that do not have far-reaching international effects are not an important concern. Moreover, many of the smaller manipulators conducted those policies at least partly to defend themselves against the larger manipulators and would probably desist if the latter did so.

Hence we recommend that any future US policy of countervailing currency intervention be limited to members of the G-20, a reasonable proxy for systemic importance (along with members of US FTAs per section above). Doing so would exclude some economies that have manipulated significantly in the past (including Hong Kong, Malaysia, Taiwan, and Switzerland), but none of them has had important systemic effects, and the first three were influenced by China's behavior. The United States could always broaden the scope if any of them began to loom large in terms of economic impact and political concerns in this country.[17]

---

16. The ESF can swap the foreign exchange it acquires to the Fed to acquire dollars to temporarily finance further operations (Henning 2008).

17. The Trade Facilitation and Trade Enforcement Act of 2015 also limits the applicability of its currency sanctions by requiring that target countries be "major trading partners of the United States," which the Treasury Department interpreted in 2016 to mean economies with which the United States had bilateral trade (exports plus imports) of more than $55 billion. This group includes only a dozen economies—a smaller and slightly different list from the G-20.

Fifth, how much actual countervailing currency intervention might be required if competitive intervention by other countries were to resume on anything like the scale of the "decade of manipulation"? Our best guess is that the number is approximately zero if the ESF had enough borrowing authority to be fully credible. If the United States made clear that it could and would respond in kind to any competitive nonappreciation, no matter how large, it seems highly unlikely that even the largest potential manipulators would proceed, especially in light of the new Trade Facilitation and Trade Enforcement Act of 2015 authorities (ideally augmented, as suggested below) and the lurking threat of further action (including by Congress) on trade policy. If they did, private investors would presumably move against them along with, or even in anticipation of, official US counterintervention, helping limit the resources the US authorities would have to deploy. The United States might have to fire off a few salvos to demonstrate its resolve and establish its credibility, but far-reaching tests seem improbable. The best deterrent is one that never needs to be used; countervailing currency intervention quite likely falls into that category if threatened intervention is large enough that no one dares test it.

Large-scale countervailing currency intervention by the United States would shatter the longstanding conventional view of the dollar as the unique and passive "nth currency" in the global system. It need not reduce the attractiveness of the dollar for international invoicing and investing, however, as long as the Federal Reserve maintains its credibility in ensuring domestic price stability.

Countervailing currency intervention would in fact be a logical extension of actions the United States has taken for many decades when it concluded that dollar overvaluation had become too costly. It broke the link with gold and applied an import surcharge in 1971. It pushed very hard to get its chief allies to adopt the locomotive strategy at the Bonn summit of 1978. It initiated the Plaza Agreement in 1985. It pushed Japan hard throughout the early 1990s and China over the past decade to permit substantial appreciation of their currencies. It bought yen in 1998 and euros in 2000 when it was clear that these currencies had become too weak.[18]

Adoption of countervailing currency intervention would be a further, and more orderly, step in that direction. To allay concerns that the United States was going unilateral, however, it should simultaneously propose changes in the practices of the IMF that would explicitly encourage the practice. It should not wait for those changes to be adopted, however, before announcing the new policy and deploying it as needed.

---

18. A useful history of US intervention can be found in Bordo, Humpage, and Schwartz (2015).

An alternative tactic would be to simply start conducting such intervention without any announcement. The "just do it" option would have the advantage of leaving the administration more flexibility in carrying out the policy, which might be especially valuable if Congress did not provide the additional borrowing authority needed for the ESF to become fully credible. However, the traditional (and proper) US focus on transparency, plus the need for full congressional buy-in if the policy is to work in the long run, argue for the more straightforward and powerful technique of preparing and then announcing the policy, as discussed in chapter 6.

Imposition of Capital Controls

Another option is to restrict or tax purchases of US assets by currency manipulators. This tool could be used against any manipulator. It would avoid the risk engendered by countervailing currency intervention of holding sovereign bonds and other assets in countries with uncertain future policy regimes. This option would provide only partial deterrence, however, because manipulators could intervene in a currency other than the dollar (especially the euro) and/or invest the proceeds of that intervention in another currency. The dollar's dominant role in international financial markets, however, makes it hard for a large manipulator to avoid investing in dollar assets altogether.

Under the International Emergency Economic Powers Act (IEEPA), the president of the United States has broad authority to restrict foreign ownership of US assets in cases of "unusual and extraordinary threat, which has its source in whole or substantial part outside the United States, to the... economy of the United States." These powers have been used to good effect against terrorist organizations and the countries that sponsor them, such as Iran. US and foreign financial institutions are required to assist in enforcement of such restrictions by ensuring that targeted governments and institutions do not hide behind third parties.

A variant of this approach would be to remove the exemption on withholding taxes for US financial assets owned by the governments or government-controlled entities of currency manipulators (Gagnon and Hufbauer 2011). Alternatively, the United States could impose a transaction tax or a "market access charge" on new purchases of US assets by currency manipulators, as Brazil does on purchases of certain assets by all foreign residents.[19] For countries with which it has a tax treaty, including China, the United States might have to provide advance notice, and Congress might

---

19. For a discussion of the market access charge, see John Hansen, "How the MAC Would Help Restore American Manufacturing," at abcdnow.blogspot.com, May 25, 2016.

have to change some elements of the tax code. These requirements make these policy options less flexible than some other options, but they could still send a strong signal to manipulators, although in a world of multiple reserve currencies manipulators, particularly smaller manipulators, could avoid the dollar.

Some observers argue that it is not in the interest of the US government to restrict or tax purchases of US bonds, because doing so could raise the market-clearing rate of interest on them, perhaps in a disruptive manner. This argument ignores the role of the Federal Reserve in setting interest rates as needed to keep the US economy growing steadily with low inflation. The primary effect of restricting or taxing foreign purchases of US assets would be to reduce the value of the dollar in terms of foreign currency—precisely what is desired to counter manipulation. Should the boost to the US economy from a cheaper dollar threaten to raise inflation above its desired rate, the Fed would need to raise interest rates, but such an outcome would be encouraging. It is possible that the Fed would not calibrate its response appropriately, but this risk is present in Fed responses to all economic developments. The more important cost is probably that the invocation of capital controls by the United States could throw financial business to other currencies and countries.

Currency manipulation is the official purchase of another country's financial assets. Any action that stops currency manipulation will reduce foreign government purchases of US financial assets, including US Treasury securities. For several months from mid-2011 through early 2012, and again since the middle of 2015, China ceased its net purchases of US Treasury securities and became a net seller. There was no discernible effect on US interest rates.

Capital controls run counter to traditional US principles and policy, especially the untrammeled international use of the dollar, although weak versions of them (the interest equalization tax, voluntary limits on short-term outflows) were deployed to defend the dollar in the 1960s. A major cost of selective capital controls targeted at manipulators is the administrative cost of enforcing them, including costs borne by US and foreign financial institutions. A major drawback is the fact that controls cannot be turned on and off quickly. Countervailing currency intervention is a much more flexible and direct approach to countering manipulation.

Imposition of Unilateral Import Controls

The financial policy options for responding to currency manipulation are nondistortionary across sectors, consistent with international law, and much more effective than the trade policy options. If those strategies are deemed undesirable or infeasible, however, trade policy alternatives may need to be considered. Trade policy measures could also be useful supplements to the preferred financial alternatives.

We have already considered the multilateral route for adopting trade policy responses to currency manipulation by mobilizing the WTO (along with the IMF, which would also have to be involved in such a strategy) to authorize import surcharges or countervailing duties. Here we elaborate on two trade policy devices that the United States could use unilaterally.

Exchange rates that are undervalued artificially make exports less expensive and imports more expensive than they would otherwise be. They thus represent a subsidy to exporters and to firms that compete with imports. When an exchange rate is undervalued because of intervention by a foreign government rather than market forces, counterintervention is justified. Indeed, the "theory of the second best" suggests that intervention by government B is *required* to counter intervention by government A to achieve an outcome as nearly equivalent as possible to a market result unfettered by governmental involvement.

Unfortunately, legal structures do not always accurately reflect economic principles, at both the national and international levels. The US Commerce Department, for example, has traditionally taken the view that its authorizing statute does not permit it to treat currency misalignments as subsidies subject to countervailing duties, even if they are clearly the result of currency manipulation. The ASCM contains a series of criteria that, although they have never been tested for currency misalignments, might or (more likely, according to Hufbauer, Wong, and Sheth 2006) might not pass muster.

Both legal structures could be tested and might prove more responsive than conventionally believed. In addition, the United States could immediately change its domestic situation. A president or secretary of commerce could simply reinterpret current law and authorize countervailing duties against currency manipulation, defending that revised interpretation in both domestic and international (WTO) court against the inevitable challenges.[20]

Congress could also amend current trade law to specifically authorize such action. Such was the central thrust of a bill that passed the House of Representatives in 2010, a bill that passed the Senate in 2011, and the Schumer Amendment that was included in the Senate version of the Trade

---

20. Some proposals would apply countervailing duties against all exports that benefit from undervalued currencies, whether that undervaluation was caused by manipulation by a country's authorities or by market forces. Their use should be limited to the former case since market forces do not represent a government subsidy.

Facilitation and Trade Enforcement Act of 2015 (the "customs bill") but dropped in the conference committee with the House.

Countervailing duties offer a sector-specific, microeconomic response to the across-the-board, macroeconomic problem of currency manipulation. Countervailing duties now in force in the United States cover only $39 billion of imports, a tiny share of total imports of about $3 trillion, although many countervailing duties completely block imports, so it is impossible to gauge their full impact. Coverage would probably remain modest even if manipulation became an eligible criterion, because, as with any countervailing duties, petitioning firms or industries would have to demonstrate that they were injured by the imports and incur the sizable cost of bringing a case. (The US government can also self-initiate cases.) Moreover, the countervailing duty process has on occasion been captured by rent-seeking industries with clever lawyers. Hence they are less than an ideal solution (Bown 2016).

Countervailing duties would offer a remedy to industries and firms that were most adversely affected by manipulation (and could prove that they were injured as a result). Their adoption, ideally by other importing countries as well as the United States, would send a signal that manipulation would no longer be costless to the perpetrators' economies and their relations with key trading partners. Such duties could constitute one part of a comprehensive policy package that sought to persuade manipulators to cease and desist.

A much larger trade response would be the imposition of import surcharges covering all or most imports against countries deemed to be currency manipulators. Such measures would still apply to only half the trade account, however; they would have no direct bearing on US exports to those countries or to US exports to third countries that are adversely affected by the currency manipulation.

The United States applied a surcharge of 10 percent on its dutiable imports (about half of total imports) for four months in 1971, as part of the "New Economic Policy" announced by President Nixon in August of that year that imposed wage-price controls and ended the convertibility of dollars into gold for foreign monetary authorities.[21] Secretary of the Treasury John Connally reportedly wanted to leave the surcharge in place for at least another year, through the elections of 1972, because it was so popular domestically, but its goal and main benefit were to prod the Europeans and Japan to agree to the initial postwar devaluation of the dollar. Such an ag-

---

21. Temporary import surcharges were also adopted by Canada in 1962, the United Kingdom in 1964–66, and France (very briefly) in 1968.

gressive measure would have the similar purpose today of inducing manipulators to cease manipulating and let their currencies appreciate.

There appears to be ample domestic legal authority for a president to apply an import surcharge (Hufbauer 2016). After the Nixon surcharge in 1971, Congress included in the Trade Act of 1974 authority for imposition of a surcharge of up to 15 percent for a maximum of 150 days. After that period, the president could invoke Section 201 of the Act as a basis for retaliation against a currency manipulator. In extremis he or she could also use the powers provided by IEEPA or even the Trading with the Enemy Act of 1917.

Import surcharges are legal under the international rules of the WTO, but only for a country that has a major balance-of-payments problem, as certified by the IMF. The United States has run persistent current account deficits for more than 30 years, but the dollar has appreciated steadily since 2011, indicating that the overall balance of payments is strong. It is highly doubtful that the IMF would deem the United States eligible to apply an import surcharge under the WTO.

In addition, under WTO rules any such surcharge must be applied equally against all of a country's trading partners, as the United States largely did in 1971, on the cardinal nondiscrimination principle of the global trading system; there is no provision for applying a surcharge against an individual country or group of countries. Targeted countries would clearly be within their rights to retaliate against the United States (and any other surcharge appliers), and at least some, including China, could be expected to do so. This option would thus escalate both the "currency war" and "trade war" rhetoric and reality and would be especially risky as long as the world economy and international economic cooperation remain fragile.

An import surcharge might become legal if the United States and any allies could demonstrate that currency manipulators were violating their own obligations under Article XV (4) of the WTO not to "by exchange action, frustrate the intent of the provisions of the Agreement." The coalition could attempt to seize the moral high ground on the issue by taking manipulators to the WTO at the same time they applied any unilateral controls (or await its decision before applying any retaliatory across-the-board trade actions).

Quantitatively, these trade policy options range from very modest (countervailing duties on a case-by-case basis) to potentially quite substantial (across-the-board import surcharges). Procedurally, they range from reactive (countervailing action and import surcharges) to preventative (chapters in new trade compacts). Legally, they could be implemented unilaterally with full recognition that they are incompatible with international law (import surcharges against specific currency violators); implemented unilaterally but based on the premise that they are justifiable under WTO rules (surcharges under an Article XV case); or positioned for possible future implementation by writing new international rules (in new trade agreements or by amending the current WTO provisions on countervailing duties under the ASCM). Combinations of these alternative approaches are also possible, especially over longer periods.

In sum, trade policy can play a supportive role in fashioning a strategy to address both the immediate economic and political, and the structural systemic, dimensions of the currency manipulation problem. Multilateral remedies are highly preferable to unilateral actions. Hence we recommend that the United States and its allies bring WTO cases against future manipulators. Winning the cases would strengthen their hands enormously in prosecuting all other remedies and would, in a second WTO step, determine permissible remedial action, adding to the arsenal of policy instruments available to them. Losing the cases would dramatize the need for reform of the WTO rules and place the issue on the agenda for either a future round or a stand-alone negotiation. Whatever the outcome, the United States (and its coalition) would have made every effort to use the existing rules and institutions and thus have demonstrated its fealty to the international system as well as to the pursuit of US national interests.

Efforts should also be made to include the manipulation issue in future trade agreements at all levels (multilateral, regional, and bilateral). Pursuit of these avenues would have the desirable side effect of breaking down the institutional barriers between monetary and trade policies, which would be beneficial in dealing with future issues when the two need to be related more effectively. Import surcharges should be eschewed, because of their flagrant violation of the international rules, unless authorized by the WTO under a successful appeal to Article XV.

Conclusion

The status quo produces a gaping hole at the heart of the global economic order in its failure to effectively address currency manipulation, the contemporary manifestation of the age-old problem of currency conflict. The bifurcation between the monetary and trading systems that so greatly exacerbates the problem must be overcome. The economic costs of inaction on this issue are extremely high, especially during a prolonged period of slow growth and high unemployment like the recent Great Recession. The domestic political reaction to these failures demonstrably contributes importantly to the backlash against open trade, and globalization more broadly, threatening an open US foreign economic policy and thus the global trading system.

Having considered the policy options, we turn finally to a summary of the main conclusions of our analysis and to a series of action recommendations. Our goal, as indicated at the outset, is to deter the risk of future currency conflict and the domestic political impact of continuing failure to address it effectively. We believe that goal is achievable and will now set out our proposals for doing so.

6

Conclusions and Recommendations

The Currency Problem

The threat of currency conflict represents a substantial risk to the world economy and to the United States. For most of the first 15 years of the 21st century, a number of countries, mostly but not solely emerging-market economies led by China, intervened excessively in the foreign exchange markets, by an average of more than $600 billion annually to limit the rise of their currencies. This competitive nonappreciation produced substantial undervaluation of their exchange rates, greatly strengthening their competitive positions and generating large current account surpluses despite their rapid growth and its usual association with current account deficits. This manipulation shifted an annual average of $300 billion of production to their own economies from the rest of the world, especially from the United States and Europe but also from a wide range of other countries—what Bhalla (2012) calls "stolen growth." During and after the Great Recession, when macroeconomic policy was unable or unwilling to achieve full employment in the major advanced economies and some others, currency manipulation cost them several million jobs, including more than 1 million in the United States alone.

The currency conflicts of the early 21st century exposed two sources of unsustainability at the heart of the world economy. The first was the sharp rise in current account imbalances, which reached levels far in excess of any previously recorded. The surplus of China rose to almost 10 percent of its GDP, and the surpluses of other manipulators were even larger in cumulative dollar terms. The deficit of the United States escalated to a record 6

169

percent of GDP, more than twice the level that triggered the large currency adjustment of the Plaza Accord two decades earlier. These imbalances made an important contribution to the onset of the Great Recession and the sluggishness of the recovery from it.

The second was the domestic political unsustainability of the currency misalignments and resulting imbalances, especially in the United States, with its acute risks for the future of international trade. When the Obama administration asked Congress to approve its major trade liberalization initiatives in 2015–16 (first by providing Trade Promotion Authority for two major upcoming negotiations and subsequently by authorizing the megaregional Trans-Pacific Partnership [TPP]), Congress pushed back, in large part because it viewed the currency manipulation of the previous decade as an unfair trade practice that severely hurt the US economy and must be curtailed before further trade expansion should be pursued.

Both presidential candidates, and several other contenders for their parties' nominations, raised similar questions as part of their unprecedented attack on globalization during the campaigns of 2016. Evidence suggests that the "China shock" to the US economy, of which perhaps a third can be attributed to currency manipulation, played a decisive role in the election of Donald Trump (Autor et al. 2017), whose rejection of the TPP and past US trade agreements could presage a sea change in the global trading system. Currency issues once again became a major driver of US trade policy, as they were in the mid-1980s, threatening at a minimum to block new liberalization and possibly leading to backsliding into protectionism, with major systemic consequences.

Considerable progress was made in addressing these misalignments and imbalances over the past decade. The US external deficit was cut in half (though it has begun to rise again and is likely to approach $1 trillion, or nearly 5 percent of GDP, in the next few years). China's exchange rate eventually rose by 35 percent against the dollar at its peak in 2015, and its external surplus declined to about 2 percent of GDP. The G-7, G-20, and TPP countries all agreed to new norms against manipulation. Congress passed legislation that spelled out objective criteria for identifying manipulation and strengthened US resistance to the practice, with the US Treasury placing five economies (China, Germany, Japan, Korea, and Taiwan) on a "monitoring list" in 2016. Manipulation largely subsided into remission in 2015 and 2016, as the exchange rates of many emerging-market economies (including China) weakened as a result of market forces, and the revenues of oil exporters fell sharply along with energy prices.

However, markets could reverse course at any time; former manipulators could resume the practice when upward pressures on their exchange rates return, especially if their economies (and the world economy) are weakening at the time. Further use of expansionary monetary policy by advanced countries, especially when they rely heavily on negative interest rates, could exacerbate the currency conflict.

Whatever happens, it is likely that US trade policy—and thus the global trading system—will be able to regain momentum only with a firm resolution of the currency problem (and a number of others). The domestic political aspect of the issue in the United States is decidedly not in remission. Hence it has become imperative to erect effective deterrents to manipulation to avoid new currency conflicts and their trade policy and financial implications.

These developments reveal two glaring gaps in the global economic architecture: the absence of effective mechanisms to discipline surplus countries in general (and currency manipulators in particular) and the inability to link monetary and trade components into a functioning governance system. Ironically, the international economic order and its institutions were set up at the end of World War II largely to prevent just such beggar-thy-neighbor policies, which had had devastating effects in the 1930s. The system includes clear rules against such policies, especially at the IMF but also in the WTO, but it has failed to address the problem successfully. So have the United States and the other major countries.

At least 20 economies actively manipulated their currencies during the first 15 years of this century, as described in chapter 4. Their excessive intervention in the foreign exchange markets—beyond what was needed to build adequate reserves or, in the case of resource exporters, to save for the future—peaked at more than $1 trillion in 2007, with China alone gaining $250 billion in net exports and the United States losing $235 billion.

In the context of the Great Recession and the weak recovery from it, several million jobs were transferred from deficit to surplus countries, underlining the deflationary bias of current global economic arrangements. Sterilized intervention, at least when large amounts of resources are devoted to it, is clearly effective in achieving its goals. Not all of the intervening economies have global impact, but a number of them, especially members of the G-20, are systemically important.

China was by far the most active manipulator, piling up more than $4 trillion of official holdings (including its sovereign wealth fund) as a result of intervention that averaged $1 billion to $2 billion per *day* for a number of years. Manipulation fully explained its external surpluses, which peaked at 10 percent of GDP in 2007 (see figure 4.3). Several other Asian economies—most notably Hong Kong, Korea, Singapore, and Taiwan—behaved similarly at least some of this time, partly to emulate China and avoid losing competitive position to it.

A number of oil-exporting countries also intervened heavily and accumulated large stocks of foreign exchange. So did a couple of European countries on the fringes of the euro area, most notably Switzerland, which temporarily became the world's largest manipulator in 2012. Japan, which had been an aggressive manipulator in earlier periods, did not intervene after 2004, except in 2011, in response to safe-haven inflows after the Fukushima nuclear tragedy (and orally in late 2012).

Intervention in foreign exchange markets is not necessarily harmful. "Leaning against the wind" to reduce disorderly and reversible movements is fully acceptable. Deficit countries can intervene defensively to resist unjustified strengthening of their currencies. Countries with inadequate levels of reserves can buy foreign currencies to augment their safety nets.

Nor have manipulators necessarily set out primarily to divert economic activity away from other countries. Some have used the exchange rate as a tool, even the primary tool, for managing their monetary policies. Some have seen it as an integral element of development policy. Some, especially smaller countries, have defensively shadowed the currencies of large neighbors to avoid losing competitive position to them. Different agencies within a government may have different motives: The central banks of Switzerland and even China have seen currency policy as a way to preserve financial, and thus economic and price, stability while their economic ministries have been more concerned with mercantilist trade objectives.

It is thus imperative to focus on the impact rather than the intent of countries' policies. Intervention that resists adjustment of underlying surpluses constitutes manipulation, which can raise major economic and political problems. When conducted by large and important countries, notably members of the G-20 steering committee for the world economy, it can threaten international monetary stability and the trading system. We propose a set of new policy responses to help deter manipulation in the future and prevent such problems.

The United States has felt by far the largest impact of currency manipulation. The manipulators intervened largely in dollars, effectively setting the exchange rate between their currencies and the dollar as the United States remained passive in the exchange markets. Foreign manipulation accounted for one-quarter to one-third of the average US external deficit, which peaked at a record 6 percent of its GDP in 2006 and has remained near 3 percent since. During the five years from 2009 through 2013, the United States lost about 1 percent of GDP each year and a million jobs or more as a result of these trade effects.

These distortive currency policies also had highly negative economic effects before the Great Recession. The manipulators invested most of their hundreds of billions of dollars of annual intervention in the United States, contributing to the loose financial conditions that helped create the housing bubble whose collapse brought on the financial crisis and the Great Recession. China's undervalued currency was also the cause of about a third of the accelerated loss of manufacturing production and employment attributed to rising US imports from China between 2001 and 2007 (Autor, Dorn, and Hanson 2016).

The US administration complained continually (but mainly privately) to China (and a few others) throughout this period. China let the renminbi gradually rise (by 35 percent against the dollar and by more than 50 percent on a trade-weighted basis by 2015), cutting its external surplus to as little as 2 percent of its GDP. But China and the other manipulators got away with a great deal of beggar-thy-neighbor activity for more than a decade.

The inadequacy of the global system meant that there was never an effective international response to the problem. The US authorities chose not to respond more forcefully—despite the clear analyses of Bergsten (2005, 2007), Goldstein (2004), Goldstein and Lardy (2008), and others—for several reasons: (1) many Americans gained from the cheaper imports and lower interest rates generated by China's undervalued exchange rate; (2) most large US companies, especially those that had invested in China, did not want to confront the Chinese; (3) the authorities believed, rightly or wrongly, that a more aggressive public stance would be counterproductive in terms of eliciting Chinese cooperation on the exchange rate itself; (4) they feared that doing so would add a major new element of instability to the world economy, especially during the Great Recession and subsequent euro crisis, when Chinese cooperation on broader economic issues was needed; (5) they believed that publicizing China's manipulation would encourage rather than contain protectionism at home; (6) the United States had its own broad foreign policy agenda with China; and (7) the authorities were simply not aware of the heavy price America was paying through the large influx of foreign capital (although Ben Bernanke was already talking about the "global savings glut") and the huge hit to manufacturing employment later identified by Autor, Dorn, and Hanson (2016).

The United States was the largest loser from the recent currency conflict. But manipulation also adversely affected many other countries. The euro area lost $50 billion to $100 billion of annual output and associated employment as a result of manipulation during and after the Great Recession. The enhanced competitive position of the Asian manipulators undermined the weaker economies of the European periphery and helped trigger the euro crisis, the second phase of the global meltdown. The United Kingdom lost $15 billion to $30 billion per year, and there is evidence that its version of the China shock played an important role in the Brexit vote in 2016.[1]

Many emerging markets that compete with the Asian manipulators, such as Mexico and Turkey, took substantial hits as well. Other developing countries, such as Brazil and India, intervened defensively to protect themselves from running even larger external deficits than they already did. Some of these countries complained publicly about manipulation and made occasional approaches to China on it, but virtually all of them limited their policy responses to defensive intervention of their own and offered very little support to the United States, even when it periodically decided to pursue the issue more vigorously.

As a result of the adverse effects on the US economy, the recognition that currency manipulation represented a massively unfair trade practice, and the perceived inadequacy of administration policy, bipartisan congressional efforts to counter the practice escalated steadily. Congressional threats of retaliation in the years just before and immediately after the Great Recession were key in persuading China to let its currency appreciate to at least a degree (while still intervening constantly to limit that appreciation) and thereby ultimately reduce its global surplus. When the administration needed legislative approval for its ambitious program of trade negotiations, via Trade Promotion Authority in 2015, Congress took the opportunity to press for a substantial toughening of US currency policy. The most far-reaching part of that effort, which would have required the inclusion of "enforceable disciplines" in the TPP and all future FTAs, narrowly failed to win voting majorities. Several significant changes were made in the relevant legislation, however, supplementing the traditional judgmental determination of manipulation with objective criteria that can be readily identified and very specific policy options that must be pursued against recalcitrant manipulators. These actions placed substantial pressure on future administrations to adopt more forceful responses to any substantial resumption of manipulation.

Domestic politics have traditionally been a more serious constraint on US trade deficits, and thus currency policy, than the country's ability to finance those deficits internationally. Indeed, the dollar overvaluation that spawns those deficits has been among the most accurate predictors of protectionist trade policies. This political backlash was partly the case in 1971, when President Nixon implemented an across-the-board import

---

1. Support for Brexit was significantly higher in British localities with industries that faced rising Chinese import competition (I. Colantone and P. Stanig, "Brexit: Data Shows that Globalization Malaise, and Not Immigration, Determined the Vote," *Bocconi Knowledge*, July 12, 2016, www.knowledge.unibocconi.eu/notizia.php?idArt=17195).

surcharge after the House of Representatives passed far-reaching legislation in the first major outbreak of trade protectionism in the postwar period and threatened more. It was wholly the case in 1985, when Secretary of the Treasury James Baker launched the Plaza Accord, in response to a widespread outbreak of protectionism, some by the administration itself but especially in Congress, sponsored by the leadership of both the House and the Senate, that threatened to disrupt the global trading system.

Similar unsustainability loomed on this latest occasion, contributing in a major way to the far-reaching attack on open trade policies and globalization more broadly in the 2016 political campaigns and ultimately to the election of Donald Trump that sealed the demise of the pending new US trade agreements themselves (including the Transatlantic Trade and Investment Partnership [TTIP] as well as the TPP). If the unwillingness of the United States to move forward toward new trade liberalization presages a new backsliding toward protectionism by the traditional leader of the global trading system, as it has in the past, and especially if the United States explicitly repudiates past agreements such as NAFTA, the world economic order is at risk.

The most fundamental political problem is probably the absence of adequate worker retraining programs and domestic safety nets to help people adversely affected by trade (and other forms of economic change). But the currency issue is also an important source of backlash in the United States. The Obama administration was forced to recognize and respond to the currency aggression of other countries, defend its stance with Congress, and try to keep its trade program intact by accepting tougher legislative mandates and negotiating an unprecedented side agreement to the TPP to address macroeconomic and currency issues. These steps did not satisfy the critics, however; pressure for more forceful action increased in 2016 and 2017.

These widespread policies of direct intervention in the foreign exchange markets to maintain competitive nonappreciation of a large number of important currencies went largely into remission in 2015–16. Some countries, including China, experienced problems in their own economies that led them to intervene on the other side of the market—selling dollars to limit depreciation of their currencies. The cumulative and escalating impact of US, including congressional, criticism of manipulation, and the related adoption of new norms on the issue by the G-7 and G-20 may also have begun to generate concern in the offending countries that they would pay a price for resuming those policies. Today only a few smaller economies could be indicted for manipulation; intervention by the largest manipulators of the past, including China and Japan, has disappeared, at least for a while.

Widespread currency manipulation could return in the near future, however. If China's reform efforts falter or its growth rate slides, it might be tempted to return to the export-led model, which relied heavily on currency undervaluation. If Abenomics fails to revive the Japanese economy, Japan might be tempted to do so, especially if the strengthening of the yen that occurred in early 2016 resumes. If India decides to aim for rapid export expansion to boost its growth rate, it could resume its heavy intervention of past years. If any or all of these Asian giants reverted to competitive depreciation, or even competitive nonappreciation, most of the rest of Asia would probably follow.

The North Atlantic countries may be susceptible to such impulses as well. Europe could seek to boost its slow growth by running even larger external surpluses. The United Kingdom already sharply weakened its currency via its Brexit decision. A more aggressive US administration, with greater doubts about globalization than its predecessors and thus less willingness to provide the global public goods of open markets and an overvalued exchange rate, could join the competitive race (especially if its main foreign partners were to go down these routes). If secular stagnation becomes the "new normal" for the world economy, many countries could seek to escape via currency depreciation and stronger trade balances—as they did in the 1930s.

The failure of the global rules and institutions to deal with this issue effectively remains a major source of discontent with the entire system. It thus remains imperative, and indeed urgent, to erect new barriers to currency manipulation, at least by the systemically important countries that affect global outcomes.

The situation is complicated by the adoption of unconventional monetary policy, by the United States and United Kingdom in 2009 and later by Japan (2013) and the euro area (2014), which led to suspicions that the large high-income countries were seeking to stimulate their own economies by weakening their currencies. Each currency in turn did weaken substantially, including against the currencies of emerging-market economies as well as against one another, as they adopted their new monetary stances.

There is a fundamental difference between manipulation of currency markets and unconventional monetary policy, however, as noted in chapter 2. Manipulation works via intervention in *foreign* currencies to directly alter the *external* price of the domestic currency. Unconventional monetary policy, like conventional monetary policy, is implemented via operations in *domestic* financial markets with *domestic* instruments. The former affects exchange rates directly and as its main intent; the latter does so only indirectly and as a byproduct of its basic goal of expanding the domestic economy.

International rules, embedded in the IMF Articles of Agreement, make a clear distinction between domestic and external policies. Countries are allowed free rein to choose domestic policies, even when those policies have spillovers; they face limits on their external policies. Because external poli-cies have greater spillover, this legal distinction makes economic sense; it informs the statements of the G-7 and G-20 that encourage countries to use macroeconomic policy to achieve sustainable growth while promising to avoid using exchange rate policy to gain competitive advantage. But emerging-market and developing countries that feel disadvantaged by un-conventional monetary policy in rich countries will undoubtedly continue to complain, sustaining at least the appearance of currency conflict and un-derlining the need for both better international understanding of the issue and more effective policy tools to head it off.

Several key analytical distinctions underlie the fashioning of a construc-tive and sustainable policy response to the threat of renewed currency con-flict. The current period, during which most of these conflicts (but not the domestic political reaction to them in the United States and elsewhere) are in remission, would be a propitious time to start implementing responses, because they could be taken without indicting individual countries as "ma-nipulators" and thus inflaming the effort. Indeed, it may be essential to move expeditiously on the issue to overcome the risk that the domestic po-litical reaction in the United States will seriously disrupt the global trading system. We address the key analytical issues in turn and indicate how each could be resolved as part of a comprehensive policy package.

Self-Insurance versus Manipulation

The central theme of this study is that direct intervention by surplus coun-tries in the foreign exchange markets to keep their currencies from appre-ciating in value is the most important currency issue of the current era. But many countries that intervene excessively justify their action on the grounds that they need to accumulate large amounts of foreign exchange to protect themselves against future downward pressure on their currencies that could disrupt their economies. They argue that their intervention is motivated by self-insurance goals rather than by competitive mercantilist objectives. The issue reduces largely into the question of the level of reserves that countries need to defend themselves in a world of globalized econo-mies and high capital mobility. Such concerns have always been present but were underlined for Asian countries by their experience with the region's financial crisis in 1997-98, when countries ran short (or out) of reserves and thus had to borrow from the IMF and accept its policy recommenda-tions, many of which they despised. This experience taught them, and many other countries, that they must hold much larger reserves than they had in the past. The rapid growth in both the value and volatility of interna-tional capital flows over the succeeding two decades reinforced those views in many countries.

There is no widely agreed upon measure of the "proper" level of a country's reserves, including the holdings of its sovereign wealth funds, as discussed in chapter 4. The number may differ sharply from country to country. Some extremes can be ruled out: The level of China's official assets (including its sovereign wealth fund) was clearly excessive when it exceeded $4 trillion at the peak and is still far too high today (at about $3 trillion). But there will inevitably be prolonged debates over whether legitimate defensive motives or competitive intent drive countries' intervention.

There is thus a need for clear new rules of the road with respect to reserve adequacy. The old norm of the equivalent of three months of imports of goods and services is not appropriate for all countries, particularly countries with open financial markets. We thus propose a two-part threshold of three months' equivalent of imports or 100 percent of short-term foreign currency liabilities, whichever is larger. Purchases of foreign exchange up to those levels should be tolerated even when a country already has a current account surplus. Larger holdings would be permitted, but significant purchases toward that goal would be prohibited when a country runs a substantial current account surplus. Exporters of nonrenewable resources would be permitted to save a reasonable fraction of their resource earnings in foreign official assets even when they have large surpluses.

Offensive versus Defensive Intervention

We have defined currency conflict primarily in terms of direct intervention in the foreign exchange markets by countries that buy foreign currency (usually dollars) in order to keep their currencies from rising in value. Not all intervention needs to be banned. Intervention to smooth disorderly short-term market fluctuations has traditionally been acceptable. Even countries that let their exchange rates float freely, such as the United States, have intervened in this way. Such intervention should be readily detectable (if the relevant data are made available) as occurring on both sides of the market, with little net effect on total reserves. Intervention is also justified for a country with low reserves that wants to build its holdings to the level indicated in the previous section.

Intervention is also permissible in two other sets of circumstances. One is where deficit countries are experiencing appreciation of their exchange rates that increase those deficits and push them away from sustainable equilibrium. Such appreciation, especially in emerging markets but also in the United States, can result from capital inflows triggered by an easing of monetary policy abroad, especially in advanced economies, and by hot money flows in response to market or other uncertainties. It can also result from direct intervention by manipulators, as it has in the United States.

Intervention to limit, or even reverse, such disequilibrating currency movements is defensive in nature and wholly appropriate. Brazil and other deficit countries have deployed such policies in recent years. More active use of such defensive intervention could be part of a comprehensive response to currency aggression, by the international community as a whole under a reference rate system or by the United States unilaterally under the heading of countervailing currency intervention, both of which were described in chapter 5 and are addressed below. Such intervention does not exacerbate international currency conflict; indeed, if carried out consistently and on a sufficient scale, it could deter it, by eliminating any gains to the manipulators themselves.

Another permissible, indeed laudable, type of intervention occurs when surplus countries buy their own currencies to keep them from weakening and thus promoting even larger surpluses in their current accounts. Downward pressure on the exchange rates of surplus countries that is sufficient to motivate them to take countervailing action is infrequent but does occur, as it did in China during 2015 and 2016, when doubts arose over both the future of its economy and the competence of its management.

More ambitiously, reference rate proposals for international monetary reform would encourage, or in their strong forms require, surplus countries to push their currencies upward toward equilibrium levels to correct persistent misalignments. They would bar countries from intervening to push their rates away from equilibrium levels, making existing imbalances even worse, as with competitive nonappreciations. We strongly support the adoption of such reforms and believe they should be pursued on their own or in tandem with any unilateral steps the United States might decide it needs to adopt to start resolving the issue.

The Special Case of Key Currency Countries

The key currencies play a special role in the currency conflict narrative, because they are the primary vehicles for manipulation: In intervening to keep their currencies from appreciating, manipulators buy key currencies directly and/or switch into them to diversify their growing levels of reserves. Most intervention, especially by China and other Asian economies, is believed to take place in dollars. Considerable intervention, especially by Switzerland and other manipulators in or near Europe, takes place in euros. A smattering apparently takes place in other currencies, including the yen, as revealed in 2011, when Japan complained publicly about Chinese purchases of yen bonds (when Japan was unable to reciprocally purchase Chinese bonds).

Much of the uniqueness of the reserve currency countries comes from the fact that the informal but powerful conventions of the international monetary system have precluded their intervening to counter the intervention of others. The implicit "grand bargain" underlying the Bretton Woods system, whether under the original "fixed" or subsequent "floating" exchange rate regimes, is that nonreserve countries can use the dollar as their intervention and reserve medium in return for financing the external deficits the United States runs as a result. Global liquidity, and reserves to finance increasing levels of trade and economic activity, rise as a consequence.

All parties widely accepted this "deal" for most of the postwar period, even after the United States abrogated gold convertibility for foreign monetary authorities in 1971, though it has frequently created perceptions around the world that it favors the United States and allows it to run "deficits without tears" and dominate global finance. In reality, the arrangement is a mixed blessing for the United States. It does earn modest amounts of seigniorage and a good deal of global prestige from the international use of the dollar, and the central role of the dollar in global markets enhances the ability of the United States to enforce financial sanctions.

But the United States also bears two major costs. One is that "deficits without tears" produce a steady buildup of net foreign debt for the United States that now exceeds $8 trillion. If left unchecked, this deficit will cause major problems, both for the United States and for the world economy, as described in chapter 3, by exempting both from normal disciplinary effects of the adjustment process.

A second cost is that other countries, rather than the United States itself, set the exchange rate of the dollar, virtually ensuring its chronic overvaluation and explaining much of the external US deficits that have prevailed throughout the postwar period. The mechanism is straightforward: China and other manipulators buy dollars, pushing (or holding) the exchange rate up and short-circuiting the corrective realignment that would occur under normal market conditions.[2] The willingness of the United States to accept dollar appreciation and overvaluation—and the resulting large trade and current account deficits—was essential if the currency manipulation was to succeed.

The reality is thus the opposite of the conventional wisdom: The rest of the world benefits greatly from the international role of the dollar, and the impact on the United States itself is uncertain at best and arguably quite negative. The United States provides a major global public good (from which it, of course, benefits as well) by permitting the dollar to play

---

2. Dooley, Folkerts-Landau, and Garber (2004) called this regime of managed exchange rates, led by China, the Bretton Woods II monetary system.

its key currency role—including by letting other countries enjoy export-led growth. Though they occasionally grumble about the alleged "exorbitant privilege," other countries have been largely content to adhere to the implicit rules of the game. But the costs of dollar overvaluation from foreign manipulation are extremely large for the United States. They include almost $200 billion of annual output and more than a million jobs during and after the Great Recession, sizable macroeconomic costs in the run-up to that period, and lasting distortions of the composition of the economy (see chapter 4).

The overarching questions for both the global system and the United States itself are whether the United States should permit this arrangement to continue and whether its domestic politics will allow it to do so. The attack on globalization in general and on new trade agreements in particular that arose in the congressional debates in 2015, the political campaigns of 2016, and especially the Trump administration raise serious questions about the viability of the traditional US stance. The future of the open international trading and financial system is at stake.

We conclude that the United States must take steps to eliminate the asymmetries in the current system, preserve global stability and prosperity, and protect its own economic interests—preferably with widespread international support. The most straightforward way to do so, as outlined in chapter 5 and elaborated on below, is to adopt a policy of countervailing currency intervention, through which the United States intervenes to counter the manipulation of other countries. If, for example, Japan buys $1 billion of dollars to keep the yen from rising, the United States would buy $1 billion of yen to offset and neutralize the Japanese move. Just announcing such a policy should deter intervention by other countries, which would recognize that such actions would become futile in affecting market exchange rates.

In adopting a policy of countervailing currency intervention, the United States should seek the support of the other key currency countries. The euro area has suffered substantially from manipulation and, as the second international currency, has a major interest in deterring the practice. Japan, which has manipulated in the past itself, was at least temporarily the target of Chinese intervention and is already severely constrained by US monitoring of its policies and G-7 accords. All of the world's largest economies, as members of the G-20, have effectively agreed to restraints on currency manipulation. The United States should propose the creation of a Special Drawing Rights (SDR) Council, preferably within the IMF, that would bring together the issuers of the five key currencies (China, the euro area, Japan, the United Kingdom, and the United States) that make up the

SDR as part of its new initiative on these issues and contribute inter alia to the further evolution of international norms against manipulation.[3]

The United States has elicited very little support from other countries for its efforts to address the currency (or broader surplus country) issue. The lack of support partly reflects the inertia of current international monetary arrangements, under which the United States essentially agrees to run deficits and provide liquidity in return for its "automatic financing" by others. It also partly reflects the mercantilistic predilections of other key countries, as manifested for some by the currency manipulation itself. Some of it is because the United States has not been more energetic itself—for example, never formally labeling China a "currency manipulator" despite the requirements of its own law. Hence it is likely that the United States will have to take unilateral action to galvanize the reform process, as it did in 1971, when the "Nixon shock" eventually produced the seismic (and highly desirable) shift from fixed to flexible exchange rates. It should nevertheless attempt to multilateralize the strategy as much as possible, as discussed below.

Rules versus (Lack of) Enforcement

The international rules that address currency issues are a mixed bag. The IMF's Articles of Agreement, and their interpretive guidelines, explicitly ban the manipulation and competitive devaluation of exchange rates. They require countries that plan to intervene to consult with other relevant countries, especially those in whose currencies they plan to operate.

However, manipulation and competitive devaluation are banned only if they are undertaken "in order to prevent effective balance of payment adjustment or gain unfair competitive advantage," raising the issue of intent. Many manipulators deny that their goals are mercantilist, arguing that their intervention is aimed at preserving financial stability or other purposes. Hence the IMF rules are imperfect. They are universally agreed on and frequently reiterated, however, and go far toward achieving the purposes we have in mind. We thus use them as the basis for our proposals, hoping and expecting that the qualifying caveats that undermine their practical utility will recede into irrelevance as the process is amended.

The frequent invocations of the IMF rules suggest that international currency norms may be evolving in a way that will help prevent future conflicts. The G-7 has gone farthest, pledging to avoid any intervention except after consultation within the group. The G-20 has not advanced that far, but it has emphasized its commitment to "not target our exchange rates for competitive purposes" (G-20 2016). The (now defunct) TPP side agree-

---

3. We are indebted to Robert Zoellick for this suggestion.

ment broke new procedural ground via its association with a trade pact and required some of its members to significantly increase the transparency and accountability of their current practices. The new US legal framework adds to this normative evolution, even though it is a purely US construct. This phenomenon may at least partly explain the recent remission in manipulation.

No effective enforcement mechanism supports the IMF rules, however. Hence its rules do not function as effective deterrents, and the Fund's toolkit is limited to hortatory "name and shame" efforts, which have some impact but cannot be counted on to induce countries to change policies they regard as important for their economies. Moreover, the IMF can pursue even these limited sanctions only through a decision-making process that is highly politicized and thus unlikely to be used against a major power. (It has used them only twice on the currency issue, against Korea and Sweden in the 1980s.) The IMF has therefore been unable to play any significant role on an issue that was supposed to be at the very top of its agenda of responsibilities.

The US government and some other governments of deficit countries have thus become enormously frustrated with the IMF. This frustration has permeated the Congress, much of which is already skeptical of international institutions. Congressional ire has been directed not just at the IMF but also at the Treasury Department and others in the executive branch who defend the IMF despite its ineffectiveness on this issue. The US authorities have been unable to rely on the IMF to address the currency problem and have concluded that they must look elsewhere, especially to their own unilateral devices, for meaningful action.

The WTO has a parallel rule on exchange rates, but it is more ambiguous than its IMF counterpart and has never been tested. There is considerable controversy among scholars concerning its applicability to cases of manipulation, with most doubting its utility. Moreover, the WTO must rely on IMF judgments concerning the substance of currency issues. The difficulties at the Fund thus compound those at the WTO (and the two institutions are frequently unable to work effectively together).

Unlike the Fund, the WTO can deploy effective trade sanctions when its rules are violated and could potentially contribute to a multilateral response to the problem. The irony is thus that the IMF has good rules but no teeth while the WTO has lots of ammunition but no action triggers in this domain. Any serious effort to develop new multilateral mechanisms to combat international currency conflict should draw on the comparative advantage of each institution. The management of the IMF should push hard for its membership to reach expeditious judgments by simple majority vote of its board of directors on the merits of currency complaints. The WTO should then be asked under its Article XV (4) to authorize its member countries to deploy trade sanctions against countries that violate its currency rules.

The key requirement is to reach agreement on practical operational criteria to implement the IMF's laudable goals. In addition to the norm on reserve adequacy suggested above, only two others are needed: definitions of a "substantial" current account surplus and "persistent one-sided intervention" in the foreign exchange markets. We suggest that any surplus above 3 percent of a country's GDP qualify as "excessive" and that net intervention that totals more than 2 percent of a country's GDP over the previous 12 months should activate that criterion. Table 4.1 shows the country coverage from our criteria in recent years.

Congress took a useful step in the direction of establishing such objective criteria when, working with the administration, it passed the Trade Facilitation and Trade Enforcement Act of 2015. The act requires the administration to undertake "enhanced engagement" with countries that meet a set of criteria that are conceptually similar to those suggested here (as originally suggested in Bergsten and Gagnon 2012). In its initial report under that legislation in May 2016, Treasury defined a "material" current account surplus as one that exceeds 3 percent of a country's GDP and "persistent one-sided intervention" as exceeding 2 percent of a country's GDP over the previous 12 months.[4] The new law requires Treasury to address countries that are "major trading partners of the United States," which it defines as exceeding $55 billion in exports plus imports in 2015. This group includes only a dozen countries. We would focus on systemically important currency manipulators (SICMs) and thus the slightly larger membership of the G-20.

The Trade Facilitation and Trade Enforcement Act of 2015 also requires a target country to run a "significant" bilateral trade surplus with the United States, which Treasury defines as exceeding $20 billion in 2015. We would drop this criterion as irrelevant in a world of multilateral trade and payments. The new law does not include a criterion for "adequate reserves," which we use to exclude countries where self-insurance is still justified. (See chapter 4 and Bergsten and Gagnon 2016 for more details on the new law and the Treasury report.)

Reflecting the widespread remission of manipulation, Treasury correctly concluded that no country currently met the standards of the new

---

4. In its October 2016 report, Treasury added language that gave it flexibility to apply the criterion of "persistent one-sided intervention" when the amounts totaled less than 2 percent of GDP, because the numbers resulting from that metric would be very high for large countries such as China and Japan.

law requiring "enhanced engagement" as it defines them. It did, however, place on a new "monitoring list" five economies that met three of its four key criteria: China, Germany (which could be branded a manipulator only as part of the euro area, because it does not have its own currency), Japan, Korea, and Taiwan.

The new US legislation, like the similar course of action suggested here, represents a major conceptual advance by substituting a set of objective criteria for the subjective judgments of "currency misalignment" and "intent to manipulate" that have been central to the issue in the past. Efforts to determine the extent of misalignments are fraught with huge intellectual difficulties, even before getting to the politics of trying to reach international agreement on them. We therefore suggested previously (Bergsten and Gagnon 2012) that the concept should be replaced with one that could be implemented objectively. Likewise, Treasury's interpretation that countries could be designated as manipulators only with proof of their intent to manipulate became an insurmountable hurdle even when Treasury's own analyses showed that a country was clearly engaging in such practices. The application of standards in this highly contentious policy area will always be difficult, but we believe that the new conceptual foundations represent major progress toward meaningful action where very little has transpired heretofore.

The 2015 legislation seeks to ensure enforcement of its norms by requiring the administration to take one or more specific actions against countries that meet its criteria (as several would have in past years under Treasury's [and our] standards) and fail to remedy their practices within a year. These actions include (1) denying Overseas Private Investment Corporation (OPIC) programs, (2) denying US government procurement (except for countries that are members of the Government Procurement Agreement in the WTO), (3) proposing to the IMF that it dispatch a "special consultation" to the country to discuss the problem, and (4) "taking into account" the country's currency policy in determining whether to pursue a trade agreement with it. The last of these actions might have had some deterrent effect vis-à-vis countries that would have liked to join an expanded TPP (such as Korea and even China) or might now envisage a bilateral agreement with the United States (such as Japan), but the four-part menu does not add much firepower to the battle against currency aggression, especially with the demise of the TPP. A highly desirable improvement would be the addition of countervailing currency intervention and submission of cases to the WTO under its Article XV (4), as described in chapter 5 and below, to the list of alternative remedies an administration would be required to take against continued manipulation.

Currency Policy and Trade Policy

This discussion indicates the need to think about currency policy and trade policy together. The United States, however, has seen trade and currency largely through separate lenses. The conceptual reason has been economic. Exchange rates have been seen primarily as driving the trade *balance*, a macroeconomic issue largely reflecting underlying economic fundamentals, such as the relationship between domestic saving and investment. In a world of flexible exchange rates, trade policy is viewed as affecting the *level* and *composition* of trade flows but not the overall balance.

The second and probably more powerful operational reason for this bifurcation has been institutional: At both the national and international levels, different agencies handle trade and currency. In the United States, the US Trade Representative is responsible for trade, and the Treasury Department is mainly responsible for macroeconomic, and especially direct currency (including intervention), issues. Most other countries maintain similar distinctions. Internationally, the IMF handles macroeconomic issues, including exchange rates, while the WTO is responsible for trade (its leadership has repeatedly rejected any direct role on currency topics).

This distinction is no longer tenable. It has already proven unviable at key points when the United States had to confront major trade imbalances brought on by currency misalignments. In 1971 President Nixon deployed a temporary import surcharge as leverage to negotiate dollar devaluation. In 1985 rampant protectionist pressure in Congress forced the Reagan administration to abandon the benign neglect of the dollar of its first term and negotiate a substantial depreciation via the Plaza Agreement. In 2015 Congress conditioned its willingness to pass new trade legislation (Trade Promotion Authority) on more aggressive efforts by the administration to counter currency manipulation. Both Donald Trump and Hillary Clinton couched their opposition to the TPP (and globalization more broadly) importantly in terms of unfair manipulation. Indeed, many political leaders have insisted that currency provisions be embedded directly in all new US trade agreements.

For both sound economic and practical political reasons, an effective US response to the currency problem should encompass both macroeconomic/monetary policy and trade policy tools. We turn now to a discussion of what those tools might look like.

A Proposed Strategy for the United States

The main goal of the new US policy should be to deter future currency conflict by creating credible policy mechanisms that would sanction manipulators with sufficient force to dissuade them from undertaking such activities. The targets should be countries that are systemically important, which we define as members of the G-20 steering committee for the world economy.[5] Manipulators should be identified through the application of a set of simple and objective criteria: current account surpluses exceeding 3 percent of their GDPs over the previous year coupled with annual intervention exceeding 2 percent of GDP over the previous year on top of reserves already exceeding the equivalent of three months' worth of imports or 100 percent of their short-term external liabilities in foreign currencies, whichever is larger, plus a reasonable amount of foreign saving by resource exporters.

We have already suggested that the most effective policy response to the risk of future currency aggression would be an announcement by the United States that it would henceforth carry out countervailing currency intervention against any G-20 country that met the relevant criteria and sought to prevent appreciation of its exchange rate by intervening directly in the foreign exchange markets. Such an announcement should, by itself, deter most if not all future manipulation, by promising to neutralize its impact and thus render it ineffectual in strengthening the manipulators' competitiveness. The announcement should work like the famous statement by European Central Bank President Mario Draghi in August 2012 to do "whatever it takes" to avoid a crisis of the euro, which immediately calmed markets and ended the crisis without action having had to be implemented. It should thus preempt the threat of "currency wars."

Unlike countervailing duties or other trade policy sanctions that apply only to imports, the new policy would address both sides of the trade balance. It would be very different from import controls, even wide-ranging ones, whose depressing impact on imports would probably be offset by corresponding dollar appreciation that would limit any net benefits for the US economy.

Countervailing currency intervention would, of course, have to be credible in market terms to have the desired deterrent impact. China's intervention over the past decade reached $500 billion in some years. Some other countries intervened at the same time, adding to the total the United States would have had to counter had it been implementing countervailing currency intervention (see box 5.2).

---

5. Avoidance of manipulation by G-20 countries would probably prevent manipulation as well by smaller countries that feel compelled to emulate their larger neighbors. A number of China's neighbors in Asia, for example, move their currencies in tandem with the renminbi (Kessler 2012) and have thus intervened at least partly to avoid losing competitive position to it. We do not include Switzerland as a potential target, despite its frequent manipulation and near G-20 size, but it could reasonably be included.

It is highly unlikely that manipulation, which is now largely in remission, would resume at anything like these levels—if at all—in the face of an announced US policy of countervailing currency intervention. In addition, private investors would almost certainly counter efforts by manipulators to place artificial ceilings on their currencies once the US government declared its intention to do so.

As described in chapter 5, however, countervailing currency intervention would maximize its credibility—and limit the likelihood that it would actually have to be used in practice—by assembling the largest possible stock of ammunition.

The Exchange Stabilization Fund (ESF) of the Treasury Department possesses assets of about $100 billion. Under the usual 50-50 sharing of responsibilities for currency operations, the Federal Reserve would probably provide another $100 billion. The "war chest" at present would thus amount to about $200 billion. It would be desirable to augment this total to make sure that the deterrent was sufficient. Congress should therefore be asked to authorize a large amount, perhaps $500 billion (which the Fed would presumably match, for a total of $1 trillion), of additional borrowing authority to bring the total to a "Powell doctrine" level of overwhelming force.

Such borrowing authority would not represent a charge to the US budget even if the resources had to be used (although any actual borrowings by the ESF would count against the debt ceiling). The dollars sold by the ESF would be fully offset by the foreign currencies that were bought in an "exchange of assets," to use the agreed budgetary terminology.[6] In terms of future revenues, the exchange should make money for the United States, which would by definition be buying foreign currencies when they are undervalued.[7] The Federal Reserve does not operate with authorized or appropriated funds, so its participation would raise no budgetary issues (though it, too, would probably enjoy increased profits that, under standard oper-

---

6. In its assessment of the budgetary cost of US funding of the IMF, the Congressional Budget Office opined that there is no budgetary cost arising from the exposure to foreign currency risk, because any difference in interest earned on foreign-currency versus domestic-currency assets is likely to be equal and opposite in sign to any expected change in the dollar value of foreign currencies (CBO 2016).

7. The US government would have made substantial profits from the sizable subsequent appreciation of the renminbi had it bought renminbi when countervailing currency intervention was first proposed, in the mid-2000s (see C. Fred Bergsten, "Muzzling Our Economic Negotiators," *Washington Post*, September 10, 2003; "The Chinese Exchange Rate and the US Economy," statement before the Senate Committee on Banking, Housing and Urban Affairs, January 31, 2007; "We Can Fight Fire with Fire on the Renminbi," *Financial Times*, December 17, 2010; and box 5.2 in chapter 5 of this book).

ating procedures, would be remitted annually to the Treasury and thus help reduce the budget deficit).

There are several possible objections to countervailing currency intervention. Chapter 5 addresses some objections of a technical nature. One objection of principle—cited by some in the Obama White House and Treasury when the idea was raised with them informally by members of Congress—is that it would be inconsistent for the United States to undertake currency intervention when it was urging other countries to avoid it. But there is nothing wrong with intervention per se. The problem is with intervention that *impedes* needed adjustment. The goal of countervailing currency intervention would be to *promote* needed adjustment, by providing a much more muscular deterrent to that particular form of intervention—one that ideally would not have to be used much if at all. Theory posits that the harm from foreign official distortion of exchange rates is optimally rectified by intervention in the opposite direction. Committed supporters of markets and opponents of government intervention should thus be the strongest proponents of countervailing currency intervention.

There is also an understandable concern that countervailing currency intervention could have unforeseen consequences. For example, US interest groups with parochial objectives could capture its implementation, as has sometimes happened with countervailing and antidumping duties. Congress and others could exert pressure to use the tool for blatantly protectionist purposes. Other countries could emulate the new US posture in less rigorous ways, and it could even be turned against the United States itself (e.g., versus a renewed use of quantitative easing, despite its clear analytical difference from manipulation, as outlined above). Fearing they might be targeted, countries could reduce or even reverse the liberalization (and increased transparency) of their own capital markets to reduce their vulnerability to countervailing currency intervention. They could look for more indirect and opaque ways to conduct intervention that could not be readily traced. If implementation of the new policy were mishandled, especially if it were applied too frequently, it could escalate rather than counter the risk of currency conflict and roil markets as a result. None of these concerns are dispositive, but it must be acknowledged that, like any major new policy instrument, this tool could trigger unintended consequences that could affect its impact on the US and world economies.

The most fundamental objection to countervailing currency intervention is that it would overturn the implicit bargain at the heart of the dollar-based monetary system: that the United States would provide this global public good, even as it led to dollar overvaluation and US external deficits, in return for which other countries would finance those deficits without grumbling too much. This bargain has provided adequate liquidity for the world economy. It has largely prevented external financial unsustainability for the United States (although it has failed to preserve domestic political sustainability and thus threatened an open US trade policy and, through it, the global trading system). A US effort to weaken its exchange rate would also run counter to the "strong dollar" rhetoric of the last two decades and perhaps be viewed as an explicit repudiation of its traditional systemic leadership role.

It is doubtful, however, that countervailing currency intervention would do much, if anything, to dent the role of the dollar in the world economy. Empirically, neither of the two previous US initiatives to weaken the dollar substantially, in 1971 and 1985, cut into the dollar's international role (though the sharp market-driven fall in the dollar in 1978 did so to a modest extent for a short while). Nor did the extended efforts to promote a stronger yen, in the 1980s and 1990s, and a stronger renminbi more recently. The continued absence of any significant rival to US currency leadership in the short to medium run underlies the age-old adage that "you cannot beat something with nothing" (Prasad 2014). Hence we believe that the United States could adopt a policy of countervailing currency intervention—or more broadly a strategy of responding much more firmly to currency aggression by others—without jeopardizing the international role of the dollar (for better or worse).

A side benefit of countervailing currency intervention, to the extent it was actually implemented, is that it would enable the United States to start building a meaningful reserve of foreign exchange of its own. US reserves of $40 billion are very meager compared with the $300 billion to $600 billion held by Hong Kong and Singapore, much less the trillions of dollars held by China and Japan. The rationale is that the United States does not need to build international reserves because it can borrow unlimited amounts in private capital markets. Moreover, its external liabilities, though large, at about $30 trillion, are denominated in its own currency, so it could not be forced into a currency crisis; the floating dollar would simply depreciate—and improve the US competitive position—if a sharp fall of confidence were ever to occur.

This logic has several flaws. The United States might not always welcome a sharp decline in the dollar if, as in 1978, when it had to mount a major rescue operation, the result was a sharp increase in inflation and/or interest rates. Numerous undesirable events, including another rating downgrade or a sequence of policy missteps, could trigger such a decline. A US reversion to protectionism or isolationism more broadly, which now seems all too possible, could drive down the currency, just as the Brexit vote led to a sharp fall in the value of the pound. Hot money could flow out of the United States the next time it is the epicenter of a global crisis. Over time the rise of China or recovery of the euro area could lead to international portfolio diversification out of the dollar. If the United States needed to intervene to support the dollar in such circumstances, especially on short notice, it would not have the wherewithal to do so. Hence it should build at least a modest war chest of foreign currency holdings. Countervailing currency intervention would generate just such an asset buildup if the United States actually needed to buy foreign currencies to offset their issuers' purchases of dollars for competitive reasons.

Germany and other members of the euro area (or any currency union) pose problems for countervailing currency intervention because they do not have their own national currencies. For this reason, currency unions must be analyzed on a consolidated basis for purposes of assessing currency manipulation. The euro area in any case would not be a target of countervailing currency intervention in the near future, because it is not accumulating official foreign assets. The United States and other countries, both inside and outside the euro area, should instead continue to press Germany to use its strong economic and budget position to adopt more expansionary fiscal policies in an effort to stimulate stronger growth and smaller surpluses in Europe as a whole, with consequent benefits for the world economy.

Countervailing currency intervention is clearly legal, in both domestic and international terms. We believe that a US administration could implement it without any need for new congressional authorization. Such intervention would simply be an adaptation of the intervention in currency markets that the United States has carried out, usually through joint action by the Treasury Department (via the Exchange Stabilization Fund) and the Federal Reserve System, on thousands of occasions in the past.

However, congressional authorization for additional borrowing would be needed to equip the ESF with adequate resources to provide full credibility for any intervention that might be needed; such authorization would also add weight and permanence to the new US policy. Countervailing currency intervention could, perhaps most expeditiously, be added to the inadequate list of remedies included in the currency chapter of the Trade Facilitation and Trade Enforcement Act of 2015. Adding it would serve a useful domestic political purpose in providing a tangible response, for which Congress could properly take credit, to widespread concerns over currency policy that Congress has expressed in recent years. The Senate passed a currency bill that included countervailing currency intervention, which it called "remedial currency intervention," in 2011. Passage of currency legislation, with the support or even lead of the administration, might be extremely helpful (or even necessary) to win support for any future trade agreements. Hence we recommend that Congress pass new legislation to authorize and fund countervailing currency intervention, either as an amendment to the currency chapter of the Trade Facilitation and Trade Enforcement Act of 2015 or on a stand-alone basis.

The United States could also adopt a trade policy tool to complement the monetary tool of countervailing currency intervention. One possibility would be the imposition of countervailing duties against imports subsidized by currency manipulation. Such duties could be imposed either through administrative reinterpretation of current legislation or, more definitively, through congressional authorization of the additional criterion for countervailing duties (as the House did in 2010 and the Senate did in 2011 and 2015).

However, countervailing duties would not be a very effective policy instrument. They would cover only the import side of the equation, and trade coverage would probably be modest, as industries would still have to petition for relief and demonstrate injury as a result of the affected imports (and pay the considerable legal fees involved). Moreover, any reduction in imports would probably lead to an offsetting appreciation of the dollar, which would preclude much, if any, net improvement in the current account balance.

In addition, countervailing duties against currency undervaluation are probably not compatible with US obligations under the WTO. No such case has ever been tested, but most trade lawyers believe that the WTO rules do not cover exchange rate issues. Target countries might therefore be able to legally retaliate against the United States, nullifying any net benefits from the tool. Adoption of such a policy would also cede some of the moral high ground that the United States could otherwise command on the issue and feed perceptions that the United States itself was launching a trade war rather than merely defending itself and seeking to deter economic conflict.

It would be desirable, however, to launch an effort in the WTO to add currency manipulation to the list of export subsidies subject to the application of countervailing duties under the Agreement on Subsidies and Countervailing Measures (ASCM). The United States should also initiate WTO cases against major manipulators under Article XV (4), which could authorize the adoption of import surcharges against such countries, if such manipulation begins again, as discussed in chapter 5 and below. The United States should also initiate new efforts to add currency provisions to FTAs, as outlined below.

Multilateralizing the Strategy

The unilateral nature of countervailing currency intervention, through which the United States would act as both judge and jury, would undoubtedly generate suspicion and opposition from other countries—especially economies that saw themselves as possible future targets, notably China and some other Asian economies. All economies have committed themselves not to manipulate through their membership in the IMF, some of them repeatedly through declarations of the G-20 and other groups. Most or all know that they have manipulated, but some genuinely believe that their actions were justified and would surely argue that unilateral enforcement of their multilateral obligations by the United States could sanction them arbitrarily and unfairly. Moreover, one of the primary goals of this entire strategy is to plug a gaping hole in the global financial architecture. Hence the United States should try to multilateralize the initiative, in at least three ways.

First, it should encourage the other key currency countries—the euro area, the United Kingdom (whose currency was the dominant key currency before the dollar), and Japan, as well as China now that the renminbi has officially attained reserve currency status as part of the SDR—to adopt similar countervailing currency intervention policies and offer to implement the policy in conjunction with them. To engage China, which could help greatly in achieving the deterrence objective, the United States should propose the creation of an SDR Council in the IMF to consult with the other four key currency issuers inter alia on implementation of the new policy. Other top economies, especially the euro area, have experienced substantial economic losses from manipulation. They should therefore be willing, despite their past reluctance, to join a "coalition of the willing" to curtail the practice.

Second, the United States should seek to engage the IMF and WTO to the maximum possible extent. The IMF's guidelines already include the key objective criteria that determine when a member country is guilty of manipulation (a substantial current account surplus and protracted, sizable one-way intervention in the currency markets). Definitions of *substantial, protracted,* and *sizable* would have to be negotiated as part of any new procedures at the Fund, to avoid the current problem of doing so ad hoc on each individual case that arises; we recommend the interpretations outlined above. The other major addition would be an informal new Fund agreement, perhaps initially by the proposed SDR Council, under which its members would be encouraged to apply countervailing currency intervention against designated manipulators.

More broadly, the United States should propose IMF adoption of a system of currency reference rates. Such rates would commit all participants to avoid destabilizing intervention and require, or at least encourage, them to undertake stabilizing intervention as well. The first part of the scheme would reinforce the countervailing currency intervention approach and greatly enhance its legitimacy, adding an enforcement dimension to the proscription of reference rates (and current IMF rules) against intervention to achieve competitive nonappreciation. The second part would add a proactive dimension to the adjustment process, along the lines of what China has already been doing recently to resist further depreciation of the renminbi.

The United States could likewise seek to use the relevant WTO rules to authorize trade policy measures against manipulators. One step would be to seek the addition of currency manipulation to the list of export subsidies prohibited by the ASCM and thus subject to countervailing duties. A broader and therefore more desirable possibility would be to seek interpretation of Article XV (4) as including currency manipulation as a monetary practice that "frustrates the intent" of the agreement and thus calls for across-the-board retaliatory action, presumably import surcharges, by bringing a case against a major manipulator if such circumstances arise again.

Third, the United States could propose including currency provisions in its future trade agreements. The TTIP or the proposed bilateral FTA with the post-Brexit United Kingdom would be natural vehicles to begin this approach, as manipulation has harmed most Europeans. The euro area and the United Kingdom operate floating exchange rates, in which manipulation (or indeed any intervention) is highly unlikely. They are thus natural collaborators with the United States in applying countervailing currency intervention. The euro area (let alone the entire European Union) has never decided how to handle currency policy, however, and is not equipped to do so; the United Kingdom, with its long history of currency policy, might therefore be a better prospect. Perhaps more important, Germany has strongly opposed the adoption of rigorous disciplines on surplus countries (within the European Union as well as internationally). It might well oppose the idea and carry the entire European Union with it (other European countries have also been unresponsive to earlier US proposals on this topic).

If the TPP were ever revived, an immediate question would be its renegotiation to include a currency chapter, as sought by numerous members of Congress as a condition for approving it even before President Trump jettisoned it. Such inclusion could be done by folding the agreed upon side arrangement on exchange rates into the TPP itself, tightening and binding the currency obligations and subjecting them to its dispute settlement mechanism, or converting that agreement into a set of binding commitments with its own dispute settlement mechanism. Either alternative would be difficult in light of the complex tradeoffs that were negotiated in the original TPP deal and the fact that the parliaments of several member countries have already approved it. It may, however, turn out to be necessary for the agreement to win US assent. This alteration of the TPP could be of considerable practical importance if Korea, possibly Taiwan, and especially

China were to participate at some point. The same issues would arise in any renegotiation of NAFTA.

FTAs should rely primarily on two remedies to deter and, if necessary, counter violation of any currency obligations they might include (see chapter 5). The most natural is the snapback of benefits provided to the violator under the FTA itself, the standard remedy for violations of any of a country's commitments. A superior alternative would be countervailing currency intervention, which would cover the exports as well as imports of all partner countries (and could be carried out by all aggrieved countries on a shared basis or simply by the United States as part of its broader countervailing currency intervention policy, as proposed here).

The broader point of multilateralizing the strategy is that unilateral action, especially by the most powerful individual country, has often proven to be essential to reforming the multilateral system. The clearest historical precedent was the brutal action by the United States in 1971 that terminated gold convertibility for foreign monetary authorities and applied an across-the-board import surcharge. That action eventually produced the seismic shift from the "fixed" exchange rates of the original Bretton Woods system to floating exchange rates. Virtually all observers, even those who excoriated the US action at the time (including one of the authors of this volume), subsequently agreed that the reform was highly desirable and that it would not have happened, at least for a very long time, without unilateral US action.

A similar dynamic occurred on trade policy a decade later, when newly aggressive US implementation of its authority to impose unilateral sanctions, under Section 301 of the Trade Act of 1974, beginning in 1985 induced the membership of the GATT, through the Uruguay Round of multilateral negotiations, to dramatically strengthen its dispute settlement mechanism. That mechanism became the core of the new WTO almost a decade later.

Aggressive action by the United States along the lines proposed here would inevitably lead to widespread outcries that it was igniting new currency conflicts rather than deterring them. The United States is still the world's largest economy. It has traditionally been the leader of an open multilateral trading and financial system and the chief defender of the global economic institutions. The dollar is the world's key currency. Other countries have become so accustomed to US provision of major global public goods, most notably its open markets and willingness to run sizable external deficits, that they will instinctively balk at any substantial changes in those arrangements.

The Trump administration's early expressions of skepticism about multilateral institutions and cooperation more broadly, including with respect to the European Union, and the "America First" rhetoric of the president's inaugural address, have heightened anxieties around the world over the unilaterialist tendencies of the United States, which are always present to some extent. Our proposals for a much more activist US approach to currency manipulation, especially the unilateral adoption and implementation of countervailing currency intervention, could reinforce these concerns if they are not handled with the necessary sensitivity.

Such major alterations in global economic arrangements should therefore be negotiated in a cooperative manner, without crises or heavy-handed pressure from the most powerful country. The inability of the system to adopt even modest and incremental steps to respond to currency problems, however, let alone the substantial reforms that are required to deal with them decisively, suggest that this path is not available. Unilateral action by the United States, while distasteful to many, will therefore almost certainly be necessary. But the United States should simultaneously offer to pursue multilateral steps, such as those indicated here, to give other countries an opportunity to participate in the process if they are willing to do so constructively.

Currency Conflict and Foreign Policy

The United States should be able to forge a wide-ranging "coalition of the willing" to counter currency manipulation. Manipulation has hurt a number of deficit countries and even some surplus countries that have never manipulated. The euro area alone was losing $50 billion to $100 billion of net exports a year at the height of manipulation. A number of emerging-market countries, including Brazil, India, Korea, and Mexico, have complained publicly about China's currency policy.

But US foreign policy objectives often complicate such a task. Some of the most active manipulators have also been close US allies that Washington would not want to alienate. Some of them may want to preserve the option of manipulating in the future—especially if their alternative growth strategies falter. To support very large current account surpluses, for example, Japan, Korea, and Taiwan, whose friendship with the United States has long been important, could (or still do) intervene at levels that exceed our criteria. Singapore and Switzerland also continue to intervene massively.

All of these economies have been hurt by the manipulation of others—Japan and Korea by each other, all of them by China.[8] The United States should be able to win their support for a strategy that is based on a credible

---

8. Japan tried to conduct a variant of countervailing currency intervention in 2011, when it objected to the appreciation of the yen prompted by Chinese purchases of yen bonds and asked China to let it purchase an equivalent amount of renminbi bonds to provide an offset.

policy of reacting strongly to any future instances of manipulation while convincing these trading partners that they could no longer benefit from the practices anyway.

An additional foreign policy complication arises from the fact that Germany, Sweden, and other surplus countries may be leery of the idea, whether or not they have manipulated. They have tended to place the onus of adjustment responsibility on deficit countries and have resisted proposals on exchange rates or other parts of the adjustment process that would limit their flexibility.

An additional concern in forging a consistent policy is that many potential supporters fear getting into a conflict with China and other target countries (EU countries, especially in the euro area, also worry about antagonizing Germany). Even countries that have assailed past intervention by China, such as India and Korea, might be reluctant to enter a coalition that was implicitly aimed against Beijing. Even Brazil, seeking to balance political imperatives with economic concerns, felt compelled to criticize the United States (for quantitative easing) and China alike while decrying the "currency wars" allegedly driving up its exchange rate and disrupting its economy.

Oil-exporting countries provide a special case of mixing foreign policy and economic concerns. Several oil exporters met our criteria as currency manipulators during the decade of manipulation. But only the United Arab Emirates and possibly Norway are likely to be saving excessively in the future and thus exceed our criteria for currency manipulation.

A final important foreign policy consideration stems from the perception that the proposed new US policy would be aimed primarily at China, despite its not manipulating since 2014, reinforced by the reversal of its currency policy to resist depreciation of the renminbi over the past year or so. Despite the lack of reason to take any action against China now, the proposed new US policy could stir tensions with Beijing.

Washington cannot ignore China's rise as an economic (and overall) superpower and the consequent need to integrate it into the leadership structure of the world economy. As China becomes the world's largest economy and trading nation, benefiting from the open trading and financial regimes, it must take greater responsibility for preserving and strengthening the system, especially as the renminbi becomes increasingly recognized as a global currency. This will be particularly essential if the United States abandons, or even significantly weakens, its role as the traditional leader and defender of globalization and the rules and institutions that govern it.

China's decision to stop manipulating its currency, although driven primarily by market forces, may signal Beijing's coming to terms with its global role and suggest a greater willingness to cooperate with the United States to avoid future currency conflict. China's long-stated intention to shift from export-led to consumption-led growth suggests that it does not plan to return to past manipulation policies.

For now China and the United States are benefiting from an interlude free of direct confrontation over the issue, making it timely for the United States to enter a conversation over currency issues, perhaps through the new SDR Council as well as bilaterally, after having adopted a firm new policy of its own on the topic: This would be essential to persuade China that the United States was serious and could not be deterred from proceeding. In the spirit of applying the G-2 concept of US-China leadership (Bergsten 2005) in the international monetary space, the United States should offer to take full account of Chinese views on how best to prevent future currency conflict and thus how to carry out its new plans.

The other major potential targets of a more muscular US policy toward currency manipulation are also mainly in Asia: Japan and Korea, and, if the policy extended beyond our recommendation to focus on the G-20, Taiwan and Singapore, and perhaps Hong Kong and Malaysia. Questions thus arise concerning the consistency of the policy with the "pivot to Asia" (or rebalancing strategy) that has driven US policy toward the region—and indeed overall US foreign policy—during the past several years, especially with the rejection of the TPP by the Trump administration. This adds to the case for multilateralizing the new US strategy to the maximum extent possible.

Remission of manipulation by China and others has reduced the sense of urgency for the issue. The Treasury Department has avoided designating any economy for "enhanced engagement" under its interpretation of the new currency legislation passed by Congress in February 2016. Other countries pressed on this issue by the United States might simply argue that no practical problem now exists.

To counter that resistance, the United States should argue that the problem is likely only in remission and that countries will inevitably be tempted to defend current account surpluses when their currencies resume appreciation. The United States will hardly be free of domestic political pressures if that happens. The absence of effective policy responses to currency manipulation (and the failure of surplus countries to contribute to the adjustment process) thus remains perhaps the biggest single gap in today's international financial architecture. A period of remission should not be an excuse for inaction. In fact, it is ideal for instituting the new policy, because no countries would be indicted and the United States, and ideally others, could establish their new countervailing currency intervention (and perhaps other) policies with less risk of pushback because they would not have to implement them. This period is an ideal time to seek a systemic remedy. We thus strongly advocate proceeding as soon as possible to take advantage of it.

Conclusion

The systemic failure to deter and deal effectively with past currency manipulation—and its sizable economic costs to the United States and other countries—justify a major new initiative to help prevent its recurrence. The domestic politics of trade policy and of globalization more broadly in the United States require a much tougher stance on this issue to avoid far-reaching threats to the global trading system. Erection of effective deterrents justifies the acceptance of some economic risks and foreign policy costs vis-à-vis China, traditional allies, and third parties.

In light of the realities of international negotiations, however, the United States will inevitably have to rely primarily on unilateral initiatives, at least initially. Maximum efforts should be made to persuade at least a few like-minded countries, particularly in Europe, to adopt parallel if not concerted measures and to engage China in a conversation to explore all possibilities for proceeding together. Success on those fronts should not be expected, however, unless the United States takes convincing steps first. Neither the IMF nor the WTO is going to be reformed in the needed directions within any reasonable period of time unless they are jolted by unilateral US initiatives, as in 1971-73, when the "Nixon shocks" ultimately moved most of the world from fixed to flexible exchange rates.

The United States should therefore launch a new initiative to deter currency manipulation and the risk of future currency conflict. The key step is to announce a policy of countervailing currency intervention, under which the United States will henceforth match (and thus neutralize) sizable and persistent one-sided intervention by G-7 and G-20 countries that have adequate levels of foreign exchange reserves and are running substantial global current account surpluses. This policy would build on and reinforce the commitments that G-20 countries have already undertaken to avoid currency manipulation.

This single step might suffice to resolve the problem. Announcement of such a policy alone should have enormous deterrent impact; like any successful deterrent, the policy itself might never need to be implemented (except perhaps for a few early salvos to demonstrate its credibility). Congress, and the domestic political process more broadly, should be assuaged that deliberate currency distortions would no longer create an unlevel international playing field and undermine the benefits of trade agreements and globalization more broadly. Implementation of such a policy could help counter the antiglobalization sentiment that suffused the political campaigns in 2016 and may well characterize the Trump administration.

The United States should pursue two additional steps through the IMF to attempt to multilateralize the process on the monetary side. First, it should propose the creation of a new SDR Council that would bring together the five issuers of key currencies that now constitute the SDR basket of the Fund to consult on the new set of policies and the problems of intervention and manipulation more broadly. Second, it should seek a new agreement in the Fund on reference rates for at least the main currencies, to reinforce its unilateral effort to deter national policies that block exchange rates from moving toward their equilibrium levels. Over time application of these principles should be extended beyond the G-20 to include all advanced and upper-middle-income countries.

In addition, the United States should adopt several new trade policies. The most important is to include currency provisions in its future FTAs. The administration should also launch an effort in the WTO to include currency manipulation as an export subsidy that can be countered by countervailing duties under the ASCM and prepare to bring a case under its Article XV (4) if a major country meets the criteria for currency manipulation.

Rollout of the new policy should be carefully orchestrated. Congressional leaders must be fully consulted and invited to provide legislative authorization for countervailing currency intervention, as the Senate did in 2011. Such authorization would also provide the most appropriate vehicle to obtain adequate funding for the ESF at Treasury to carry out any countervailing intervention that might actually be needed. Potential foreign partners in the initiative should be consulted, with priorities for Germany vis-à-vis the euro area and China both bilaterally and via the proposed SDR Council. All potential target economies should be assured that no early implementation of the new policy is envisaged and that none would be needed as long as they did not revert to manipulation. The management and governing bodies of the key international institutions, especially the IMF and the WTO, should be fully consulted and invited to multilateralize the initiative to the maximum extent possible through corresponding reforms in both.

Risk of renewed currency conflict calls for a major new US policy initiative. The substantial economic costs of past manipulation to the United States and other countries, the huge gap in the international systemic architecture, and especially the domestic political costs of the status quo in the United States—with their threat to the open global trading system—all call for such action. We recommend that the new administration and Congress move in these directions as promptly as possible.

Appendix A
Data Sources and Annual Data on Currency Manipulation

Table A.1 shows the net official stocks, the net official flows, and the current account as a percent of GDP from 2000 through 2016 for the 20 economies that engaged in currency manipulation for at least one year between 2003 and 2016.

The principal sources of data for this book are the IMF's *Balance of Payments* (BOP), *International Financial Statistics* (IFS), *International Reserves* (RES), and *World Economic Outlook* (WEO) databases and the World Bank's *World Development Indicators* (WDI) database. The primary source for aggregate international assets and liabilities is the External Wealth of Nations (EWN) database of Lane and Milesi-Ferretti (www.imf.org/external/pubs/ft/wp/2006/data/update/wp0669.zip). The primary source for the indicator of capital mobility is Aizenman, Chinn, and Ito (2015). We filled in missing observations with data from alternate sources where available.

Most data are annual. Higher-frequency data are obtained from Haver Analytics where necessary.

We updated all data in October 2016, with the exception of the 2016 foreign exchange reserves (RES) data, which we updated in January 2017.

Net official assets are the sum of foreign exchange reserves and nonreserve official foreign assets minus official foreign liabilities. For advanced economies (as defined by the IMF) official foreign liabilities are assumed to be in local currency and are not subtracted from official foreign assets. Holdings and purchases of net official assets affect the exchange rate only to the extent that the government changes the net supply of foreign currency in the market.

The primary source for foreign exchange reserves is "Reserve Assets, Other Reserve Assets, US Dollars" from the BOP database. This series excludes gold, special drawing rights (SDRs), and accounts at the IMF. We filled in missing observations with data from the same series in local currency converted by the end-of-period exchange rate or by subtracting gold, SDRs, and IMF accounts from total reserves where available. We also used "Official Reserve Assets, Foreign Currency Reserves (converted to dollars from SDRs)" and "Total Reserves Excluding Gold, Foreign Exchange, US Dollars" data from the IFS database. Where no measure of reserves that focuses on foreign exchange was available, we sometimes used broader measures, namely the IFS series on "Total Reserves Excluding Gold" or "Official Reserve Assets."[1] Where data were available, we added long forward and futures positions to reserves and subtracted short positions.[2] Forward and futures positions come from the RES database. We estimated data for 2016 using the most recent observation (June, September, October, November, or December 2016) and extrapolating at a constant monthly growth rate to December.

Where available, nonreserve official foreign assets are the sum of "portfolio assets," "other assets," and "financial derivatives" held by the central bank or general government.[3] For observations in which the central bank category was missing, we used the equivalent entry under "monetary authority" if available. We defined nonreserve official liabilities in a similar way (for nonadvanced economies). We used the highest levels of aggregation where available; where higher-level data were not available, we aggregated data at lower levels.[4] When aggregating over lower-level categories, some of which are missing for some countries, we assumed missing values were equal to zero. Net nonreserve official assets are the difference between gross assets and liabilities. We filled in missing data for 2015 by adding 2015 nonreserve flows to 2014 stocks where available. We set estimates for 2016

---

1. We backcast Guatemalan reserve data before 2005 using reserve flows.

2. We did not include forward positions for the United States, Japan, and the euro area, because they are significant only for periods in which central bank currency swaps were active. The accounting treatment of these swaps does not appear consistent across central banks. Because the swaps involved exactly offsetting short and long positions, they do not affect the net positions of these institutions and are thus excluded from both reserves and nonreserve official assets. The swaps do not appear to have distorted the official data of other central banks.

3. Nonreserve official assets are small in the euro area and Japan except for the swap lines. We set them equal to zero. We set the central bank portion of nonreserve assets to zero in the United States for the same reason.

4. We backcast nonreserve stocks for Barbados before 2008 and for Suriname before 2011 using nonreserve flows.

equal to 2015 values (i.e., we assumed 2016 nonreserve flows were zero, except for Norway, for which we used Ministry of Finance data).

Reporting of the nonreserve official categories of foreign assets and liabilities is missing or incomplete for many countries. In general, we used external public debt data from the World Bank to fill in official liabilities of many developing economies. We used information on sovereign wealth funds (SWFs) from various sources to fill in official assets of countries with such funds.

We filled in missing values of nonreserve official liabilities with the value of WDI public and publicly guaranteed (PPG) external debt. For the following countries, we replaced all observations of net nonreserve official assets with –1 times WDI PPG external debt, because the BOP data had gaps and/or appeared to be incomplete: Angola, Bangladesh, Belize, Bhutan, Botswana, Brazil, Cambodia, Cameroon, Costa Rica, the Dominican Republic, Ecuador, Fiji, Georgia, Indonesia, Jamaica, Lebanon, Mexico, Nicaragua, Nigeria, Sri Lanka, Tajikistan, Turkey, and Zambia. For Benin we used WDI data starting in 2014. In Sudan the BOP data start in 2003 but appear to be more complete than the WDI data; to avoid a break in the series, we set the net nonreserve official assets as missing before 2003.

For Taiwan we obtained foreign exchange reserves from the central bank and assumed net nonreserve official assets to be zero.

Several countries have SWFs that are not included in the official BOP asset data. For the following countries, we set net nonreserve official assets equal to estimates of foreign assets held by SWFs from Stone and Truman (2016) for 2015 and the Sovereign Wealth Center (www.sovereignwealthcenter.com) for 2002, 2007, 2012, and 2014 (where available): Bahrain, Brunei, Malaysia, New Zealand, Oman, Qatar, and the United Arab Emirates. We interpolated missing observations between 2002 and 2015. These countries had no reported external public debt.

Algeria, Hong Kong, and Russia include assets of SWFs in reserves. Chile moved SWF assets out of reserves in 2006; before 2006 nonreserve assets are zero.

Saudi Arabia moved SWF assets into reserves in 2005; reported nonreserve stocks and flows are zero from 2005 on. We used reserve stock and flow data to construct a nonreserve stock in 2004 and the perpetual inventory method with nonreserve flows to fill in earlier dates.

Azerbaijan reports SWF assets in BOP data for 2007–08 only. We constructed values for other years using the perpetual inventory method on BOP nonreserve official flows.

We constructed nonreserve assets for Botswana and Kazakhstan using the Stone and Truman (2016) estimate for 2015 and the perpetual inventory method on nonreserve flows. These flows appear to reflect only SWF purchases and not official borrowing. We took nonreserve liabilities from WDI PPG external debt.

We constructed net nonreserve assets for Kuwait and Libya from the Stone and Truman (2016) estimates for 2015 and the perpetual inventory method on nonreserve flows.

China established an SWF in 2007. We took estimates of its value in 2007, 2012, 2014, and 2015 from Stone and Truman (2016) and the Sovereign Wealth Center, interpolating the missing values between 2007 and 2015. The People's Bank of China reports "other foreign assets" that are not included in the SWF (Setser and Pandey 2009). We added them to, and subtracted WDI PPG external debt from, net nonreserve assets.

The Singapore Ministry of Finance at one time reported total financial assets of the Singapore government for March 2010 of SGD 650 billion.[5] We subtracted Temasek's reported local assets of SGD 60 billion as of the same date (www.temasek.com.sg) and converted the figures using the end-2009 exchange rate to get an estimate of end-2009 net foreign assets. We subtracted reserves to get net nonreserve assets in 2009 and used the perpetual inventory method to construct net nonreserve assets in other years.[6]

We used total assets of the Pension Fund Global as our estimate of net nonreserve official assets of Norway, based on data from Norges Bank.

We took reserve assets for Trinidad and Tobago from the central bank website. The country set up an SWF in 2007. We took estimates for 2007, 2012, 2014, and 2015 from Stone and Truman (2016) and the Sovereign Wealth Center, interpolating missing values.

Net official flows are the sum of foreign exchange reserve flows and net nonreserve official flows. Consistent with our treatment of official assets, for advanced economies (as defined by the IMF), we assumed that official foreign liability flows are in local currency and did not subtract them from official foreign asset flows.

Financial flows are defined to include purchases and sales of assets, extension and repayment of loans, and reinvested income earned on assets. This definition of flows ensures that the current account equals the financial account in principle. Flows do not include changes in the market valuation of existing assets. However, to fill in missing observations, we some-

---

5. This balance sheet is no longer available on the ministry's website, but we kept a paper copy.

6. The resulting estimate for Singapore net official assets in 2015 ($571 billion) is consistent with Stone and Truman's (2016) estimate of Singapore SWF holdings of $502 billion, considering that Singapore's SWF holdings include an undisclosed fraction of its foreign exchange reserves of $281 billion. Thus we would expect to find net official assets somewhere between $502 billion and $787 billion.

times used the approximation that flows equal the change in stocks or that stocks can be estimated over time from the cumulated flows. In its *External Sector Reports*, the IMF model of global current account balances uses the change in the stock of foreign exchange reserves as its estimate of net official flows. The IMF approach ignores the effects of nonreserve official flows.

The primary source for foreign exchange reserve flows is BOP "Financial Account, Reserve Assets, US Dollars." Where available, we took missing observations from BOP "Supplementary Items, Reserves and Related Assets, US Dollars," BOP "Financial Account, Reserve Assets with Fund Record, US Dollars," and IFS "Supplementary Items, Reserve Assets with Fund Record." Where data were available, we added changes in long forward and futures positions to reserve flows and subtracted changes in short positions.[7] Forward and futures positions come from the RES database. We estimated data for 2016 using the most recent available observation (June or September 2016), extrapolating at a constant monthly growth rate to December.

We took nonreserve official flows from "portfolio flows," "other flows," and "financial derivatives flows" for the central bank and general government, analogously to the nonreserve official stocks described above. We removed debt relief, as measured by BOP "Capital Account, Capital Transfers, Net," from central bank and government flows.[8]

Coverage of nonreserve official flows is somewhat better than for nonreserve official stocks, including for countries with SWFs. We filled in missing values of net nonreserve official flows with changes in net nonreserve official stocks.

We assumed that Norway's net nonreserve official flows are equal to the sum of government transfers into and earnings on the assets in the Pension Fund Global, as reported by the Norwegian Ministry of Finance in the annual budget.

Data on the *current account* are from BOP. We filled in missing values with data from IFS or WEO.

Data on *gross domestic product* (in US dollars, nominal local currency, and real local currency) are from WEO.

Data on the *fiscal balance* (defined as general government net lending/borrowing as a percentage of GDP) are from WEO.

Tariff rate data are from WDI. They are the simple mean (in percent) of the tariff rates on all products a country imports.

---

7. We did not include changes in forward positions for the United States, Japan, and the euro area because they are significant only for periods in which central bank currency swaps were active. See footnote 2.

8. Debt relief data for Liberia and Madagascar were missing from the capital account data. We set net nonreserve flows equal to zero for Liberia in 2008-11 and for Madagascar in 2006.

Data on the *consumer price index* (CPI) are from WEO.

Data on the *unemployment rate* are from WEO.

Money market interest rates are from Haver. The exact definition varies by country and is listed in each figure.

10-year government bond yields are from Haver.

Real housing indices are from Haver. The exact definition varies by country and is listed in each figure. All housing indices are deflated by the all-items CPI for each country.

Real equity indices are from Haver. The exact definition varies by country and is listed in each figure. All equity indices are deflated by the all-items CPI for each country.

Exchange rates (annual average) are from the WEO as the primary source. They are generated by dividing current prices GDP in national currency by current prices GDP in dollars. We used the dollar-euro exchange rate from IFS for the euro area for 1999–2015. We filled in missing data with data from IFS or EWN where available.

The primary source for end-of-period exchange rates is IFS national currency per dollar. We filled in missing data using the reciprocal of the IFS dollar per national currency figure or data from EWN where available. We set remaining missing values equal to the annual average exchange rate.

The WEO data for Liberia and Myanmar's exchange rate included errors. We replaced the average exchange rate for the period with end-of-period values for all years for Liberia and 1998–2011 for Myanmar.

Real effective exchange rates (REERs), based on the CPI, are from IFS. We extrapolated them for 2016 using the JPMorgan Chase CPI-based REER from Haver. Korea's REER is missing for all years in the IFS; we used the JPMorgan Chase REER.

The *net international investment position* is the difference between a country's external financial assets and its liabilities. The primary source is EWN. We filled in missing values using BOP data.

Data on *external liabilities, portfolio debt liabilities,* and *other investment liabilities* are from EWN. We filled in missing values using BOP data.

Data on *goods and services exports and imports* are from BOP goods and services credits and debits, respectively. We filled in missing data by adding up goods and services separately or using data in local currency, where available, and by using data from IFS. We extrapolated data for 2014 and 2015 based on WDI merchandise trade where necessary.

We took data for Argentina, Brazil, Egypt, and Taiwan from national central bank websites. Data for Trinidad and Tobago for 2012–15 are missing. Its central bank website shows little change in net services trade over this period, so we extrapolated both exports and imports using WDI data on merchandise trade.

Data on the *money supply* are based on the M2 definition from WDI. We filled in missing data using IFS, including local currency data or the M3 definition where necessary. Data for Canada, Norway, and the euro area are from Haver. Data for Israel are from the Federal Reserve Bank of St. Louis FRED database. Data for Taiwan are from the central bank. We corrected an error for Zambia in 2001–02.

Net energy exports are from WDI energy exports and imports as a share of merchandise trade times the value of merchandise trade. We replaced some apparent errors for Bahrain, Kuwait, and the United Arab Emirates by interpolating between years with correct data. Data for Trinidad and Tobago are from the central bank website. Data for Angola, Gabon, and Libya are from the Gagnon et al. (2017) dataset, which is based on an earlier vintage of the WDI data.

Data on *capital mobility* are from Aizenman, Chinn, and Ito (2015).

Financial integration is constructed from BOP data. It is the sum of the absolute value of gross private financial flows relative to the absolute values of gross private financial flows and gross current account flows.

Table A.1   Net official stocks, net official flows, and the current account balance of currency manipulators, 2000–16

Country/ year	Net official stocks		Net official flows		Current account	
	Billions of US dollars	Percent of GDP	Billions of US dollars	Percent of GDP	Billions of US dollars	Percent of GDP
Manufacturing exporters						
China						
2000	80	7	14	1	21	2
2001	131	10	51	4	17	1
2002	209	14	75	5	35	2
2003	332	20	108	6	43	3
2004	532	27	187	10	69	4
2005	748	32	257	11	132	6
2006	997	36	286	10	232	8
2007	1,619	45	621	17	353	10
2008	2,108	46	550	12	421	9
2009	2,531	49	370	7	243	5
2010	2,980	49	473	8	238	4
2011	3,304	44	378	5	136	2
2012	3,445	40	107	1	215	3
2013	4,023	42	499	5	148	2
2014	4,059	38	113	1	277	3
2015	3,480	31	−337	−3	331	3
2016	3,123	27	−357	−3	271	2
Israel						
2000	23	17	1	0	−2	−2
2001	25	19	1	1	−2	−2
2002	25	21	1	1	−1	−1
2003	28	22	2	2	1	1
2004	28	21	1	1	7	5
2005	28	20	−1	−1	4	3
2006	29	19	1	1	7	4
2007	28	16	−1	0	6	3
2008	43	20	14	6	3	1
2009	59	29	17	8	8	4
2010	70	30	10	4	8	3
2011	74	28	4	2	7	3

Table A.1   Net official stocks, net official flows, and the current account balance of currency manipulators, 2000–16 *(continued)*

Country/ year	Net official stocks		Net official flows		Current account	
	Billions of US dollars	Percent of GDP	Billions of US dollars	Percent of GDP	Billions of US dollars	Percent of GDP
Manufacturing exporters						
Israel *(continued)*						
2012	75	29	1	0	1	1
2013	80	27	6	2	10	3
2014	85	27	4	1	12	4
2015	89	30	5	2	14	5
2016	98	31	9	3	10	3
Japan						
2000	347	7	49	1	131	3
2001	386	9	40	1	86	2
2002	449	11	46	1	109	3
2003	652	15	187	4	139	3
2004	822	18	161	3	182	4
2005	825	18	22	0	170	4
2006	874	20	32	1	175	4
2007	943	22	37	1	212	5
2008	998	21	31	1	142	3
2009	999	20	27	1	146	3
2010	1037	19	44	1	221	4
2011	1219	21	177	3	130	2
2012	1190	20	−38	−1	60	1
2013	1204	25	39	1	46	1
2014	1192	26	8	0	36	1
2015	1179	29	5	0	136	3
2016	1162	25	−17	0	176	4
Korea						
2000	96	17	24	4	10	2
2001	103	19	8	1	3	1
2002	121	20	12	2	5	1
2003	155	23	26	4	12	2
2004	201	26	40	5	30	4

(table continues)

Table A.1   Net official stocks, net official flows, and the current account balance of currency manipulators, 2000–16 *(continued)*

Country/year	Net official stocks Billions of US dollars	Net official stocks Percent of GDP	Net official flows Billions of US dollars	Net official flows Percent of GDP	Current account Billions of US dollars	Current account Percent of GDP
Manufacturing exporters						
Korea *(continued)*						
2005	249	28	49	5	13	1
2006	278	27	20	2	4	0
2007	301	27	13	1	12	1
2008	208	21	–72	–7	3	0
2009	287	32	84	9	34	4
2010	350	32	74	7	29	3
2011	344	29	3	0	19	2
2012	366	30	31	3	51	4
2013	396	30	43	3	81	6
2014	427	30	47	3	84	6
2015	420	30	10	1	106	8
2016	414	29	–6	0	102	7
Malaysia						
2000	10	10	0	0	8	8
2001	6	6	–3	–3	7	7
2002	9	8	–3	2	7	7
2003	18	15	9	7	13	11
2004	44	33	26	20	15	11
2005	41	28	–5	–3	21	14
2006	50	30	4	3	26	16
2007	79	40	22	11	30	15
2008	50	21	–22	–9	39	17
2009	53	25	1	1	31	15
2010	64	25	0	0	26	10
2011	92	31	33	11	32	11
2012	94	30	–3	–1	16	5
2013	82	25	–2	–1	11	3
2014	65	19	–10	–3	15	4
2015	89	30	–5	–2	9	3
2016	93	31	3	1	4	1

Table A.1   Net official stocks, net official flows, and the current account balance of currency manipulators, 2000–16 *(continued)*

Country/ year	Net official stocks		Net official flows		Current account	
	Billions of US dollars	Percent of GDP	Billions of US dollars	Percent of GDP	Billions of US dollars	Percent of GDP
Manufacturing exporters						
Sweden						
2000	19	7	−1	0	12	4
2001	18	8	1	1	15	6
2002	23	9	1	1	12	5
2003	27	8	2	1	23	7
2004	31	8	2	0	25	7
2005	28	7	4	1	26	7
2006	32	8	3	1	35	8
2007	36	7	4	1	43	9
2008	48	9	21	4	45	9
2009	48	11	−8	−2	25	6
2010	48	10	−2	0	29	6
2011	50	9	1	0	34	6
2012	55	10	3	0	32	6
2013	68	12	13	2	35	6
2014	64	11	7	1	31	5
2015	60	12	4	1	28	6
2016	61	12	1	0	26	5
Taiwan						
2000	107	32	1	0	9	3
2001	122	41	15	5	19	6
2002	162	52	39	13	26	9
2003	207	65	45	14	31	10
2004	242	69	35	10	20	6
2005	253	67	12	3	18	5
2006	266	68	13	3	26	7
2007	270	66	4	1	35	9
2008	292	70	21	5	27	7
2009	348	89	56	14	42	11
2010	382	86	34	8	40	9
2011	386	79	4	1	40	8

(table continues)

Table A.1 Net official stocks, net official flows, and the current account balance of currency manipulators, 2000–16 *(continued)*

Country/ year	Net official stocks		Net official flows		Current account	
	Billions of US dollars	Percent of GDP	Billions of US dollars	Percent of GDP	Billions of US dollars	Percent of GDP
Manufacturing exporters						
Taiwan *(continued)*						
2012	403	81	18	4	47	10
2013	417	81	14	3	53	10
2014	419	79	2	0	63	12
2015	426	81	7	1	76	15
2016	440	85	14	3	78	15
Thailand						
2000	19	15	–4	–3	9	7
2001	23	19	1	1	5	4
2002	34	25	2	3	5	3
2003	48	31	4	2	5	3
2004	36	21	4	2	3	2
2005	38	20	5	3	–8	–4
2006	74	33	16	7	2	1
2007	107	41	32	12	16	6
2008	119	41	12	4	1	0
2009	154	55	32	11	21	7
2010	192	56	29	9	10	3
2011	207	56	9	2	9	2
2012	206	52	–9	–2	–1	0
2013	190	45	–6	–2	–5	–1
2014	180	45	1	0	15	4
2015	168	42	–2	–1	32	8
2016	199	51	32	8	38	10
Financial centers						
Hong Kong						
2000	102	60	13	7	8	4
2001	105	62	4	2	10	6
2002	107	64	–1	–1	13	8
2003	112	70	0	0	17	11
2004	116	69	2	2	17	10

Table A.1   Net official stocks, net official flows, and the current account balance of currency manipulators, 2000–16 *(continued)*

Country/ year	Net official stocks		Net official flows		Current account	
	Billions of US dollars	Percent of GDP	Billions of US dollars	Percent of GDP	Billions of US dollars	Percent of GDP
Financial centers						
Hong Kong *(continued)*						
2005	114	63	−2	−1	22	12
2006	127	65	10	5	25	13
2007	139	66	8	4	28	13
2008	166	76	31	14	33	15
2009	245	115	77	36	21	10
2010	257	112	8	3	16	7
2011	270	109	11	4	14	6
2012	301	114	24	9	4	2
2013	311	113	7	3	4	2
2014	328	113	18	6	4	1
2015	359	116	36	12	10	3
2016	381	121	22	7	9	3
Macao						
2000	3	n.a.	0	n.a.	n.a.	n.a.
2001	4	52	0	3	n.a.	n.a.
2002	4	52	0	4	2	32
2003	4	53	1	9	2	31
2004	6	52	1	11	4	33
2005	7	57	1	12	3	24
2006	9	62	2	15	2	15
2007	13	72	4	20	4	22
2008	16	76	2	11	3	16
2009	18	85	2	10	6	28
2010	24	84	5	17	11	39
2011	34	93	10	27	15	41
2012	22	51	11	26	17	39
2013	16	31	9	17	21	40
2014	22	40	10	18	19	34
2015	27	59	5	10	13	28
2016	27	62	0	0	12	28

(table continues)

**Table A.1   Net official stocks, net official flows, and the current
account balance of currency manipulators, 2000–16**
(continued)

Country/ year	Net official stocks		Net official flows		Current account	
	Billions of US dollars	Percent of GDP	Billions of US dollars	Percent of GDP	Billions of US dollars	Percent of GDP
Financial centers						
Singapore						
2000	170	177	12	13	10	11
2001	162	182	–4	–4	12	14
2002	169	184	1	1	12	13
2003	197	203	21	21	22	23
2004	231	202	30	26	21	18
2005	248	194	26	20	28	22
2006	316	214	65	44	37	25
2007	379	211	55	31	47	26
2008	371	193	–6	–3	28	15
2009	421	219	47	24	33	17
2010	495	209	80	34	56	24
2011	573	208	82	30	62	23
2012	598	207	29	10	52	18
2013	603	201	9	3	54	18
2014	579	189	–2	–1	54	17
2015	571	195	–4	–2	58	20
2016	582	196	11	4	57	19
Switzerland						
2000	36	13	–3	–1	34	12
2001	37	13	0	0	24	9
2002	45	15	–3	–1	27	9
2003	53	15	–1	0	47	13
2004	63	16	0	0	60	15
2005	76	19	–9	–2	58	14
2006	81	19	0	0	64	15
2007	98	21	2	0	51	11
2008	82	15	–61	–11	17	3
2009	151	28	122	23	44	8
2010	247	43	126	22	87	15
2011	282	40	26	4	53	8

Table A.1   Net official stocks, net official flows, and the current account balance of currency manipulators, 2000–16 *(continued)*

Country/ year	Net official stocks		Net official flows		Current account	
	Billions of US dollars	Percent of GDP	Billions of US dollars	Percent of GDP	Billions of US dollars	Percent of GDP
Financial centers						
Switzerland *(continued)*						
2012	499	75	213	32	69	10
2013	522	76	13	2	76	11
2014	539	77	35	5	62	9
2015	618	93	100	15	76	11
2016	699	106	81	12	61	9
Resource exporters						
Algeria						
2000	−11	−21	8	14	9	17
2001	−3	−5	6	11	7	13
2002	2	3	5	9	4	8
2003	11	16	10	14	9	13
2004	23	27	10	12	11	13
2005	41	39	20	19	21	21
2006	74	63	29	25	29	25
2007	106	79	30	22	30	22
2008	140	82	37	22	34	20
2009	144	105	4	3	0	0
2010	158	98	15	10	12	8
2011	178	89	20	10	18	9
2012	187	90	12	6	12	6
2013	191	91	0	0	1	1
2014	176	83	−6	−3	−10	−4
2015	141	85	−28	−17	−27	−16
2016	141	84	0	0	−25	−15
Kuwait						
2000	63	167	13	35	15	39
2001	70	199	7	19	8	24
2002	72	190	3	8	4	11
2003	77	161	12	26	9	20
2004	84	142	10	16	16	26

(table continues)

Table A.1 Net official stocks, net official flows, and the current account balance of currency manipulators, 2000–16 *(continued)*

Country/ year	Net official stocks		Net official flows		Current account	
	Billions of US dollars	Percent of GDP	Billions of US dollars	Percent of GDP	Billions of US dollars	Percent of GDP
Resource exporters						
Kuwait *(continued)*						
2005	98	122	21	26	30	37
2006	120	118	39	38	45	45
2007	139	121	30	26	42	37
2008	156	105	37	25	60	41
2009	163	154	20	19	28	27
2010	173	150	40	34	37	32
2011	191	124	49	32	66	43
2012	212	122	69	40	79	45
2013	301	173	57	33	69	40
2014	371	228	43	26	54	33
2015	372	326	1	1	6	5
2016	374	338	2	1	4	4
Libya						
2000	11	30	5	14	6	16
2001	14	40	1	3	3	10
2002	13	64	1	6	1	3
2003	18	70	5	20	3	13
2004	24	74	6	18	5	14
2005	38	81	14	29	15	32
2006	80	146	19	35	22	40
2007	109	161	28	42	29	42
2008	130	149	22	25	36	41
2009	142	225	12	19	9	15
2010	150	201	12	16	17	22
2011	158	457	6	18	3	9
2012	178	217	19	23	24	29
2013	179	271	−2	−3	0	0
2014	153	345	−26	−58	−12	−28
2015	138	348	−15	−39	−17	−42
2016	133	339	−5	−12	−19	−47

Table A.1   Net official stocks, net official flows, and the current account balance of currency manipulators, 2000–16 *(continued)*

Country/ year	Net official stocks		Net official flows		Current account	
	Billions of US dollars	Percent of GDP	Billions of US dollars	Percent of GDP	Billions of US dollars	Percent of GDP
			Resource exporters			
Norway						
2000	70	41	20	12	25	15
2001	91	52	27	16	28	16
2002	118	60	24	12	24	12
2003	163	72	20	9	28	12
2004	211	80	28	11	33	12
2005	252	82	42	14	50	16
2006	341	99	62	18	56	16
2007	434	108	58	15	50	12
2008	380	82	88	19	73	16
2009	503	130	38	10	45	12
2010	578	135	42	10	50	12
2011	601	121	63	13	66	13
2012	735	144	71	14	64	12
2013	883	169	64	12	53	10
2014	928	185	58	11	60	12
2015	903	233	23	6	34	9
2016	902	240	13	3	26	7
Oman						
2000	6	31	6	31	3	17
2001	8	43	3	17	2	11
2002	10	52	2	8	2	10
2003	11	52	1	5	1	7
2004	11	47	1	5	1	4
2005	14	45	5	15	5	17
2006	16	46	4	12	6	16
2007	18	43	3	7	2	6
2008	24	41	7	11	5	8
2009	24	51	0	0	−1	−1
2010	30	54	7	13	5	9
2011	42	63	12	18	9	13

(table continues)

Table A.1   Net official stocks, net official flows, and the current account balance of currency manipulators, 2000–16 *(continued)*

Country/ year	Net official stocks		Net official flows		Current account	
	Billions of US dollars	Percent of GDP	Billions of US dollars	Percent of GDP	Billions of US dollars	Percent of GDP
Resource exporters						
Oman *(continued)*						
2012	27	36	−14	−19	8	10
2013	41	53	25	32	5	7
2014	52	64	12	15	4	5
2015	51	80	−2	−3	−11	−17
2016	59	99	8	13	−13	−21
Russia						
2000	−21	−8	29	10	45	16
2001	−12	−4	23	7	32	10
2002	−1	0	25	7	27	7
2003	26	6	35	8	33	7
2004	83	13	50	8	59	9
2005	142	17	90	11	84	10
2006	262	25	135	13	92	9
2007	437	31	156	11	72	5
2008	387	22	−39	−2	104	6
2009	376	29	4	0	50	4
2010	402	25	35	2	67	4
2011	409	20	12	1	97	5
2012	404	19	1	0	71	3
2013	384	17	−32	−1	33	1
2014	296	15	−93	−5	58	3
2015	284	21	9	1	69	5
2016	291	23	7	1	39	3
Trinidad and Tobago						
2000	2	20	0	5	1	7
2001	2	24	1	6	0	5
2002	2	25	0	0	0	1
2003	3	23	0	2	1	9
2004	3	25	1	6	2	14
2005	5	34	2	11	4	24

Table A.1 Net official stocks, net official flows, and the current account balance of currency manipulators, 2000–16 *(continued)*

Country/ year	Net official stocks		Net official flows		Current account	
	Billions of US dollars	**Percent of GDP**	**Billions of US dollars**	**Percent of GDP**	**Billions of US dollars**	**Percent of GDP**
Resource exporters						

Trinidad and Tobago *(continued)*

Country/ year	Billions of US dollars	Percent of GDP	Billions of US dollars	Percent of GDP	Billions of US dollars	Percent of GDP
2006	6	35	1	8	7	39
2007	9	40	3	15	5	24
2008	11	40	2	8	8	30
2009	12	61	1	5	2	9
2010	13	58	1	6	4	19
2011	14	54	1	3	3	11
2012	14	54	0	1	1	3
2013	16	60	2	7	2	7
2014	17	61	1	3	1	5
2015	16	64	−1	−4	−1	−5
2016	15	66	−1	−4	−2	−9
United Arab Emirates						
2000	14	13	3	3	27	26
2001	14	14	1	1	15	15
2002	176	160	1	1	7	6
2003	199	160	23	19	9	8
2004	231	156	32	21	13	9
2005	308	170	77	43	31	17
2006	429	193	122	55	50	22
2007	508	197	79	31	32	13
2008	532	169	23	7	22	7
2009	540	213	8	3	8	3
2010	553	193	13	4	12	4
2011	599	172	47	13	44	13
2012	677	181	78	21	74	20
2013	863	222	185	48	74	19
2014	963	240	101	25	40	10
2015	1228	332	264	71	12	3
2016	1213	323	−15	−4	4	1

n.a. = not available

References

Acemoglu, Daron, David Autor, David Dorn, Gordon Hanson, and Brendan Price. 2016. Import Competition and the Great US Employment Sag of the 2000s. *Journal of Labor Economics* 34, no. S1: S141–98.

Adler, Gustavo, Noemie Lisack, and Rui Mano. 2015. *Unveiling the Effects of Foreign Exchange Intervention: A Panel Approach.* IMF Working Paper 15/130. Washington: International Monetary Fund.

Ahearne, Alan, Joseph Gagnon, Jane Haltmaier, Steve Kamin, and others. 2002. *Preventing Deflation: Lessons from Japan's Experiences in the 1990s.* International Finance Discussion Paper No. 729. Washington: Board of Governors of the Federal Reserve System.

Aizenman, Joshua, Menzie Chinn, and Hiro Ito. 2015. The Trilemma Indexes. Available at http://web.pdx.edu/~ito/trilemma_indexes.htm.

Andrle, Michal, Patrick Blagrave, Pedro Espaillat, Keiko Honjo, Benjamin L. Hunt, Mika Kortelainen, René Lalonde, Douglas Laxton, Eleonora Mavroeidi, Dirk Muir, Susanna Mursula, and Stephen Snudden. 2015. *The Flexible System of Global Models (FSGM).* IMF Working Paper 15/64. Washington: International Monetary Fund.

Armington, Paul S. 1969. *A Theory of Demand for Products Distinguished by Place of Production.* IMF Staff Paper 16, no. 1: 159–78. Washington: International Monetary Fund.

Autor, David H., David Dorn, and Gordon Hanson. 2016. *The China Shock: Learning from Labor Market Adjustment to Large Changes in Trade.* NBER Working Paper 21906. Cambridge, MA: National Bureau of Economic Research.

Autor, David H., David Dorn, Gordon Hanson, and Kaveh Majlesi. 2016. *Importing Political Polarization? The Electoral Consequences of Rising Trade Exposure.* NBER Working Paper 22637. Cambridge, MA: National Bureau of Economic Research.

Autor, David H., David Dorn, Gordon Hanson, and Kaveh Majlesi. 2017. A Note on the Effect of Rising Trade Exposure on the 2016 Presidential Election. Appendix to *Importing Political Polarization? The Electoral Consequences of Rising Trade Exposure.* NBER Working Paper 22637. Cambridge, MA: National Bureau of Economic Research.

Autor, David H., David Dorn, Gordon Hanson, and Jae Song. 2014. Trade Adjustment: Work-Level Evidence. *Quarterly Journal of Economics* 129, no. 4: 1799–860.

Ball, Laurence, Joseph Gagnon, Patrick Honohan, and Signe Krogstrup. 2016. *What Else Can Central Banks Do?* Geneva Report on the World Economy 18. Geneva and London: International Center for Monetary and Banking Studies and Centre for Economic Policy Research.

Bayoumi, Tamim, Joseph Gagnon, and Christian Saborowski. 2015. Official Financial Flows, Capital Mobility, and Global Imbalances. *Journal of International Money and Finance* 52 (April): 146–74.

Bayoumi, Tamim, and Franziska L. Ohnsorge. 2013. *Do Inflows or Outflows Dominate? Global Implications of Capital Account Liberalization in China.* IMF Working Paper 13/189. Washington: International Monetary Fund.

Berg, A., E. Borensztein, G. M. Milesi-Ferretti, and C. Pattillo. 2000. *Anticipating Balance of Payments Crises: The Role of Early Warning Systems.* IMF Occasional Paper 186. Washington: International Monetary Fund.

Berg, A., R. Portillo, S. Yang, and L. F. Zanna. 2012. *Public Investment in Resource-Abundant Developing Countries.* IMF Working Paper 12/274. Washington: International Monetary Fund.

Bergsten, C. Fred. 1996. *Dilemmas of the Dollar: Economics and Politics of United States International Monetary Policy.* New York: Council on Foreign Relations.

Bergsten, C. Fred. 2002. The Correction of the Dollar and Foreign Intervention in Currency Markets. Testimony before the US House of Representatives, Washington, June 25.

Bergsten, C. Fred. 2005. *The United States and the World Economy: Foreign Economic Policy for the Next Decade.* Washington: Institute for International Economics.

Bergsten, C. Fred. 2007. The Chinese Exchange Rate and the US Economy. Testimony before the Senate Committee on Banking, Housing and Urban Affairs, Washington, January 31.

Bergsten, C. Fred. 2014. *Addressing Currency Manipulation through Trade Agreements.* PIIE Policy Brief 14-2. Washington: Peterson Institute for International Economics.

Bergsten, C. Fred. 2015. The Revenge of Helmut Schmidt. *International Economy* (Spring). Available at www.international-economy.com/TIE_Sp15_Bergsten.pdf.

Bergsten, C. Fred. 2016. Time for a Plaza II? In *International Monetary Cooperation: Lessons from the Plaza Accord after Thirty Years,* ed. C. Fred Bergsten and Russell A. Green. Washington: Peterson Institute for International Economics.

Bergsten, C. Fred, and Joseph E. Gagnon. 2012. *Currency Manipulation, the US Economy, and the Global Economic Order.* PIIE Policy Brief 12-25. Washington: Peterson Institute for International Economics.

Bergsten, C. Fred, and Joseph E. Gagnon. 2016. The New US Currency Policy. RealTime Economic Issues Watch blog, April 29. Washington: Peterson Institute for International Economics.

Bergsten, C. Fred, and Russell A. Green, eds. 2016. *International Monetary Cooperation: Lessons from the Plaza Accord after Thirty Years.* Washington: Peterson Institute for International Economics.

Bergsten, C. Fred, Gary C. Hufbauer, and Sean Miner. 2014. *Bridging the Pacific: Toward Free Trade and Investment Between China and the United States.* Washington: Peterson Institute for International Economics.

Bergsten, C. Fred, and John Williamson. 1983. Exchange Rates and Trade Policy. In *Trade Policy in the 1980s*, ed. William Cline. Washington: Institute for International Economics.

Bhalla, Surjit S. 2012. *Devaluing to Prosperity: Misaligned Currencies and Their Growth Consequences.* Washington: Peterson Institute for International Economics.

Blanchard, Olivier J., Gustavo Adler, and Irineu de Cavalho Filho. 2015. *Can Foreign Exchange Intervention Stem Exchange Rate Pressures from Global Capital Flow Shocks?* NBER Working Paper 21427. Cambridge, MA: National Bureau of Economic Research.

Blustein, Paul. 2012. *Off Balance: The Travails of Institutions That Govern the Global Financial System.* Waterloo, ON: Centre for International Governance Innovation.

Bordo, Michael D., Owen F. Humpage, and Anna J. Schwartz. 2015. *Strained Relations: US Foreign Exchange Operations and Monetary Policy in the 20th Century.* Chicago and London: University of Chicago Press.

Bown, Chad. 2016. *Should the United States Recognize China as a Market Economy?* PIIE Policy Brief 16-24. Washington: Peterson Institute for International Economics.

CBO (Congressional Budget Office). 2016. *The Budgetary Effects of the United States' Participation in the International Monetary Fund* (June 16). Washington.

Cherif, R., and F. Hasanov. 2012. *Oil Exporters' Dilemma: How Much to Save and How Much to Invest.* IMF Working Paper 12/4. Washington: International Monetary Fund.

Chinn, Menzie D., and Eswar S. Prasad. 2003. Medium-Term Determinants of Current Accounts in Industrial and Developing Countries: An Empirical Exploration. *Journal of International Economics* 59, no. 1: 47–76.

Cline, William. 2005. *The United States as a Debtor Nation.* Washington: Institute for International Economics.

Cline, William R. 2016. *Estimates of Fundamental Equilibrium Exchange Rates, November 2016.* PIIE Policy Brief 16-22. Washington: Peterson Institute for International Economics.

Cline, William, and John Williamson. 2008. *New Estimates of Fundamental Equilibrium Exchange Rates.* PIIE Policy Brief 08-7 (July). Washington: Peterson Institute for International Economics.

Cline, William, and John Williamson. 2012. *Updated Estimates of Fundamental Equilibrium Exchange Rates.* PIIE Policy Brief 12-23 (November). Washington: Peterson Institute for International Economics.

Destler, I. M. 2005. *American Trade Politics,* 4th ed. Washington: Institute for International Economics.

Dominguez, Kathryn. 2003. Foreign Exchange Intervention: Did It Work in the 1990s? In *Dollar Overvaluation and the World Economy,* ed. C. Fred Bergsten and John Williamson. Washington: Institute for International Economics.

Dooley, Michael B., David Folkerts-Landau, and Peter Garber. 2004. *The Revived Bretton Woods System: The Effects of Periphery Intervention and Reserve Management on Interest Rates & Exchange Rates in Center Countries.* NBER Working Paper 10332. Cambridge, MA: National Bureau of Economic Research.

Edison, Hali. 1993. *The Effectiveness of Central Bank Intervention: A Survey of the Literature after 1982.* Princeton Studies in International Economics. Princeton, NJ: Department of Economics, Princeton University.

Eichengreen, Barry. 1992. *Golden Fetters: The Gold Standard and the Great Depression.* New York: Oxford University Press.

Ethier, Wilfred J., and Arthur I. Bloomfield. 1975. *Managing the Managed Float.* Princeton Essays in International Finance no. 112. Princeton, NJ: Princeton University.

European Commission. 2012. *Current Account Surpluses in the EU.* European Economy Series 9/2012. Brussels: Directorate-General for Economic and Financial Affairs.

Frankel, Jeffrey. 2008. Equilibrium Exchange Rate of the Renminbi. In *Debating China's Exchange Rate Policy*, ed. Morris Goldstein and Nicholas R. Lardy. Washington: Peterson Institute for International Economics.

Freund, Caroline L. 2000. *Current Account Adjustment in Industrialized Countries.* International Finance Discussion Paper 692. Washington: Board of Governors of the Federal Reserve System.

Freund, Caroline L. 2005. Current Account Adjustment in Industrial Countries. *Journal of International Money and Finance* 24, no. 8: 1278-98.

Gagnon, Joseph E. 2007. Productive Capacity, Product Varieties, and the Elasticities Approach to the Trade Balance. *Review of International Economics* 15, no. 4: 639-59.

Gagnon, Joseph E. 2011. *Flexible Exchange Rates for a Stable World Economy.* Washington: Peterson Institute for International Economics.

Gagnon, Joseph E. 2012. *Global Imbalances and Foreign Asset Expansion by Developing Economy Central Banks.* PIIE Working Paper 12-5. Washington: Peterson Institute for International Economics.

Gagnon, Joseph E. 2013. *The Elephant Hiding in the Room: Currency Intervention and Trade Imbalances.* PIIE Working Paper 13-2. Washington: Peterson Institute for International Economics.

Gagnon, Joseph E. 2014. *Alternatives to Currency Manipulation: What Switzerland, Singapore, and Hong Kong Can Do.* PIIE Policy Brief 14-7. Washington: Peterson Institute for International Economics.

Gagnon, Joseph E. 2016. Foreign Exchange Intervention since the Plaza Accord. In *International Monetary Cooperation: Lessons from the Plaza Accord after Thirty Years*, ed. C. Fred Bergsten and Russell A. Green. Washington: Peterson Institute for International Economics.

Gagnon, Joseph, Tamim Bayoumi, Juan M. Londono, Christian Saborowski, and Horacio Sapriza. 2017. Direct and Spillover Effects of Unconventional Monetary and Exchange Rate Policies. *Open Economies Review* 28: 191-232.

Gagnon, Joseph E., and Gary C. Hufbauer. 2011. Taxing China's Assets: How to Increase U.S. Employment without Launching a Trade War. *Foreign Affairs* (April 25).

Goldstein, Morris. 1998. *The Asian Financial Crisis: Causes, Cures, and Systemic Implications.* Policy Analysis in International Economics 55. Washington: Institute for International Economics.

Goldstein, Morris. 2004. *Adjusting China's Exchange Rate Policies.* Working Paper 04-1. Washington: Institute for International Economics.

Goldstein, Morris. 2006. The IMF as Global Umpire for Exchange Rate Policies. In *C. Fred Bergsten and the World Economy*, ed. Michael Mussa. Washington: Peterson Institute for International Economics.

Goldstein, Morris, and Mohsin Khan. 1985. Income and Price Effects in Foreign Trade. In *Handbook of International Economics*, vol. 2, ed. R. W. Jones and P. B. Kenen, 1041–105. Amsterdam: Elsevier.

Goldstein, Morris, Graciela Kaminsky, and Carmen Reinhart. 2000. *Assessing Financial Vulnerability: An Early Warning System for Emerging Markets*. Washington: Institute for International Economics.

Goldstein, Morris, and Nicholas R. Lardy, eds. 2008. *Debating China's Exchange Rate Policy*. Washington: Peterson Institute for International Economics.

Gourinchas, Pierre-Olivier, and Hélène Rey. 2007. From World Banker to World Venture Capitalist: US External Adjustment and the Exorbitant Privilege. In *G7 Current Account Imbalances: Sustainability and Adjustment*, ed. Richard Clarida. Cambridge, MA: National Bureau of Economic Research.

G-20 (Group of Twenty). 2013. G-20 Leaders' Declaration, St. Petersburg Summit, September 5–6.

G-20 (Group of Twenty). 2016. G-20 Leaders Communiqué, Hangzhou Summit, September 4–5.

Hellebrandt, Tomáš, Jacob Kirkegaard, Nicholas Lardy, Robert Lawrence, Paolo Mauro, Silvia Merler, Sean Miner, Jeffrey Schott, and Nicolas Véron. 2015. *China's Economic Transformation: Lessons, Impact, and the Path Forward*. PIIE Briefing 15-3. Washington: Peterson Institute for International Economics.

Henning, Randall C. 2008. *Accountability and Oversight of United States Exchange Rate Policy*. Washington: Peterson Institute for International Economics.

Hills, Carla A., Peter G. Peterson, and Morris Goldstein. 1999. *Safeguarding Prosperity in a Global Financial System: The Future International Financial Architecture*. Report of an Independent Task Force Sponsored by the Council on Foreign Relations. New York: Council on Foreign Relations.

Hufbauer, Gary C. 2016. *Could a President Trump Shackle Imports?* PIIE Policy Brief 16-6. Washington: Peterson Institute for International Economics.

Hufbauer, Gary, Y. Wong, and K. Sheth. 2006. *US-China Trade Disputes: Rising Tide, Rising Stakes*. Policy Analyses in International Economics 78. Washington: Institute for International Economics.

IMF (International Monetary Fund). 2009. *Cooperation between the IMF and the WTO*. Background Document 2. Washington: Independent Evaluation Office.

IMF (International Monetary Fund). 2011a. *Assessing Reserve Adequacy*. Monetary and Capital Markets, Research, and Strategy, Policy, and Review Departments (February 14). Washington.

IMF (International Monetary Fund). 2011b. *Consolidated Spillover Report: Implications from the Analysis of the Systemic 5* (July 11). Washington.

IMF (International Monetary Fund). 2012a. *External Balance Assessment (EBA): Technical Background of the Pilot Methodology* (August 3). Washington.

IMF (International Monetary Fund). 2012b. *IMF Survey: IMF Adopts Institutional View on Capital Flows* (December). Washington.

IMF (International Monetary Fund). 2013a. *Assessing Reserve Adequacy: Further Considerations*. IMF Policy Paper (November 13). Washington.

IMF (International Monetary Fund). 2013b. *Greece: Ex-Post Evaluation of Exception Access under the 2010 Stand-by Arrangement* (May 2). Washington.

IMF (International Monetary Fund). 2014. *People's Republic of China: Staff Report for the 2014 Article IV Consultation* (July 30). Washington.

IMF (International Monetary Fund). 2015a. *Assessing Reserve Adequacy: Specific Proposals.* IMF Policy Paper (April). Washington.

IMF (International Monetary Fund). 2015b. *Switzerland: Staff Report for the 2015 Article IV Consultation* (May 4). Washington.

IMF (International Monetary Fund). 2015c. Exchange Rate and Trade Flows, Disconnected? In *World Economic Outlook: Adjusting to Lower Commodity Prices* (October). Washington.

IMF (International Monetary Fund). 2016. *World Economic Outlook* (October). Washington.

Irwin, Douglas A. 2011. *Trade Policy Disaster.* Cambridge, MA: MIT Press.

Jeanne, Olivier, and Romain Rancière. 2008. *The Optimal Level of International Reserves for Emerging Market Countries: A New Formula and Some Applications.* CEPR Discussion Paper 6723. Washington: Center for Economic Policy Research.

Kamin, Steven B., Mario Marazzi, and John W. Schindler. 2006. The Impact of Chinese Exports on Global Import Prices. *Review of International Economics* 14, no. 2: 179–201.

Kessler, Martin. 2012. *The Renminbi Bloc Is Here: Asia Down, Rest of the World to Go?* PIIE Working Paper 12-19. Washington: Peterson Institute for International Economics.

Krugman, Paul. 1989. Differences in Income Elasticities and Trends in Real Exchange Rates. *European Economic Review* 33, no. 5: 1031–46.

Laeven, Luc, and Fabián Valencia. 2012. *Systemic Banking Crises Database: An Update.* IMF Working Paper 12/163. Washington: International Monetary Fund.

de Lima-Campos, Aluisio, and Juan Antonio Gaviria. 2012. A Case for Misaligned Currencies as Countervailable Subsidies. *Journal of World Trade* 4, no. 5: 1017–44.

Marquez, Jaime. 2002. *Estimating Trade Elasticities.* Boston: Kluwer Academic Press.

Menon, Ravi. 2014. Economic Overview and Challenges. Remarks at the MAS Annual Report 2013/14 Press Conference, Singapore, July 24.

Obstfeld, Maurice, and Kenneth Rogoff. 2007. The Unsustainable US Current Account Position Revisited. In *G7 Current Account Imbalances: Sustainability and Adjustment*, ed. Richard Clarida. Cambridge, MA: National Bureau of Economic Research.

Ostry, Jonathan D., Atish R. Ghosh, Karl Habermeier, Luc Laeven, Marcos Chamon, Mahvash S. Qureshi, and Annamaria Kokenyne. 2011. *Managing Capital Inflows: What Tools to Use?* IMF Staff Discussion Note 11/06. Washington: International Monetary Fund.

Pierce, Justin R., and Peter K. Schott. 2016. The Surprisingly Swift Decline of US Manufacturing Employment. *American Economic Review* 106, no. 7: 1632–62.

Posen, Adam S. 2011. Monetary Policy, Bubbles, and the Knowledge Problem. *Cato Journal* 31, no. 3: 461–71.

Prakken, Joel, and Chris Varvares. 2016. *Trump Stimulus in the Forecast?* Macro Focus (December 9). Macroeconomic Advisors.

Prasad, Enwar S. 2014. *The Dollar Trap: How the U.S. Dollar Tightened Its Grip on Global Finance.* Princeton, NJ: Princeton University Press.

Primus, Keyra. 2016. *Fiscal Rules for Resource Windfall Allocation: The Case of Trinidad and Tobago.* IMF Working Paper 16/188. Washington: International Monetary Fund.

Rajan, Raghuram. 2014. Competitive Monetary Easing: Is It Yesterday Once More? Remarks at the Brookings Institution, April 10. Available at www.brookings.edu/wp-content/uploads/2016/07/rajan_remarks_at_brookings.pdf (accessed on April 17, 2017).

Rasmussen, Chris. 2016. *Jobs Supported by Exports 2015: An Update.* April 8. Washington: Office of Trade and Economic Analysis, International Trade Administration, Department of Commerce.

Saborowski, Christian, and Milan Nedeljkovic. 2017. *The Relative Effectiveness of Spot and Derivatives-Based Intervention: The Case of Brazil.* IMF Working Paper 17/11. Washington: International Monetary Fund.

Setser, Brad W., and Arpana Pandey. 2009. *China's $1.5 Trillion Bet: Understanding China's External Portfolio.* Center for Geoeconomic Studies Working Paper (May). New York: Council on Foreign Relations.

Stockton, David J. 2016. The Global Economy: A Driverless Car in the Slow Lane. Presentation at the Peterson Institute for International Economics, Washington, September 29.

Stone, Sarah, and Edwin Truman. 2016. *Uneven Progress on Sovereign Wealth Fund Transparency and Accountability.* PIIE Policy Brief 16-18. Washington: Peterson Institute for International Economics.

Taylor, John B. 2016. A Rules-Based Cooperative International Monetary System for the Future. In *International Monetary Cooperation: Lessons from the Plaza Accord after Thirty Years,* ed. C. Fred Bergsten and Russell A. Green. Washington: Peterson Institute for International Economics.

US Department of the Treasury. 2016. *Foreign Exchange Policies of Major Trading Partners of the United States. Report to Congress* (April). Washington.

Volcker, Paul A., and Toyoo Gyohten. 1993. *Changing Fortunes: The World's Money and the Threat to American Leadership.* New York. Three Rivers Press.

Wei, Shang-Jin, and Xiaobo Zhang. 2011. The Competitive Saving Motive: Evidence from Rising Sex Ratios and Savings Rates in China. *Journal of Political Economy* 119, no. 3: 511–64.

Williamson, John. 2007. *Reference Rates and the International Monetary System.* Policy Analyses in International Economics 82. Washington: Peterson Institute for International Economics.

Williamson, John. 2016. *International Monetary Reform: A Specific Set of Proposals.* London: Routledge.

Williamson, John, and Marcus H. Miller. 1987. *Targets and Indicators: A Blueprint for the International Coordination of Economic Policy.* Washington: Institute for International Economics.

WTO (World Trade Organization). 1999. *India—Quantitative Restrictions on Imports of Agricultural, Textile and Industrial Products.* Report of the Panel (April 6). Geneva.

Index

China
  bond market, 157
  consumer price inflation, 98, 98f
  currency manipulation by, 3, 8–10
    decline in, 119, 135, 170, 175
    domestic effects of, 132
    extent of, 74–75, 156, 171
    foreign policy and, 196–98, 200
    private diplomacy about, 133–35
    retaliation against, 156–57,
      158b–159b
  current account surplus, 38–40, 39f, 208t
    during decade of manipulation, 88,
      89f, 97–100, 97f, 173
    extent of, 169
    norms for, 54
    persistence of, 49, 148
    projected, 120–22, 121t
    recent, 119–20, 121t
    unsustainability of, 47, 92, 170
  fixed exchange rate, 38
  GDP growth, 98, 98f
  government budget balance, 99, 99f
  import competition from, 69, 95
  interest rates, 99, 100f
  as key currency country, 179–82, 193
  mini-devaluation, 13
  private diplomacy with, 133–38
  real effective exchange rate, 97, 97f
  reserves, 8, 9, 132, 178, 190
  saving rate, 49, 99
  unconventional monetary policy, 11
  US complaints about, 9, 11, 135, 138–39,
    144, 174
China shock, 1, 8, 93–95, 136, 170, 174
Clinton, Hillary, 95, 138, 186
COFER (Currency Composition of Official
    Foreign Exchange Reserves) data,
    86–87
competitive devaluation, 3–4, 151, 169
competitive nonappreciation, 2, 6
Connally, John, 138n, 165
consumer price index (CPI)
  China, 98, 98f
  data sources, 206
  Japan, 101, 102f
  Korea, 106, 106f
  Singapore, 114, 115f
  Switzerland, 110, 110f

corporate tax rates, 60
countervailing currency intervention,
    156–62
  announcement of, 16, 153, 162, 187, 199
  against China, 157–60, 158b–159b
  in European Union, 156
  extent of, 161, 181–82
  as FTA remedy, 195
  international rules, 157
  legality of, 191–92
  multilateralization of, 192–96, 199–200
  objections to, 189–90
  obstacles to, 191
  as proposed strategy, 186–92, 199–200
  side benefits of, 190–91
  targets of, 16, 160, 181–82, 187–88
countervailing duties, 143, 152, 156–57,
    192
CPI. See consumer price index
Currency Composition of Official Foreign
    Exchange Reserves (COFER) data,
    86–87
currency conflict
  concept of, 2–3
  foreign policy and, 196–98, 200
  history of, 1, 3–7, 169–70
  key currency countries, 179–82, 193
  recent renewal of, 7–14
  significance of, 171–74, 200
currency intervention
  authority for, 129, 148, 186
  criteria for, 150–51
  during decade of manipulation, 96–116
  illegitimate (See currency manipulation)
  indirect, 150–51
  legitimate, 63–64, 77, 172, 178–79
  offensive versus defensive, 178–79
  oral, 150–51
  remedial (See countervailing currency
    intervention)
  spillovers of, 86–87
  sterilized, 30n, 37b, 171
  unsterilized, 30n, 37b
currency manipulation. See also specific
    country
  in Asia, 9, 74–75, 171–74, 179, 198
  criteria for, 76–85, 150, 185, 187, 193
    excessive imbalance, 76–77
    mature markets, 81–84, 83t

France, 165*n*
FRB/US model, 34, 36, 91
free trade, 44
free trade agreements. *See also specific*
agreement
    currency issues included in, 145–54,
      146*b*–147*b*, 194–95, 200
    labor and environmental standards in,
      146*b*–147*b*
    plurilateral action, 130, 131*t*
    remedies, 152–53, 195

G-5, role of, 6, 130
G-7
    policy options, 96, 149, 175, 182
    private diplomacy, 133, 135
    role of, 6, 77, 130
G-20
    countervailing intervention against, 16,
      160, 181–82, 187–88
    policy options, 96, 150, 175, 182–83
    private diplomacy, 133, 135
    role of, 77, 130, 171, 172
GATT (General Agreement on Tariffs and
    Trade), 4, 148, 157, 195. *See also* World
    Trade Organization
GDP (gross domestic product), 18. *See also*
    economic growth
    China, 98, 98*f*
    data sources, 205
    exchange rate interaction with, 21–24,
      21*b*, 34
    fiscal policy and, 36
    growth rate (*See* economic growth)
    investment ratio, 47, 57–60, 59*f*
    relative to US, 27*t*, 29
GDP identity, 21*b*, 23
General Agreement on Tariffs and Trade
    (GATT), 4, 148, 157, 195. *See also*
    World Trade Organization
Germany
    currency manipulation by, 6, 170–71
    currency policy, 194, 200
    norms for, 54, 77
    role in European Union, 7, 45*b*
    sustainability analysis, 61, 62*f*
    as target of countervailing intervention,
      191

global financial crisis. *See* Great Recession
    (2007-08)
globalization, attack on, 181
"global saving glut," 173
goods trade balance, 18*n*
government bond yield
    data sources, 206
    Japan, 102, 103*f*
    Korea, 106, 107*f*
    Singapore, 116, 117*f*
    Switzerland, 111, 112*f*
government borrowing, 51, 53, 56–61, 79,
    95–96, 188
government procurement, 137, 185
Great Depression (1930s), 1, 4
Great Recession (2007-08), 8, 9
    causes of, 69
    decline in output after, 96
    free trade and, 44
    private diplomacy during, 134, 136
    quantitative easing, 2, 10–11, 13, 65–66,
      176
        current account and, 34–35,
          102–103, 353*f*
    safe havens during, 13, 109
    unemployment during, 91, 136, 169, 171,
      173, 175
    US trade policy during, 139
Greenspan-Guidotti rule, 71, 79
gross domestic product. *See* GDP
growth rate. *See* economic growth; GDP

historical background, 1, 3–7, 169–70
Hong Kong
    bond market, 157
    currency manipulation by, 75, 160, 171,
      198
    current account balance, 212*t*–213*t*
    reserves, 8, 190
hot money flows, 82–83, 190

IEEPA (International Emergency Economic
    Powers Act), 162, 166
illegitimate intervention, 64. *See also*
    currency manipulation
IMF. *See* International Monetary Fund
import competition, 69, 95
import controls, 163–67
import duties, 143, 156–57, 192

Other Publications from the
PETERSON INSTITUTE FOR INTERNATIONAL ECONOMICS

POLICY ANALYSES IN INTERNATIONAL ECONOMICS SERIES

* = out of print

World Agricultural Trade: Building a Consensus*
William M. Miner and
Dale E. Hathaway, eds.
1988   ISBN 0-88132-071-3
Japan in the World Economy*   Bela Balassa and
Marcus Noland
1988   ISBN 0-88132-041-2
America in the World Economy: A Strategy for
the 1990s*   C. Fred Bergsten
1988   ISBN 0-88132-089-7
Managing the Dollar: From the Plaza to the
Louvre*   Yoichi Funabashi
1988, 2d ed. 1989   ISBN 0-88132-097-8
United States External Adjustment and the
World Economy   William R. Cline
May 1989   ISBN 0-88132-048-X
Free Trade Areas and U.S. Trade Policy*
Jeffrey J. Schott, ed.
May 1989   ISBN 0-88132-094-3
Dollar Politics: Exchange Rate Policymaking
in the United States*   I. M. Destler and
C. Randall Henning
September 1989   ISBN 0-88132-079-X
Latin American Adjustment: How Much Has
Happened?*   John Williamson, ed.
April 1990   ISBN 0-88132-125-7
The Future of World Trade in Textiles and
Apparel*   William R. Cline
1987, 2d ed. June 1999   ISBN 0-88132-110-9
Completing the Uruguay Round: A Results-
Oriented Approach to the GATT Trade
Negotiations*   Jeffrey J. Schott, ed.
September 1990   ISBN 0-88132-130-3
Economic Sanctions Reconsidered (2 volumes)
Economic Sanctions Reconsidered: Supple-
mental Case Histories*   Gary Clyde Hufbauer,
Jeffrey J. Schott, and Kimberly Ann Elliott
1985, 2d ed. Dec. 1990   ISBN cloth 0-88132-115-X/
                          paper 0-88132-105-2
Economic Sanctions Reconsidered: History
and Current Policy*   Gary Clyde Hufbauer,
Jeffrey J. Schott, and Kimberly Ann Elliott
December 1990   ISBN cloth 0-88132-140-0
                        ISBN paper 0-88132-136-2
Pacific Basin Developing Countries: Prospects
for the Future*   Marcus Noland
January 1991   ISBN cloth 0-88132-141-9
                        ISBN paper 0-88132-081-1
Currency Convertibility in Eastern Europe
John Williamson, ed.
October 1991   ISBN 0-88132-128-1
International Adjustment and Financing: The
Lessons of 1985–1991*   C. Fred Bergsten, ed.
January 1992   ISBN 0-88132-112-5
North American Free Trade: Issues and Recom-
mendations*   Gary Clyde Hufbauer and Jeffrey J.
Schott
April 1992   ISBN 0-88132-120-6
Narrowing the U.S. Current Account Deficit*
Alan J. Lenz
June 1992   ISBN 0-88132-103-6
The Economics of Global Warming
William R. Cline
June 1992   ISBN 0-88132-132-X

US Taxation of International Income: Blueprint
for Reform*   Gary Clyde Hufbauer,
assisted by Joanna M. van Rooij
October 1992   ISBN 0-88132-134-6
Who's Bashing Whom? Trade Conflict in High-
Technology Industries   Laura D'Andrea Tyson
November 1992 ISBN 0-88132-106-0
Korea in the World Economy*   Il SaKong
January 1993   ISBN 0-88132-183-4
Pacific Dynamism and the International Eco-
nomic System*   C. Fred Bergsten and
Marcus Noland, eds.
May 1993   ISBN 0-88132-196-6
Economic Consequences of Soviet Disintegra-
tion*   John Williamson, ed.
May 1993   ISBN 0-88132-190-7
Reconcilable Differences? United States-Japan
Economic Conflict*   C. Fred Bergsten and
Marcus Noland
June 1993   ISBN 0-88132-129-X
Does Foreign Exchange Intervention Work?
Kathryn M. Dominguez and Jeffrey A. Frankel
September 1993   ISBN 0-88132-104-4
Sizing Up U.S. Export Disincentives*
J. David Richardson
September 1993   ISBN 0-88132-107-9
NAFTA: An Assessment*   Gary Clyde Hufbauer
and Jeffrey J. Schott, rev. ed.
October 1993   ISBN 0-88132-199-0
Adjusting to Volatile Energy Prices
Philip K. Verleger, Jr.
November 1993   ISBN 0-88132-069-2
The Political Economy of Policy Reform
John Williamson, ed.
January 1994   ISBN 0-88132-195-8
Measuring the Costs of Protection in the United
States   Gary Clyde Hufbauer and
Kimberly Ann Elliott
January 1994   ISBN 0-88132-108-7
The Dynamics of Korean Economic Develop-
ment*   Cho Soon
March 1994   ISBN 0-88132-162-1
Reviving the European Union*
C. Randall Henning, Eduard Hochreiter, and Gary
Clyde Hufbauer, eds.
April 1994   ISBN 0-88132-208-3
China in the World Economy   Nicholas R. Lardy
April 1994   ISBN 0-88132-200-8
Greening the GATT: Trade, Environment,
and the Future   Daniel C. Esty
July 1994   ISBN 0-88132-205-9
Western Hemisphere Economic Integration*
Gary Clyde Hufbauer and Jeffrey J. Schott
July 1994   ISBN 0-88132-159-1
Currencies and Politics in the United States,
Germany, and Japan   C. Randall Henning
September 1994   ISBN 0-88132-127-3
Estimating Equilibrium Exchange Rates
John Williamson, ed.
September 1994   ISBN 0-88132-076-5
Managing the World Economy: Fifty Years
after Bretton Woods   Peter B. Kenen, ed.
September 1994   ISBN 0-88132-212-1

Trade Liberalization and International Institutions*   Jeffrey J. Schott
September 1994   ISBN 978-0-88132-3
Reciprocity and Retaliation in U.S. Trade Policy*
Thomas O. Bayard and Kimberly Ann Elliott
September 1994   ISBN 0-88132-084-6
The Uruguay Round: An Assessment*
Jeffrey J. Schott, assisted by Johanna Buurman
November 1994   ISBN 0-88132-206-7
Measuring the Costs of Protection in Japan*
Yoko Sazanami, Shujiro Urata, and Hiroki Kawai
January 1995   ISBN 0-88132-211-3
Foreign Direct Investment in the United States, 3d ed.   Edward M. Graham and Paul R. Krugman
January 1995   ISBN 0-88132-204-0
The Political Economy of Korea-United States Cooperation*   C. Fred Bergsten and Il SaKong, eds.
February 1995 ISBN 0-88132-213-X
International Debt Reexamined*   William R. Cline
February 1995   ISBN 0-88132-083-8
American Trade Politics, 3d ed.   I. M. Destler
April 1995   ISBN 0-88132-215-6
Managing Official Export Credits: The Quest for a Global Regime*   John E. Ray
July 1995   ISBN 0-88132-207-5
Asia Pacific Fusion: Japan's Role in APEC
Yoichi Funabashi
October 1995   ISBN 0-88132-224-5
Korea-United States Cooperation in the New World Order*   C. Fred Bergsten and Il SaKong, eds.
February 1996   ISBN 0-88132-226-1
Why Exports Really Matter!*   ISBN 0-88132-221-0
Why Exports Matter More!*   ISBN 0-88132-229-6
J. David Richardson and Karin Rindal
July 1995; February 1996
Global Corporations and National Governments
Edward M. Graham
May 1996   ISBN 0-88132-111-7
Global Economic Leadership and the Group of Seven   C. Fred Bergsten and C. Randall Henning
May 1996   ISBN 0-88132-218-0
The Trading System after the Uruguay Round*
John Whalley and Colleen Hamilton
July 1996   ISBN 0-88132-131-1
Private Capital Flows to Emerging Markets after the Mexican Crisis*   Guillermo A. Calvo, Morris Goldstein, and Eduard Hochreiter
September 1996   ISBN 0-88132-232-6
The Crawling Band as an Exchange Rate Regime: Lessons from Chile, Colombia, and Israel
John Williamson
September 1996   ISBN 0-88132-231-8
Flying High: Liberalizing Civil Aviation in the Asia Pacific*   Gary Clyde Hufbauer and Christopher Findlay
November 1996   ISBN 0-88132-227-X
Measuring the Costs of Visible Protection in Korea*   Namdoo Kim
November 1996   ISBN 0-88132-236-9
The World Trading System: Challenges Ahead
Jeffrey J. Schott
December 1996   ISBN 0-88132-235-0
Has Globalization Gone Too Far?   Dani Rodrik
March 1997   ISBN paper 0-88132-241-5

Korea-United States Economic Relationship*
C. Fred Bergsten and Il SaKong, eds.
March 1997   ISBN 0-88132-240-7
Summitry in the Americas: A Progress Report*
Richard E. Feinberg
April 1997   ISBN 0-88132-242-3
Corruption and the Global Economy
Kimberly Ann Elliott
June 1997   ISBN 0-88132-233-4
Regional Trading Blocs in the World Economic System   Jeffrey A. Frankel
October 1997   ISBN 0-88132-202-4
Sustaining the Asia Pacific Miracle: Environmental Protection and Economic Integration   Andre Dua and Daniel C. Esty
October 1997   ISBN 0-88132-250-4
Trade and Income Distribution
William R. Cline
November 1997   ISBN 0-88132-216-4
Global Competition Policy   Edward M. Graham and J. David Richardson
December 1997   ISBN 0-88132-166-4
Unfinished Business: Telecommunications after the Uruguay Round   Gary Clyde Hufbauer and Erika Wada
December 1997   ISBN 0-88132-257-1
Financial Services Liberalization in the WTO
Wendy Dobson and Pierre Jacquet
June 1998   ISBN 0-88132-254-7
Restoring Japan's Economic Growth
Adam S. Posen
September 1998   ISBN 0-88132-262-8
Measuring the Costs of Protection in China
Zhang Shuguang, Zhang Yansheng, and Wan Zhongxin
November 1998   ISBN 0-88132-247-4
Foreign Direct Investment and Development: The New Policy Agenda for Developing Countries and Economies in Transition
Theodore H. Moran
December 1998   ISBN 0-88132-258-X
Behind the Open Door: Foreign Enterprises in the Chinese Marketplace   Daniel H. Rosen
January 1999   ISBN 0-88132-263-6
Toward A New International Financial Architecture: A Practical Post-Asia Agenda
Barry Eichengreen
February 1999   ISBN 0-88132-270-9
Is the U.S. Trade Deficit Sustainable?
Catherine L. Mann
September 1999   ISBN 0-88132-265-2
Safeguarding Prosperity in a Global Financial System: The Future International Financial Architecture, Independent Task Force Report Sponsored by the Council on Foreign Relations
Morris Goldstein, Project Director
October 1999   ISBN 0-88132-287-3
Avoiding the Apocalypse: The Future of the Two Koreas   Marcus Noland
June 2000   ISBN 0-88132-278-4
Assessing Financial Vulnerability: An Early Warning System for Emerging Markets
Morris Goldstein, Graciela Kaminsky, and Carmen Reinhart
June 2000   ISBN 0-88132-237-7

Foreign Direct Investment and Development: Launching a Second Generation of Policy Research, Avoiding the Mistakes of the First, Reevaluating Policies for Developed and Developing Countries   Theodore H. Moran
April 2011   ISBN 978-0-88132-600-0

How Latvia Came through the Financial Crisis
Anders Åslund and Valdis Dombrovskis
May 2011   ISBN 978-0-88132-602-4

Global Trade in Services: Fear, Facts, and Offshoring   J. Bradford Jensen
August 2011   ISBN 978-0-88132-601-7

NAFTA and Climate Change   Meera Fickling and Jeffrey J. Schott
September 2011   ISBN 978-0-88132-436-5

Eclipse: Living in the Shadow of China's Economic Dominance   Arvind Subramanian
September 2011   ISBN 978-0-88132-606-2

Flexible Exchange Rates for a Stable World Economy   Joseph E. Gagnon with Marc Hinterschweiger
September 2011   ISBN 978-0-88132-627-7

The Arab Economies in a Changing World, 2d ed.   Marcus Noland and Howard Pack
November 2011   ISBN 978-0-88132-628-4

Sustaining China's Economic Growth After the Global Financial Crisis   Nicholas R. Lardy
January 2012   ISBN 978-0-88132-626-0

Who Needs to Open the Capital Account?
Olivier Jeanne, Arvind Subramanian, and John Williamson
April 2012   ISBN 978-0-88132-511-9

Devaluing to Prosperity: Misaligned Currencies and Their Growth Consequences   Surjit S. Bhalla
August 2012   ISBN 978-0-88132-623-9

Private Rights and Public Problems: The Global Economics of Intellectual Property in the 21st Century   Keith E. Maskus
September 2012   ISBN 978-0-88132-507-2

Global Economics in Extraordinary Times: Essays in Honor of John Williamson
C. Fred Bergsten and C. Randall Henning, eds.
November 2012   ISBN 978-0-88132-662-8

Rising Tide: Is Growth in Emerging Economies Good for the United States?   Lawrence Edwards and Robert Z. Lawrence
February 2013   ISBN 978-0-88132-500-3

Responding to Financial Crisis: Lessons from Asia Then, the United States and Europe Now
Changyong Rhee and Adam S. Posen, eds
October 2013   ISBN 978-0-88132-674-1

Fueling Up: The Economic Implications of America's Oil and Gas Boom   Trevor Houser and Shashank Mohan
January 2014   ISBN 978-0-88132-656-7

How Latin America Weathered the Global Financial Crisis   José De Gregorio
January 2014   ISBN 978-0-88132-678-9

Confronting the Curse: The Economics and Geopolitics of Natural Resource Governance
Cullen S. Hendrix and Marcus Noland
May 2014   ISBN 978-0-88132-676-5

Inside the Euro Crisis: An Eyewitness Account
Simeon Djankov
June 2014   ISBN 978-0-88132-685-7

Managing the Euro Area Debt Crisis
William R. Cline
June 2014   ISBN 978-0-88132-687-1

Markets over Mao: The Rise of Private Business in China   Nicholas R. Lardy
September 2014   ISBN 978-0-88132-693-2

Bridging the Pacific: Toward Free Trade and Investment between China and the United States
C. Fred Bergsten, Gary Clyde Hufbauer, and Sean Miner. Assisted by Tyler Moran
October 2014   ISBN 978-0-88132-691-8

The Great Rebirth: Lessons from the Victory of Capitalism over Communism
Anders Åslund and Simeon Djankov, eds.
November 2014   ISBN 978-0-88132-697-0

Ukraine: What Went Wrong and How to Fix It
Anders Åslund
April 2015   ISBN 978-0-88132-701-4

From Stress to Growth: Strengthening Asia's Financial Systems in a Post-Crisis World
Marcus Noland; Donghyun Park, eds.
October 2015   ISBN 978-0-88132-699-4

The Great Tradeoff: Confronting Moral Conflicts in the Era of Globalization
Steven R. Weisman
January 2016   ISBN 978-0-88132-695-6

Rich People, Poor Countries: The Rise of Emerging-Market Tycoons and their Mega Firms   Caroline Freund, assisted by Sarah Oliver
January 2016   ISBN 978-0-88132-703-8

International Monetary Cooperation: Lessons from the Plaza Accord After Thirty Years
C. Fred Bergsten and Russell A. Green, eds.
April 2016   ISBN 978-0-88132-711-3

Currency Conflict and Trade Policy: A New Strategy for the United States   C. Fred Bergsten and Joseph E. Gagnon
June 2017   ISBN 978-0-88132-726-7

SPECIAL REPORTS

1   Promoting World Recovery: A Statement on Global Economic Strategy*   by Twenty-six Economists from Fourteen Countries
December 1982   ISBN 0-88132-013-7

2   Prospects for Adjustment in Argentina, Brazil, and Mexico: Responding to the Debt Crisis*   John Williamson, ed.
June 1983   ISBN 0-88132-016-1

3   Inflation and Indexation: Argentina, Brazil, and Israel*   John Williamson, ed.
March 1985   ISBN 0-88132-037-4

4   Global Economic Imbalances*
C. Fred Bergsten, ed.
March 1986   ISBN 0-88132-042-0

5   African Debt and Financing*   Carol Lancaster and John Williamson, eds.
May 1986   ISBN 0-88132-044-7

6   Resolving the Global Economic Crisis: After Wall Street*   by Thirty-three Economists from Thirteen Countries
December 1987   ISBN 0-88132-070-6

7   World Economic Problems*
Kimberly Ann Elliott and John Williamson, eds.
April 1988   ISBN 0-88132-055-2

Sales Representatives

In Asia, North America, and South America

Perseus Distribution
210 American Drive
Jackson, TN 38301
orderentry@perseusbooks.com

Tel. (800) 343-4499
Fax (800) 351-5073
Email: cup_book@columbia.edu

Secure online ordering is available on the CUP website at: www.cup.columbia.edu

In Africa, Europe, the Middle East, South Africa, South Asias, and the United States

Columbia University Press
c/o Wiley European Distribution Centre
New Era Estate
Oldlands Way, Bognor Regis
West Sussex PO22 9NQ

Tel. (1243) 843-291
Fax (1243) 843-296
Email: customer@wiley.com

(Delivery via Wiley Distribution Services Ltd., or you may collect your order by prior arrangement)

United States and Canada Sales and Publicity Representatives

Brad Hebel, Director of Sales and Marketing
61 West 62nd Street
New York, NY 10023

Tel. (212) 459-0600, ext. 7130
Fax (212) 459-3678
Email: bh2106@columbia.edu

Columbia University Sales Consortium Manager and Souther US

Catherine Hobbs

Tel. (804) 690-8529
Fax (434) 589-3411
Email: catherinehobbs@earthlink.net

Northeast US and Eastern Canada

Conor Broughan

Tel. (917) 826-7676
Email: cb2476@columbia.edu

Midwest US and Central Canada

Kevin Kurtz

Tel. (773) 316-1116
Fax (773) 489-2941
Email: kkurtz5@earthlink.net

Western US and Western Canada

William Gawronski

Tel. (310) 488-9059
Fax (310) 832-4717
Email: wgawronski@earthlink.net

United Kingdom and Europe

The University Press Group Ltd.
Lois Edwards
LEC 1, New Era Estate
Oldlands Way, Bognor Regis
PO22 9NQ England

Tel. 44 (1243) 842-165
Fax 44 (1243) 842-167
Email: lois@upguk.com

Ben Mitchell
U.K. Sales Manager
62 Fairford House
Kennington Lane
London SE11 4HR England

Tel. (44) 776-691-3593
Email: ben.mitchell.upg@gmail.com

Andrew Brewer
Managing Director
57 Cobnar Road
Sheffield S8 8QA England

Tel. (44) 114-274-0129
Mobile (44) 796-703-1856
Email: andrew.brewer@virgin.net

Middle East and Africa

Andrew Brewer
Managing Director
57 Cobnar Road
Sheffield S8 8QA England

Tel. (44) 114-274-0129
Mobile (44) 796-703-1856
Email: andrew.brewer@virgin.net

Asia

Brad Hebel
61 West 62nd Street
New York, NY 10023

Tel. (212) 459-0600, ext. 7130
Fax (212) 459-3678
Email: bh2106@columbia.edu

Ingram Content Group UK Ltd.
Milton Keynes UK
UKHW020808210523
422080UK00011B/321